TRAVELLERS

MALAYSIA & SINGAPORE

By
NICK HANNA

Written by Nick Hanna, updated by David Henley
Original photography by Nick Hanna, Ken Paterson and CPA Media

Published by Thomas Cook Publishing
A division of Thomas Cook Tour Operations Limited.
Company registration no. 3772199 England
The Thomas Cook Business Park, Unit 9, Coningsby Road,
Peterborough PE3 8SB, United Kingdom
E-mail: books@thomascook.com, Tel: + 44 (0) 1733 416477
www.thomascookpublishing.com

Produced by Cambridge Publishing Management Limited
Burr Elm Court, Main Street, Caldecote CB23 7NU

ISBN: 978-1-84157-996-2

Series Editor: Maisie Fitzpatrick
Production/DTP: Steven Collins

Printed and bound in Italy by Printer Trento

Cover photography: Front L-R: Guy Vanderelst/Photographer's Choice/
Getty: © David Noton/David Noton Photography/Alamy;
© Herb Schmitz/Alamy
Back: © Wayne Lawler/Corbis

Contents

Background 4–27
Introduction 4
The land 6
History 8
Politics 10
Culture 14

First steps 28–9
Impressions 28

Destination guide 30–115
Malaysia 30
Kuala Lumpur 30
Around Kuala Lumpur 37
Melaka 40
Central Highlands 46
Northwest coast 52
Pulau Pinang 54
East coast 66
Sarawak 74
Sabah 84
Singapore 94

Getting away from it all 116–25

Directory 126–89
Shopping 126
Entertainment 136
Children 144
Sport and leisure 146
Food and drink 150
Hotels and accommodation 168
Practical guide 178

Index 190–91

Maps
Southeast Asia 5
Malaysia and Singapore 31
Kuala Lumpur 32
Peninsular Malaysia 36–7
Melaka walk 44
Cameron Highlands walk 48
Georgetown walk 60
Pulau Pinang tour 62
Pulau Langkawi tour 64
Sarawak 75
Bako National Park walk 81
Sabah 85
Mount Kinabalu National Park walk 93
Singapore Island 95
Singapore city 97
Chinatown walk 110
Bukit Timah Nature Reserve walk 112
Little India walk 114
MRT system, Singapore 187
MRT system, Kuala Lumpur 188

Features
Peoples of Malaysia 12
The Straits Chinese 20
Thaipusam Festival 26
Orang Asli 38
Tea plantations 50
Coral reefs 72
Rainforests 82
Night markets 135
Malay pastimes 142
Tropical fruits 166

KEY TO MAPS

Airport
MRT station
Start of walk/tour
Mountain hut
163m Mountain
Path
Information
115 3 Road number

Introduction

At the heart of Southeast Asia, Malaysia and Singapore are two separate states linked by a common heritage that started in the days of the great sea-trading routes of the spice traders, and continued through the colonial era to their current status as neighbouring economic powers.

Malaysia

For centuries, travellers have been drawn to the shores of Malaysia, creating a melting pot of peoples and lifestyles – of Malays, Chinese, Indians and many other ethnic groups that live side by side in almost every corner of the country. For the present-day visitor, this diversity yields a rich and heady mixture of cultural attractions – of music, dance and arts from several countries, and an almost continuous calendar of festivals and feasts drawn from many different religious traditions.

In Malaysia the lifestyle is as varied as the landscape, although much of society is bound together by the common thread of Islam. The call to prayer echoes five times a day from mosques everywhere, from the bustling streets of Kuala Lumpur, the capital, to the smallest village or *kampung*, where small wooden houses on stilts are surrounded by a cooling canopy of papaya, banana and palm trees.

The mountains, rivers and rainforests of Malaysia beckon the adventurous. From jungle-trekking to scuba-diving, there are plenty of options for exploration in national parks and other wilderness areas. On the islands off the east and west coasts, you can recuperate beneath the coconut palms on coral beaches, with the choice of a luxury hotel or a simple, thatched hut to stay in. A sense of history resonates, from the smoke-filled temples of Pinang to the tribal long-houses of Sarawak, providing a range of travel experiences unparalleled in Asia.

THOMAS COOK'S MALAYSIA AND SINGAPORE

Thomas Cook first arrived in Singapore on his world tour of 1882–83. Raffles Hotel became a headquarters for Cook travellers, who subsequently travelled northwards through Malaya on the Federated Malay Railway System. The travel business in this part of the world was of such importance to Thomas Cook that a special Malay edition of the Thomas Cook magazine, *The Travellers' Gazette*, was published in 1923.

The vibrancy of Malaysia's street life will provide much to enthral and entertain. In one street you may come across a noisy and colourful celebration of a deity's birthday; in the next, a string of open-air restaurants where Indian cooks fling large circles of dough on to hot-plates to create sizzling snacks. In the markets of Sabah and Sarawak, tribal peoples display weird and wonderful fruits from the forest alongside brightly patterned basketware and other ethnic crafts.

In essence, Malaysia is a breathtaking mix of ethnic, religious, culinary, musical and literary traditions that cannot fail to stimulate. Few, if any, other countries are heir to so diverse and eclectic a mix.

Singapore

Despite recent economic growth and modernisation, the soul of the Orient is never far from the surface in Singapore. The tower blocks may be built according to the laws of structural engineering, but their design is still very much determined by the principles of Chinese geomancy or *feng shui*, which dictates where doors, windows, even furniture should be placed to ensure that good spirits and wealth stay within the building. A Singaporean executive might be trading worldwide via his mobile telephone, but his values are likely to be influenced as much by the Confucian precepts of filial piety, discipline and respect for the family as they are by currency markets.

Southeast Asia

There are a remarkable number of things to see and do in this vibrant island city state. You can take it easy browsing by daytime in what must be the world's largest bazaar or venturing out in the evening for a tour of the sights by bicycle-rickshaw. You can trace the roots of the city in the ethnic and colonial areas or catch up with today's generation in one of the many pulsating, hi-tech discos in the small hours of the morning.

Renowned for its amazing choice of restaurants, the city is a gastronomic delight for the traveller. A mouth-watering variety of ethnic and international food is available at all times of day and night, often at a surprisingly low cost. A journey through Singapore is likely to be as much an exploration of taste as it is a tour of the sights.

The land

Malaysia consists of two distinct geographical regions: Peninsular Malaysia and East Malaysia. These two regions are separated by the South China Sea. Much of both of these regions is covered by thick tropical forests, home to a vast number of endemic plants and animals. Singapore, situated 136km (85 miles) north of the equator, is an island state lying off the southern tip of the Malaysian peninsula.

Malaysia

Peninsular Malaysia extends from the Thai border down to the Selat Johor (Straits of Johor). East Malaysia comprises the states of Sarawak and Sabah on the northern half of Borneo, with the tiny country of Brunei Darussalam sandwiched between the two.

The regions of Peninsular Malaysia are defined by a mountainous spine (the Banjaran Titiwangsa) that runs down the centre of the country from the border with Thailand almost to the capital, Kuala Lumpur. The heavily forested and hilly interior is the most sparsely populated part of the peninsula. To the west of the mountains, the foothills and alluvial plains running down to the coast are carpeted in rubber and oil-palm plantations. On the eastern seaboard the coastal plains are not so extensive and rice cultivation predominates.

The most spectacular landscapes are in the East Malaysia states of Sabah and Sarawak. Sarawak is characterised by dense jungle and extensive river systems (the Rajang River flows for 563km/ 350 miles through the heart of the country). Covering some 124,500sq km (48,070sq miles), Sarawak is the largest state in Malaysia.

Bordered by Sarawak and the Indonesian state of Kalimantan to the south, Sabah covers an area of 73,700sq km (28,456sq miles). Its shores are washed by three different seas: the South China Sea to the west, and the Sulu Sea and Celebes Sea to the east. Gunung (Mount) Kinabalu, at the pinnacle of the Banjaran Crocker, is the highest peak in Malaysia.

The southern tip of Peninsular Malaysia lies at latitude 1°N, with the northern provinces extending up to latitude 7°N. Sabah and Sarawak occupy a similar range of latitude, putting the whole country firmly in the Tropical Humid belt with average annual rainfall of around 2,800mm (110 inches). *See* Climate, *pp179 & 180*, for more details.

Malaysia has a prosperous economy and is one of the world's major exporters of rubber, tin, palm oil and cocoa. With the discovery of oil deposits off the east coast in 1978, the petroleum industry has added to the country's wealth and crude oil has now outstripped tin as the major export. Manufacturing industries include textiles, electronic goods, jewellery, optical and scientific equipment, toys and sportswear. Malaysia is a major exporter of timber, principally from the eastern states of Sabah and Sarawak, a trade that continues to involve the country in considerable international controversy.

Singapore

The main island (covering some 580sq km/224sq miles) is what most people refer to as 'Singapore'; the state also encompasses around 58 smaller islands, most of which are scattered over the sea to the south in the Straits of Singapore. Singapore is a low-lying island with the capital occupying roughly a third of the total area.

At latitude 1°N, the country lies in the Tropical Humid belt and has an average annual rainfall of around 2,400mm (95 inches). *See* Climate, *pp179 & 180*, for more details.

Until the 1960s, the south of the island around the Singapore River area was the only properly developed urban area in the country, but since that period a steady construction of satellite towns and a corresponding shrinking of the original tropical rainforest have taken place. Today there are very few natural areas left on the island, the Bukit Timah Nature Reserve being a notable exception.

Over the last 40 years Singapore has undertaken a number of land reclamation projects, merging smaller islands into larger ones, creating useful areas for new industry and business. By 2030 Singapore is expected to have grown by at least another 100sq km (39sq miles).

Singapore's economy is based on tourism, trade, finance, shipping and manufacturing.

Gunung Santubong and the Santubong River at Bako National Park

History

Malaysia

38,000 BC	Primitive man inhabits the Niah caves in Sarawak.
8–6,000 BC	The first Orang Asli ('original peoples') arrive from the Andaman Islands.
7th–14th century	Seafarers from the Hindu Kingdom of Srivijaya settle the Malay Archipelago.
1398	The port of Melaka is founded.
1511	Melaka is taken by the Portuguese and becomes the focus of European power in the region.
1641	Melaka falls to the Dutch.
1786	Captain Francis Light lands on Pinang and establishes a settlement.
1824	Britain acquires Melaka.
1826	Melaka, Pinang and Singapore join to form the Straits Settlements.
1840	A young adventurer, James Brooke, helps the Sultan of Brunei crush a rebellion and is awarded control of the province of Sarawak.
1841	James Brooke is installed as Rajah of Sarawak.
1888	Sarawak and North Borneo (Sabah) become British protectorates.
1895	The Federation of Malay States is established.
1914	The Sultan of Johor accepts British protection.
1941	Japan invades Malaya on 8 December.
1948	Attacks on Europeans by the Communist Party of Malaya mark the beginning of a 12-year guerrilla war.
1957	Malaya independence granted on 31 August.
1963	Founding of Federation of Malaysia.
2006	Malaysia abandons a controversial bridge to Singapore after protests.
2008	General elections won by the ruling coalition.
2009	Najib Abdul Razak becomes Malaysia's sixth prime minister.

Singapore

13th century	Sang Nila Utama founds Temasek.
1414	Temasek is annexed to the Sultanate of Melaka.
1511	Singapore is annexed to the State of Johor.
1819	Sir Stamford Raffles persuades the British East India Company to establish a port on Singapore. The Sultan of Johor and Prince Temenggong cede Singapore.
1826	Singapore, Pinang and Melaka join to form the Straits Settlements.
1867	The Straits Settlements become a Crown Colony.
1874	Immigration from South China begins.
1877	Rubber trees are introduced to Singapore; Dunlop invents the pneumatic tyre a year later and plantations spread all over the Archipelago.
1921	Singapore's coastal defences strengthened against Japan's growing military power.
1942	Allied troops retreat and the Battle for Singapore begins. The British surrender on 15 February. Singapore is renamed Syonan-to.
1945	The Japanese surrender to Allied forces on 21 August.
1948	First legislative council elected in Singapore.
1954	Lee Kuan Yew founds the People's Action Party (PAP), seeking independence for Singapore.
1959	Singapore granted self-government. Lee Kuan Yew is the first prime minister.
1963	Founding of Federation of Malaysia, including Singapore.
1965	Singapore becomes a sovereign nation.
1990	Lee Kuan Yew succeeded by Goh Chok Tong.
2004	Lee Hsien Loong becomes Singapore's third prime minister.
2010	Singapore set to host the Youth Olympics.

Politics

Both Malaysia and Singapore are parliamentary democracies. Modern Malaysia, until 2003, was dominated by one person, Dr Mahathir Mohamad. In Singapore, politics in the post-Independence period was, until 1990, dominated by the personality of Lee Kuan Yew, the country's first prime minister. Under both these leaders, the respective countries achieved remarkable economic growth and the foundations were laid for the stable, multiracial societies that exist today.

Malaysia

Like Singapore, Malaysia has gone in for a degree of 'social engineering' to promote racial harmony and a sense of national unity. In the wake of Independence in 1957, the Chinese emerged as the main force in business and commerce in the country, leaving the *bumiputras* (literally, the 'sons of the soil' – native Malays) economically backward, even if they did hold many of the elite positions in government. After a series of bloody race riots in 1969 the government introduced the New Economic Policy, or NEP, a controversial attempt to help Malays 'catch up' and reduce economic disparities by introducing racial quotas in employment. Instead of promoting racial harmony, the NEP was a recipe for corruption and antagonised the rest of the population. It was eventually dropped in 1990. Despite ethnic tensions such as these that still bubble beneath the surface, Malaysia has enjoyed considerable stability and peace.

The ruling party is the United Malays National Organisation (UMNO). In the 2008 general election the party lost its two-thirds majority in parliament for the first time since 1969, leading to the resignation of the prime minister, Abdullah Ahmad Badawi. Najib Abdul Razak, scion of a respected political dynasty, now leads the coalition government and was sworn in as the new prime minister in April 2009.

Prior to the British colonial period, the sultans reigned supreme in their sovereign states, their power unchallenged since they were answerable only to God. Although these powers were somewhat diluted by the British, their sovereignty was eventually guaranteed in the constitution even after Independence. However, in the 1990s the position of the monarchy came under scrutiny following charges of assault on members of the public by the Sultan of Johor. In 1993 Parliament approved a bill to strip royalty of the right to immunity from prosecution that it had enjoyed for centuries.

Singapore

Lee Kuan Yew's party, the People's Action Party (PAP) has provided Singaporeans with a high standard of living, affordable housing (nearly 90 per cent of the population live in apartments built by the Housing and Development Board) and nearly full employment. These achievements have not been won without some cost to civil liberties. For 13 years (from 1968 to 1980) the PAP held every seat in Parliament, and the lack of any credible opposition meant that the government had free rein, effectively stifling criticism and silencing those few politicians who stood out against government policy. A draconian Internal Security Act has been used to imprison supposed radicals without trial. Even today, foreign publications that seek to criticise government policy are censored.

As Singapore became more affluent the government became more paternalistic, embarking on a series of campaigns to mould the nation into a well-behaved society and imposing numerous laws to further this aim. Government propaganda on how to behave, how many children to have, what languages to speak (Mandarin, not Chinese dialects) have all been backed up by lavish media campaigns. Foremost among them was the campaign to create a sense of national identity to prevent ethnic conflicts between the many racial groups in the country.

Lee Hsien Loong, Prime Minister of Singapore

The stranglehold of the PAP on parliament began to decline in the early 1980s, when for the first time an opposition member, JB Jeyaretnam, was elected. In the 1984 elections there was a 13 per cent swing against the PAP, in response to which it began a programme of 'self-renewal', looking to politicians of a younger generation to take over. After 31 years in power, Lee Kuan Yew himself stepped down in 1990 to make way for his chosen successor, Goh Chok Tong.

Under Goh's leadership the style of politics in Singapore shifted slightly, to become more flexible and open to the aspirations of the younger generation. Goh promised more consensus-style government, and greater participation in decision making at the town council level. He even allowed the showing of 'blue movies' (to which Singaporeans flocked in great numbers) to try to counter authoritarian-style government as part of a drive towards artistic creativity – an area in which the country was long lacking.

In 2004, Lee Hsien Loong, son of Lee Kuan Yew, became Singapore's third prime minister and continued Goh's policy of social liberalisation.

Peoples of Malaysia

Wander through any market in Malaysia and you will hear a babel of tongues as traders and customers converse in Chinese, Malay, Tamil and quite likely English as well. The peoples of Malaysia are a highly diverse mix of races and cultures.

The 14 million Malays comprise the majority of the population, although they are by no means a homogeneous group. Malays are sometimes referred to as the *bumiputras*, which means the Sons or Princes of the Soil. As the name implies, the *bumiputras* have traditionally been farmers or fishermen, but just as many now lead an urban life, particularly since Malays dominate in the civil service and government.

The tribal peoples of Sarawak and Sabah are also classed as *bumiputras*, as are the Orang Asli (*see pp38–9*).

There are some 7 million Chinese in the country, the largest group after the Malays. The first Chinese traders set up their warehouses in Melaka around the time of Admiral Cheng Ho's visit in the 15th century, but the majority arrived during the 19th century. Escaping hard times in China, people from the southern provinces (principally Hokkiens, Hakkas, Teochews,

Malay women, Kota Bharu

Member of a Borneo tribe

Cantonese and Hainanese) came seeking their fortunes. The Chinese constitute the majority of Malaysia's traders, merchants and industrialists.

Like the Chinese, the Indians had been coming to Malaysia for centuries, but it was not until the 19th century that they arrived in significant numbers. Most came to work on the plantations, and the majority were from southern India. Malaysian Indians mostly live on the west coast.

With over 30 different ethnic groups in Sarawak and Sabah (including Malays and Chinese), the picture is far more complex. In Sarawak, the largest group are the Iban, who number more than half a million. Although they live inland, Europeans named them 'sea dyaks' because of their frequent forays downriver to raid coastal areas. The Bidayuh, who built their houses on steep hillsides, became known as 'land dyaks'. Other tribes include the Melanau and the Orang Ulu ('up-river dwellers'), which includes the Penan, Kayan, Kenyah, Kelabit and Lun Bawan peoples.

In Sabah, the population comprises approximately 30 different ethnic groups and races, with the major indigenous peoples consisting of the Kadazan/Dusuns, the Bajau and the Murut (*see pp84–5*).

Culture

For centuries traders, immigrants and conquerors from all over the world have passed through Malaysia and Singapore, bringing with them their traditions, religions and lifestyles. The people of the region learned to change and adapt to new ways, and to live in tolerance with other races and creeds. Nowhere is this more obvious than in streets such as Jalan Tokong in Melaka, Telok Ayer Street in Singapore or Jalan Masjid Kapitan Kling in Georgetown, Pinang, in all of which you can find Taoist temples next to Islamic mosques and Hindu shrines.

Malaysia

Malaysia is a multicultural democracy, but Islam is the state religion. Malays were first converted to Islam by itinerant Arab and South Indian merchants and sailors, from the 9th century onwards, with Melaka becoming an Islamic Sultanate in 1400. As well as Malay Muslims, there are smaller numbers of Tamil, Arab and Chinese Muslims in Malaysia. Just over 60 per cent of the population of Malaysia is Muslim, amounting to around 16 million people.

Malaysian Muslims are expected to pray five times a day either at home, at work or in the *surau* – the village mosque, centre of Malay neighbourhoods. The most important event in the Islamic calendar is the month of Ramadan, during which Muslims fast from sunrise to sunset every day. At the conclusion of Ramadan, the festival of Hari Raya Puasa is a whirl of socialising and feasting.

Buddhists total around 19 per cent of the population in Malaysia, or just over five million, and are overwhelmingly Chinese.

Hinduism might once have been a Malay religion, but today its adherents are almost exclusively migrants from the Indian subcontinent, mainly from Tamil Nadu and Kerala, who have been resident in Malaysia from colonial times. The majority of the Indians in Malaysia are Hindus, and, at approximately 6 per cent of the population or just over 1.6 million people, Hinduism is Malaysia's fourth religion, after Islam, Buddhism and Christianity.

The Malaysian powers that be make a vital distinction between *bumiputra* or 'sons of the soil' and migrant peoples, even though the latter might have been established in the country for centuries. Nevertheless, the country is proud of its multi-ethnic make-up and promotes itself as 'truly Asia' because of this varied and rich cultural legacy.

The gate and minaret of the State Mosque in Kota Bharu

Singapore

Buddhism is the major religion of Singapore, with more than 40 per cent of the population, or about 1,800,000 people, professing some sort of adherence to Buddhism, usually in conjunction with Taoism, Confucianism or ancestor worship. The majority of these adherents are Chinese.

In Singapore the Chinese population contributes a wealth of festivals to the local lifestyles, the biggest one being the Chinese New Year in February. Chinese temples often combine different shrines to different gods, much as Chinese philosophy is a blend of Confucianism, Taoism and Buddhism. It is just as common to see young office workers throwing fortune sticks to divine the future as it is to see the older generation offering joss sticks, fruit and flowers to the temple gods. Luck or 'joss' is an important part of everyday life, as is ancestor worship.

In Singapore, Hindus number about 180,000 people or 4 per cent of the population, and as in Malaysia most settlers originated from South India and Sri Lanka during colonial times.

The percentage of Muslims is much lower than that found in Malaysia, amounting to about 14 per cent of the population, or 630,000 people.

CULTURAL ENCOUNTERS

Malaysia

Culture shock is likely to hit you if you arrive in Kuala Lumpur and immediately set out to see the sights, only to find yourself overwhelmed by noise and vehicle fumes from the rush-hour traffic.

Allow time to recover from jet lag – spending the first day beside a hotel swimming pool is always a good remedy – and only set out to explore when you feel full of energy again.

English is spoken in Malaysia in most of the tourist destinations, but less so outside the resorts and cities, and a few words of Bahasa Malaysia, the national language, can be helpful.

Avoiding offence

The two things most likely to cause offence in Malaysia are pointing at someone or touching them (*see p182*). If you are sitting on the floor, whether inside a house or at a village function, men can sit cross-legged but women should sit sideways, with their feet tucked under them.

Wherever or whatever you are eating, the most important thing to remember is never to handle food or eat with your left hand – or worse still, offer someone food with your left hand. Food is always eaten with the right hand (the left hand is 'unclean' since it is normally used for personal ablutions).

Chinese worshippers, Cheng Hoon Teng Temple, Melaka

What to wear

Malaysia is hot and humid for most of the year. If you are not used to the heat the best advice is to take it easy and start off by venturing out either in the early mornings or late afternoons, when temperatures are lower. An umbrella is excellent protection against both the fierce tropical sun and the sudden downpours that occur even in the so-called dry season. If you haven't brought one with you, cheap folding umbrellas can be bought in most of the larger towns and cities.

Hospitality

Malaysians of all ethnic backgrounds are very hospitable people, though it's fair to say that rural Malaysians are more welcoming than city dwellers, many of whom live busy lives commuting to work from anonymous, if comfortable, high-rise buildings. In the country especially, and in smaller towns, the Malays are quite likely to invite you into their homes, and if you show yourself to be friendly and interested, it's not at all unusual to be invited to share a meal. The same is true for Malaysian Indians – though the Malaysian Chinese, business people at heart, take a little longer to 'warm up'.

Greetings

Hand-shaking is normal when you are being introduced in Malaysia, although Malay men customarily do not shake hands with women, but instead bow respectfully. Nowadays, women do tend to shake hands more, but if you are introduced to a Malaysian woman it is best to watch her behaviour first and take your cue from that. If she clasps her hands in front of her, stick to a bow.

A man about to play *sepak bulu ayam*, a traditional Malay game, in rural Kelantan

Hassles

On the whole, Malaysia is a safe country for tourists and you are unlikely to encounter many problems, provided you take normal, common-sense precautions. Bag-snatches by thieves on motorbikes have been

Chinese god at a street shrine, Singapore

reported in Kuala Lumpur, but it is fairly unusual. The most harassment you are likely to encounter is from an overly persistent salesman. There are very few beggars in Malaysia. Foreign females may provoke verbal harassment from Malay youths (particularly in beach-resort areas), but violence is rare.

Temples and mosques

Dress politely when entering mosques or temples. Women should cover their arms and heads and avoid wearing short dresses. For men, too, shorts and T-shirts show a lack of respect, and should be avoided. Shoes should be removed when entering sacred precincts – basically, take your shoes off whenever you see the locals have done so.

Singapore

Singapore is an easy destination for the first-time visitor to Asia, with good transport links, telephones and other services that work, and a range of accommodation to suit all pockets. English is the only widely spoken western language in Singapore.

Nobody is likely to suffer culture shock on landing in Singapore unless, of course, you have been travelling elsewhere in Asia and are not prepared for a futuristic city with a first-class infrastructure, well-planned, tree-lined streets and the almost total absence of crime and litter.

This pleasant environment has not been achieved without Singaporeans – and visitors – being subjected to a barrage of laws concerning litter and public behaviour (*see* Etiquette, *p182*) of which you should be aware.

What to wear

Singapore is hot and especially humid almost the whole year. As with Malaysia, if you are not used to the heat the best advice is to take things slowly to begin with and start off by venturing outside either in the early mornings or late afternoons, when temperatures are lower. An umbrella is excellent protection against both the fierce tropical sun and the sudden downpours that occur in the city at almost any time. If you haven't brought one with you, umbrellas can be bought in almost any shopping mall.

It's tempting to keep hopping into air-conditioned restaurants or shopping malls to cool off when you find yourself flagging, but be warned that the constant change of temperature is likely to give you a cold.

Hospitality

Singapore is an urban society where the great majority of the population, of all classes and ethnic backgrounds, lives in high-rise apartments or shop houses. This means that the visitor is unlikely to be invited into private homes, at least on first acquaintance. Singaporean people also tend to be rather reserved at first, and may give the appearance of being rather aloof – perhaps more like the British than any other people in Southeast Asia. On further acquaintance, however, they can be most charming and hospitable; it's just a question of giving them time and getting to know them.

Greetings

Hand-shaking is normal amongst all ethnic communities in Singapore when you are being introduced.

Temples and mosques

As with Malaysia, dress politely when entering a mosque or Hindu temple; shoes should usually be removed. Chinese temples are less rigorous and shoes can be left on.

Serangoon Road in Little India lit up for the Deepavali (Diwali) Festival

The Straits Chinese

In the ethnic melting pot of the old Straits Settlements, one of the most unusual cultural minorities to evolve were the Straits-born Chinese, or Peranakans ('local born'). Their origins date back to the early Chinese traders and settlers who intermarried with local Malay women (particularly from the west coast around Melaka), creating a new generation with their own unique heritage.

Peranakan men are referred to as Babas, unmarried women as Nyonyas, and older, married women as Bibis (as a group, they are also known as 'Baba Nyonyas'). Over the centuries the Peranakans prospered, creating their wealth in timber, tin, spices and, later on, rubber plantations. They evolved a luxurious lifestyle that flourished as a result of combining gracious Malay pastimes with Chinese business acumen. They speak their own dialect of Malay, with the addition of many Chinese colloquialisms, and developed their own style of cooking, which relied on unusual mixtures of piquant spices, coconut milk and *belacan* (dried shrimp paste).

The Peranakans are renowned for their taste in porcelain, which used to be specially commissioned from China. Known as Nyonyaware, it is characterised by bright colours and exuberant decorative motifs. Special sets of blue-and-white ceramics were also ordered for use during times of mourning and ancestral worship. Intricate beadwork and delicate, filigree silverware are also Peranakan hallmarks.

Peranakan culture was at its height during the colonial era, from the mid-19th century onwards. Not only did they show tremendous loyalty to the British Crown (to the extent that they were also known at one time as 'the King's Chinese'), but they also emulated the British lifestyle and adopted European clothing.

The Peranakan houses that exist today give a fascinating glimpse into this unique fusion of cultures and lifestyles. Intricate Qing-dynasty tables and chairs, inlaid with mother-of-pearl, sit side-by-side with massive English-style sideboards and cupboards laden with crystal and the finest old brandies. Colonial 'planter's chairs', with their wicker seats and foot-rest extensions, share space with the ancestral altar covered in dragon carvings. Roll-top desks and pedestal-type telephones coexist with embroidered Chinese wall-hangings and mah-jong tables. The houses themselves (which were built in a style known variously as Chinese palladian or Chinese baroque) are a riot of intricately carved screens and doors overlaid with gold leaf.

Straits Chinese-Peranakan architecture, Jalan Kampung Pantai, Melaka

FESTIVALS

Malaysia

Like Singapore, Malaysia's festivals reflect its multiracial population, and the Hindu, Chinese and Muslim events similarly change dates according to the lunar calendar.

Mid-January

Ponggal This spring harvest festival marks the end of the monsoon season in India. In the early morning, a dish of *ponggal* (newly harvested rice with milk, nuts, peas and raisins) is cooked in a new pot and allowed to boil over, symbolising plenty and prosperity. Later on, rice, vegetables, sugar cane and spices are offered to the gods to the accompaniment of prayers and music in Hindu temples.

January/February

Chinese New Year The start of the Chinese lunar New Year is celebrated with colourful processions and lion dances. Unlike Singapore, firecrackers are not banned in Malaysia so you can expect it to be particularly noisy. The best places to watch all the festivities that take place are the Chinatowns of Kuala Lumpur and Pulau Pinang.

Thaipusam In Kuala Lumpur, this Hindu festival is celebrated wth a procession that culminates in spectacular fashion at the Batu Caves (13km/8 miles north of Kuala Lumpur), where devotees scale the 272 steps to the temple with their *kavadis*. Special trains and buses are laid on at this time. In Pinang, the procession starts at the Sri Mariamman Temple (entrance on Lebuh Queen) and finishes at the Nattukotai Temple on Waterfall Road.

March and September

Monkey God Festival (*See p24.*)

March/April

Ramadan The ninth month of the Islamic calendar is marked by strict fasting by Muslims from sunrise to sunset. Street-stalls selling Malay cakes and other delicacies are set up outside mosques ready for the breaking of the daily fast at nightfall.

April

Hari Raya Puasa This festival heralds the end of the fasting month of Ramadan. For several days in advance, homes are decorated and special cakes and sweetmeats prepared. On the day itself, Muslims put on their best finery and visit relatives and friends.

Easter Most notably celebrated in Melaka, with a candlelit procession to St Peter's Church.

May

Wesak Day A one-day celebration of Lord Buddha's birth, enlightenment and death, best seen in Buddhist temples in Pinang and Melaka.

Kadazan Harvest Festival
A thanksgiving festival at the end of the rice harvest celebrated by Kadazan farmers in Sabah, with feasting, buffalo races and other events.

Malaysia International Kite Festival Local and international competitors take part in this championship with their colourful *wau* (kites) at Tumpat, near Kota Bharu.

May/June

Gawai Festival Traditional *dyak* celebrations to mark the rice harvest in Sarawak. Dances, cockfights, blow-pipe competitions and much feasting and rice-wine drinking.

Dragon Boat Festival Commemorates the death of Chinese poet and statesman Qu Yuan, who committed suicide by throwing himself into the river as a protest against political corruption in his day. Legend has it that fishermen tried to save him by thrashing the water with their paddles and beating drums and gongs to prevent the fish from eating his body.

The event is now celebrated with longboat races, with the oarsmen urged on by drummers sitting in the bows. Longboats adorned with dragons' heads race through the waters around Pulau Pinang.

June/July

Kelantan International Drum Festival Another rice-harvest festival, celebrated in Kota Bharu, Kelantan with percussion competitions on the giant Kelantan drums, *rebana ubi.*

June

Birthday of HM The Yang Di Pertuan Agong Cultural shows planned weeks ahead and traditional games in Kuala Lumpur mark the birthday of the reigning Sultan.

August/September

National Day Celebrations Public holiday with parades, entertainments and stage shows to mark the gaining of Independence in 1957. Kuala Lumpur hosts the most events.

Sungai Sarawak Regatta Longboats and dragon boats compete on the river amid various celebrations in September on the Sarawak River, Sarawak.

October/November

Deepavali A national holiday to celebrate the Hindu Festival of Lights. (*See p25.*)

November/December

Kota Belud Tamu Besar Annual market festival at Kota Belud in Sabah (*see p87*). Held at the end of November, it attracts around 10,000 people who come to watch the buffalo races and competitions of horsemanship by the famed Bajau horsemen. There are also dances and cultural shows by ethnic groups (in ceremonial costumes) from all over Sabah, including the Irranuns, Dusun and Tindal from the south, the Tempasuk Dusun, the Dusun Tabiluing from the north, and Bajaus and Ubians.

December

Pesta Pulau Pinang Annual event on Pulau Pinang featuring carnivals, trade fairs and cultural and sporting activities.

Christmas (*25 Dec*) Though not as colourfully celebrated as in Singapore, Christmas is a public holiday in Malaysia.

Singapore

Given the diversity of ethnic and religious groups that make up the population of Singapore it is not surprising that there is a constant stream of festivals throughout the year. Some of these are on fixed dates, but many events celebrated by the Chinese, Hindu and Malay communities are calculated according to the lunar calendar, which changes from year to year, and it is difficult therefore to give exact dates. The most reliable source of information on specific dates and locations is the annual *Calendar of Festivals & Events* produced by the Singapore Tourist Promotion Board.

Mid-January

Ponggal The best place to watch the festivities is the Sri Sreenivasa Perumal Temple on Serangoon Road. (*See p115.*)

January/February

Chinese New Year The start of the lunar year is the most important festival of the calendar for the Chinese. Houses and shops are decorated with lights and banners (particularly along New Bridge Road and Eu Tong Sen Street) and stores sell mandarin and plum trees, both of which are considered lucky.

Traditionally, Chinese New Year is as noisy as possible, with masses of firecrackers being set off to frighten away evil spirits. Unfortunately, stray fireworks sometimes burned down a number of houses and this practice has now been banned by the government. However, plenty of noisy drum- and gong-bashing accompanies the dragon and lion dances.

Thaipusam Festival One of the most intensely dramatic Hindu festivals (*see pp26–7*). The procession starts at the Sri Perumal Temple in Serangoon Road and ends up at the Chettiar Temple in Tank Road. Procession times and route maps are published in the daily papers.

February

Chingay Procession This spectacular procession marks the end of the Chinese New Year festivities and is held on the first or the second Sunday after Chinese New Year's Day. The word *chingay* refers to the Chinese-style decorated floats that are paraded along Orchard Road.

March and September

Monkey God Festival The birthday of the Monkey God is celebrated twice a year at the Monkey God Temple in Seng Poh Road (opposite Tiong Bahru market). Mediums carry sedan chairs shoulder high, which rock and jerk if possessed by the spirit of the Monkey God. They then go into a trance and pierce their cheeks and tongues, using the blood to write special charms, which are distributed to devotees.

March/April

Ramadan (*See p22.*)

Qing Ming Chinese visit the graves of their ancestors to make offerings.

April

Hari Raya Puasa In Singapore the best place to experience Hari Raya Puasa is in and around Geylang Serai (*MRT: Paya Lebar*), where the streets are draped in festive lights for several days. (*See p22.*)

May

Vesak Day Celebration of Lord Buddha's birth, enlightenment and death, with chanting and prayers in the temples, the release of caged birds (to symbolise the freeing of the soul), and candlelit processions to mark the end of the day. The festival is celebrated in every Buddhist temple.

June

Dragon Boat Festival The Singapore event attracts top teams from all over the world. (*See p23.*)

Singapore Festival of the Arts Southeast Asia's biggest arts festival, held biennially, with performances of drama, music, arts and dance by participants from all over the world. At the same time there is a fringe festival featuring international and local talent. See the daily newspapers for details.

July/August

Festival of Hungry Ghosts Chinese festival marked by performances of *wayangs* (Chinese operas) and processions of floats.

September/October

Navarathiri Festival Hindu festival of the 'Nine Nights', dedicated to the goddesses Durga, Lakshmi and Saraswathi. Set in three cycles, the festival honours each goddess in turn, finishing up with a procession at the Chettiar Temple in Tank Road. Nightly performances of traditional dance and music take place at the Sri Mariamman Temple (South Bridge Road) and the Chettiar Temple (Tank Road).

October/November

Deepavali The 'festival of lights', during which small oil lamps are lit in temples and homes to symbolise the triumph of good over evil. Temples and streets in Little India are festooned with lights and garlands.

Festival of the Nine Emperor Gods Nine days of ceremonies and Chinese opera to honour the nine Sons of the Queen of Heaven.

Thimithi Festival Annual fire-walking ceremony, held in honour of the Hindu goddess Draupadi at the Sri Mariamman Temple. (*See p109.*)

25 December

Christmas The lighting up of Orchard Road for Christmas begins in November, when department stores and hotels compete for the most glittering and spectacular displays on the fronts of their buildings.

Thaipusam Festival

Shivering from fear as much as from the early morning cold, a young boy in thin yellow robes slides into a trance as a Hindu priest fans incense smoke across his face. The chanting in the temple changes to a higher pitch and the ringing of bells in the background becomes more insistent. The boy's body arches backwards as the trance takes hold, his eyes are tightly shut. A helper chants loudly into one ear while another steps forward and thrusts the *vel*, a 15cm (6-inch) long steel needle, through one cheek near the corner of his mouth, and then out through the other. The boy

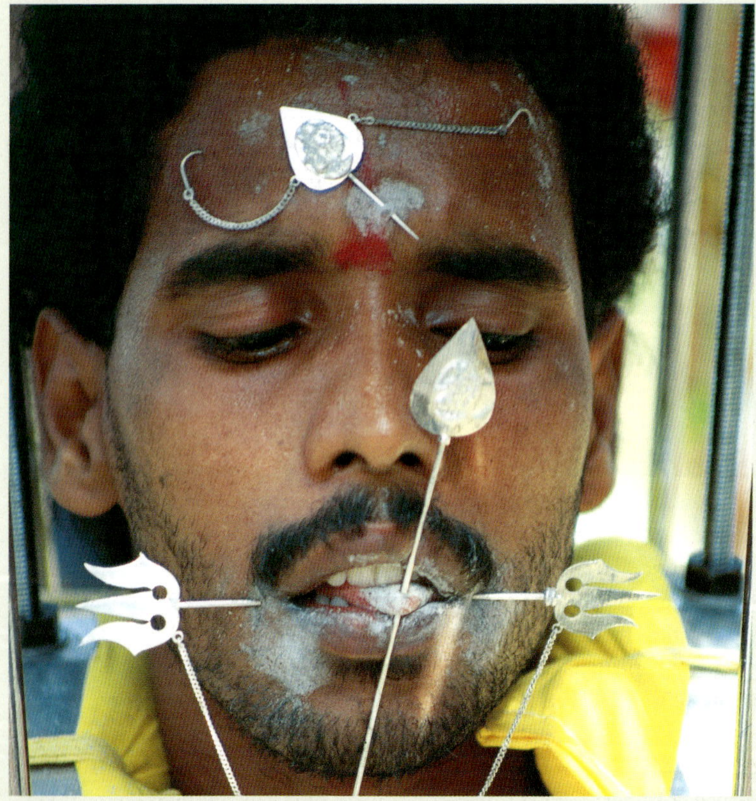

Devotees pierce their faces with the *vel*

pushes his tongue underneath the silver rod, and another is stuck through his tongue vertically.

With the chanting, the incense, the bells, the crowds, the brief cries as metal enters flesh or the sharp intake of breath as another hook goes in, the atmosphere in the temple is highly charged. It is a spell-binding and very intense experience for the onlookers; tourists' popping flashlights are totally ignored among the general mayhem.

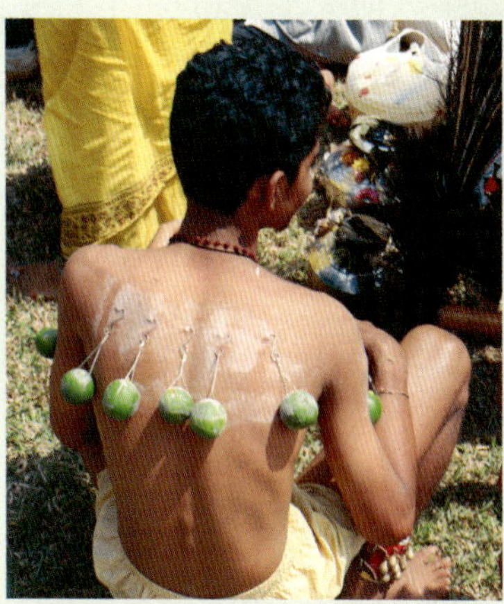

Devout Hindus also carry hooks on their backs

Outside the temple the sky is still dark: it is 6am on the second morning of the annual Thaipusam Festival. All through the first day of the festival a huge silver chariot containing the image of Lord Subramanya, drawn by white bullocks, parades through the streets. Thousands of coconuts are smashed in its path so that the wheels may pass over rivers of coconut milk, 'the purest water in the world'.

On the second day, hundreds of devout Hindus undergo ordeals such as piercing their cheeks with the *vel*, or slinging hooks into the skin of their backs and chests, hanging silver or gold chains or fresh limes from the hooks to weigh them down. Others opt to carry the *kavadi*, a heavy metal frame decorated with flowers and peacock feathers.

Hindu legend says that Lord Shiva gave Lord Mariamman the *vel*, the steel rod that pierces the flesh, in order that he might have knowledge. The devotees who take part are fulfilling a vow they made some time during the previous year – that a loved one should recover from illness, that they be blessed with children, or gain a good job.

When the devotees are ready they circle the temple and then set off through the streets – some even pulling chariots behind them, attached to the hook sunk into their backs. When the temple is reached, the priests bestow blessings and smear sacred ash upon the wounds of the devotees; as their burdens are removed and the trance subsides they claim to have felt no pain – and there are no scars.

Banned in India, Thaipusam still takes place in Singapore, Kuala Lumpur and Georgetown.

Impressions

Malaysia and Singapore are both easy destinations for first-time visitors to Asia, with good transport links, telephones and other services that work, and a range of accommodation to suit all pockets. English is the only widely spoken western language in Singapore and in the tourist destinations in Malaysia (outside the resorts and cities a few words of Bahasa Malaysia, the national language, can be helpful).

EXPLORING MALAYSIA

Kuala Lumpur

Usually referred to as simply 'KL', Kuala Lumpur is a sprawling city with a confusing street plan. From the visitor's point of view it can be roughly divided into two or three parts. Most of the international-class hotels are scattered over the eastern half of the city, with a cluster centred around Jalan Sultan Ismail. The majority of the cultural sights and tourist attractions are in the downtown area, some distance away. On the eastern side of the Klang River is Chinatown and the Central Market, while many of the city's historic buildings are on the western side of the river.

The west coast

For centuries the west coast has been the centre of commerce in Malaysia, and this has given it some of the peninsula's most intriguing historical towns and cultural sights. A popular excursion from Kuala Lumpur is to the port of Melaka on the southwest coast. Most of the country's top beach hotels are on the west-coast islands, the best known of which is Pulau Pinang. To the north of Pinang is Pulau Langkawi and, further to the south, Pulau Pangkor, both of which are quieter and more unspoiled than Pinang.

Hill resorts in the Highlands

The mountains of the Central Highlands are visible to the north of Kuala Lumpur on a clear day, beckoning those intent on exploring the wilderness. The 'hill stations' of the highlands were established in colonial times so that Europeans could benefit from the cooler climate of the mountains, and they are still popular with both visitors and locals as a cool retreat from the heat of the plains and the coast. It is a good idea to hire a car if you want to visit several of the hill resorts or explore once you are there.

The east coast

Malaysia's east coast is less developed and more traditional in character than the west coast. Here you will find miles and miles of sandy beaches linking numerous fishing villages and coconut groves. Offshore there are a number of small-scale, laid-back resorts on a string of islands which are accessible by ferries from the mainland. There is one main highway down the east coast and driving is easy, with very little traffic compared to the west coast.

Eastern Malaysia

Just over an hour's flight across the South China Sea, East Malaysia (comprising Sarawak and Sabah) is more of a challenge for the independent traveller, although package tours are available for those who don't feel confident enough to tackle it on their own. Although travel is more difficult, tourism is a fast-growing industry and there are plenty of first-rate hotels. Travelling costs are generally higher than on the peninsula.

EXPLORING SINGAPORE

City centre

The city of Singapore overlooks the Straits of Singapore on the southern side of the island. It is divided by the Singapore River. To the south of the river is the bustling area of Chinatown and the financial district.

Immediately to the north of the river is the colonial heart of Singapore, with many imposing buildings from that era centred around a large open space known as the Padang. Beyond is Raffles City, overshadowing the venerable Raffles Hotel. Continue northwards and you will reach Little India and Arab Street. Turn left and you will come to the start of Singapore's Golden Mile, the ever-open shopping malls and numerous luxury hotels centred on Orchard Road and Scotts Road.

Around the island

The majority of Singapore's residents live outside the city centre in satellite dormitory towns such as Queenstown, Kallang, Toa Payoh and Jurong. Most of Singapore's manufacturing industries are on the north coast. Many of the large theme parks, wildlife parks and similar attractions are outside the city centre to the west, in areas such as Jurong, but with comfortable, regular and cheap public transport, nowhere on the island is hard to reach. Remnants of the island's natural heritage can still be found outside the city centre. The last patch of the primary rainforest that once covered the island surrounds the highest hill, Bukit Timah.

The Kuching waterfront in Sarawak

Malaysia

Since independence from Britain in 1957, Malaysia has seen a steady, continuous rise in its fortunes. There have been one or two bumps along the road, notably confrontation with Indonesia in the early 1960s, and serious racial riots in 1969, but generally Malaysia has seen a remarkable rise in prosperity and, for many years, regular double-digit economic growth. Today's Malaysia, a patchwork of ethnic groups, is generally well educated, harmonious and go-ahead.

KUALA LUMPUR

The federal capital of Malaysia, Kuala Lumpur is a cosmopolitan city with facilities (such as deluxe hotels) to match, but it is also a city of great character with a multiracial population and an interesting mix of architectural styles, from colonial British to contemporary Islamic.

Founded in 1857 as a trading post for miners, Kuala Lumpur (roughly translated as 'muddy estuary') has grown rapidly to achieve its present status and is still expanding – although now progress is skywards. The modern high-rise buildings contrast sharply with the jumble of temples, markets and crowded streets at ground level. Now bisected by fast-moving freeways, Kuala Lumpur began as a cluster of makeshift buildings at the confluence of the Klang and Gombak rivers. The early Chinese traders found they could pole no further upriver than this point, and so established a settlement to supply the tin mines at nearby Ampang. In the first few months 70 of the original party of 87 had died of fever, but the population of Kuala Lumpur grew rapidly as more tin deposits were discovered.

The outpost developed into a boom town where gang wars, brawls and epidemics were a normal part of the pioneers' lives. The Sultan of Selangor, Abdul Samad, put the settlement under the control of Yap Ah Loy, the *Kapitan China* (Chinese headman), but it progressed little beyond a squalid shanty town.

The major change came when Frank Swettenham, the British Resident in Selangor, moved his administration to Kuala Lumpur and rebuilt it from scratch, pulling down the wooden huts and replacing them with stone and brick structures.

In 1886 a railway line was constructed to connect Kuala Lumpur to the port of Klang, and in 1896 it became the capital of the Federated States.

Wealth started to flood in from tin revenues, and the new tin millionaires

built themselves impressive mansions along Jalan Ampang. Development proceeded rapidly and the population grew – augmented by many thousands of Indians who arrived at the beginning of the 20th century to work as labourers on the rubber plantations. In 1957, after Independence, the city soon established its pre-eminent role as the business and commercial capital of Malaysia.

Getting around the city is not hard, particularly in the downtown areas, where most of the sights are within walking distance of each other. Keep in mind that a number of places may be closed on a Friday and check timings. Make sure you protect yourself from the sun and try to avoid the morning and evening rush hours, when the congestion and belching fumes make walking unpleasant. For travelling to and from your hotel, or for journeys elsewhere in the city, taxis are the best bet and are inexpensive.

Kuala Lumpur is not a city to be rushed through, so allow plenty of time.

Central Market and Central Square

Sited on the banks of the Klang River, the Central Market is one of the focal points of downtown Kuala Lumpur. Built in 1936, this handsome Art Deco building was originally a produce market until it was converted in 1984. It is now a 'festival hall' with craft shops, restaurants and cultural performances and Kuala Lumpur's main outlet for craftspeople, painters and musicians. Surrounded by pedestrianised areas, it offers a pleasant retreat from city traffic and is a good place to while away an hour or two browsing among the stalls, listening to the buskers or watching outdoor performances in the evenings. (*See p126 for more details.*) Next door is Central Square, a colourfully decorated building housing more shops, restaurants and a multi-screen cinema.

Jalan Hang Kasturi.
Tel: (03) 2274 6542.
www.centralmarket.com.my.
Open: daily 10am–10pm.
KLRT: Central Market.

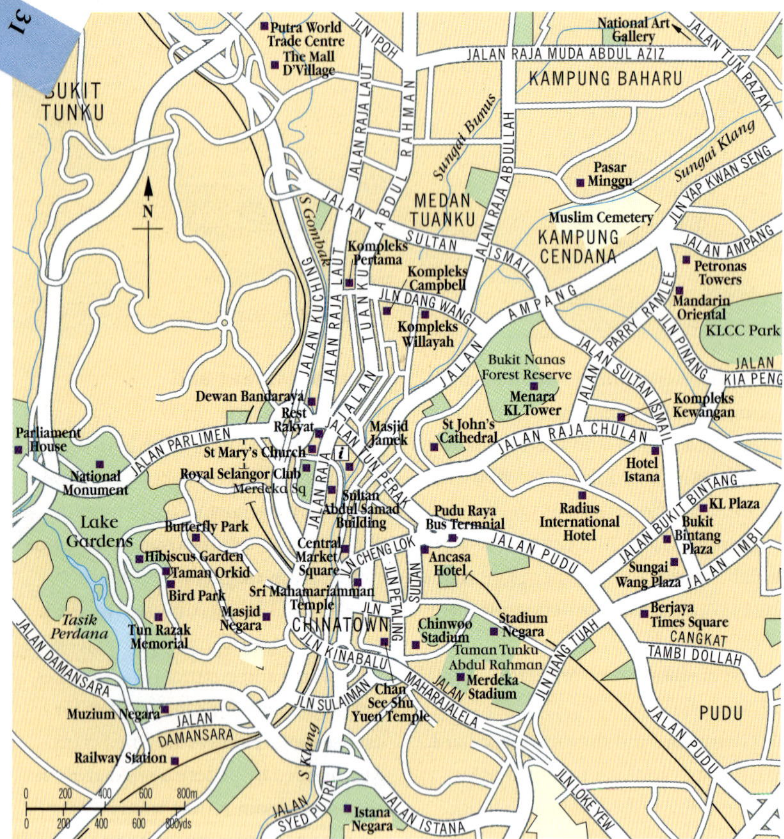

Chan See Shu Yuen Temple

This typical Chinatown clan-house and temple, built in 1906, is embellished with ornate ceramic friezes and sculptures, with wall paintings and woodcarvings inside.

172 Jalan Petaling. Open: daily. KLRT: Pasar Seni.

Chinatown

You really need to visit the bustling streets of Chinatown twice. During the day you can wander around and peer into old shop-houses where sign-painters, shoe-repairers and basket-makers carry on in time-honoured fashion. Chinatown then has to be seen by night, when the central area around Jalan Petaling is transformed into a *pasar malam* (night market), with stalls selling everything from hot chestnuts to calculators. (*Also see p128 & p135.*) *KLRT: Maharajalela.*

Jalan Ampang

Many of the grandiose mansions of the early tin magnates still survive, although few are private homes any more. Most have been taken over by foreign embassies and consulates (Jalan Ampang is also known as Ambassador's Row), while others have been converted to different uses, such as Tunku Abdul Rahman Hall, which is now the Malaysia Tourism Centre.

Lake Gardens

The Lake Gardens is the only significant swathe of greenery in Kuala Lumpur. The 90-hectare (222-acre) park, built around an artificial lake, is popular with joggers, picnickers and local families at weekends. On weekdays it is less crowded.

Set on a hilltop, the well-landscaped **Orchid Garden** (Taman Orkid) displays around 800 species of orchid, while the neighbouring **Hibiscus Garden** (Taman Bunga Raya) boasts around 500 rare and exotic blooms laid out along shaded walkways and beside cooling fountains.

Just down the hillside is the **Bird Park** (Taman Burung), where a large enclosure houses tropical species within a landscape of trees, flowering shrubs and miniature waterfalls. It houses many species of hornbill, and is steadily expanding.

The newest addition to the Lake Gardens area is the **Butterfly Park** (Taman Rama Rama), with around 150 species of butterfly housed in an environment designed to resemble the Malaysian rainforest. There are also displays of giant frogs, stick insects, millipedes and other exotica.

Across Jalan Parlimen is the massive **National Monument**, sculpted by Felix de Weldon (creator of the Iwo Jima monument in Washington, DC), which commemorates the Malay and Commonwealth forces who died fighting the Communist insurgents during the 12-year Emergency.

Also within the Lake Gardens are **Parliament House**, an 18-storey building, and the **Tun Razak Memorial**, which together house a large collection of the personal memorabilia of Malaysia's second prime minister.

Orchid Garden and Hibiscus Garden. Open: daily 9am–6pm. Free admission.
Bird Park. Open: daily 9am–7pm. Admission charge.
Butterfly Park. Open: weekdays 9am–5pm, weekends & public holidays 9am–6pm. Admission charge (extra for cameras and videos).
Tun Razak Memorial. Open: Tue–Sun & public holidays 9am–6pm. Closed: Mon; Fri noon–3pm. Free admission.
KLRT: Stesen Sentral.

Masjid Jamek

Surrounded by palm trees on a triangular spit of land at the confluence of the Klang and Gombak rivers, the Masjid Jamek lies on the site where the city of Kuala Lumpur began. Built in 1909 in classic Arabian-Moorish style, this beautiful mosque has a triple-

domed prayer hall and is surmounted by elegant minarets.
Entrance on Jalan Tun Perak. Open: daily 8.30am–12.20pm & 2.30–4pm (Fri closed 11am–2.30pm). Visitors must be suitably attired. KLRT: Masjid Jamek.

Masjid Negara (National Mosque)

Built in the 1960s, the National Mosque is one of the largest in Asia and can accommodate up to 8,000 worshippers at any one time. The main dome is in the form of an 18-point star, and within the grounds are a further 48 smaller domes and a towering, 73m (240ft) high minaret.
Jalan Sultan Hishamuddin. Open: daily 9am–noon, 3–4pm & 5.30–6.30pm (Fri closed 2.45–6.30pm). Visitors must be suitably attired. KLRT: Stesen Sentral.

Merdeka Square

Known in colonial times as the Padang, this square was formerly used as playing fields (for tennis, rugby and cricket) by the British, who built the mock-Tudor Royal Selangor Club on the western side. Appropriately, the Padang was the venue for the historic ceremony that took place on 30 August 1957, when Independence was proclaimed and the chapter closed on colonial rule. A round, black marble plaque commemorates the spot where the Union Jack was finally lowered and the Malaysian flag hoisted for the first time. The national flag now flies from a 100m (328ft) high flagpole at one end of the Padang. The square is a venue for concerts and is a popular meeting place for young Malaysians. A shopping complex is located beneath the square.
Jalan Raja. KLRT: Masjid Jamek.

Muzium Negara (National Museum)

Situated between two expressways at the foot of the Lake Gardens, the National Museum was built in 1963 to replace the old Selangor Museum, destroyed during World War II. The exterior draws on various elements of traditional Malay architecture, with the entrance flanked by mosaic murals depicting Malaysian culture and history. Inside, various displays focus on the history of Kuala Lumpur, the rubber and tin-mining industries, Malay arts and crafts and the flora and fauna of Southeast Asia. Other exhibits document Orang Asli traditions, Peranakan culture, and life at the royal courts of the Malay sultanates. The presentation is rather dated and static, but it will give you a good overview of Malaysia's culture and peoples.
Jalan Damansara/Jalan Travers (located 1km/⅔ mile from the railway station). Tel: (03) 2282 6255. www.museum.gov.my. Open: daily 9am–6pm. Admission charge. KLRT: Stesen Sentral.

National Art Gallery

Houses a permanent collection and exhibition of local and foreign art.
Jalan Temerloh, off Jalan Tun Razak. Tel: (03) 4025 4990.

www.artgallery.gov.my. Open: daily 10am–6pm. Free admission. KLRT: Titiwangsa.

Petronas Towers

The twin, 88-storey Petronas Towers constituted the world's tallest building until Taiwan's Taipei 101 edged a bit higher. Visitors can take a free ride to the viewing platform between the 41st and 42nd levels, but places are limited, and there is often a queue from 8.30am. The best exterior, close-up views of the towers are from the attractively landscaped KLCC Park immediately in front. It is difficult not to be impressed by the stainless steel and glass façade, designed to resemble motifs found in Islamic art.

KLCC, Jalan Ampang. Tel: (03) 2331 1769. www.malaysiasite.nl/twinseng.htm. Open: Tue–Sun 9am–5pm. Closed: Mon, Fri 1–2.30pm. KLRT: KLCC.

Railway station

Looking more like a mosque than a train terminus, the railway station is a riot of Moorish architecture with scalloped eaves, keyhole arches, minarets and cupolas. Designed in 1910 by architect AB Hubbock, it replaced the original station of 1885. The Malayan Railway Administration Building opposite the station is designed in a similar, although more restrained, style.

Jalan Sultan Hishamuddin. KLRT: Stesen Sentral.

Sri Mahamariamman Temple

The oldest Hindu temple in Kuala Lumpur, built in 1873, it was originally located on the site of the present railway station and moved to Chinatown in 1885. The temple has the usual decorative *gopuram* (gateway) and the interior features ornate Italian and Spanish ceramic tiles.

163 Jalan Tun HS Lee. KLRT: Pasar Seni.

Sultan Abdul Samad Building

Facing Merdeka Square, the Sultan Abdul Samad Building, with its 4m (13ft) high clock tower, is one of Kuala Lumpur's most prominent and most photographed landmarks. The Moorish-style building, completed in 1897, was originally the home of the State Secretariat. It now houses the Supreme Court and the High Courts. The courts are not open to the public, although permission can be obtained by writing in advance to the judiciary department.

Jalan Raja Laut. KLRT: Masjid Jamek.

A Malay family visiting Merdeka Square, Kuala Lumpur

Peninsular Malaysia

AROUND KUALA LUMPUR

Batu Caves

These gigantic caverns were first discovered in 1878. The main cavern is the vast Cathedral Cave, where shafts of sunlight filter through holes in the ceiling some 100m (328ft) above. In 1891, the local Hindu community erected a shrine to Lord Subramaniam inside. The best time to visit is during the annual Thaipusam Festival (*see pp26–7*). At the bottom of the hill there is a small museum of Hindu deities.

13km (8 miles) north of Kuala Lumpur, on the Ipoh Road. Open: daily 7am–9pm. Free admission. Minibus 11 or Len Sen bus 69 or 70 from Kuala Lumpur.

Orang Asli Museum

Set up in 1987 to preserve the heritage of Malaysia's Orang Asli (*see pp38–9*), this museum has exhibits ranging from jewellery to hunting equipment.

Kilometre 24, Jalan Pahang, Gombak. Tel: (03) 6189 2113. Open: Sat–Thur 9am–5pm. Closed: Fri. Check at weekends & holidays. Free admission. Bus: 174.

Templer's Park

This beautiful forest reserve offers both visitors and residents a wonderful escape from the busy city. The park, named after the last British high commissioner, contains an array of jungle ferns, trees and plants along with a number of refreshing waterfalls.

22km (14 miles) north of Kuala Lumpur on Highway 1. Tel: (03) 6091 0022. Open: daily 24 hours. Free admission. Bus: 66.

Orang Asli

Visiting Malaysia you will often be reminded that this is a multiracial society of Malays, Indians and Chinese. And yet, driving up to the Cameron Highlands or trekking in Taman Negara, you may encounter a group of people who fit none of these categories. Sitting by the roadside with the fruits of the forest spread in front of them, or quietly walking the hills with their blowpipes to hand, these are the Orang Asli, or 'original peoples'. In fact, the blanket term 'Orang Asli' is misleading, since the 83,000 people who belong to Peninsular Malaysia's indigenous minority comprise 19 different ethnic groups, each with its own language and culture.

The characteristics of Orang Asli vary greatly from tribe to tribe, as do their occupations and lifestyles. Some are easily identifiable, such as the distinctive Negrito peoples, with their dark skin and frizzy hair. They are the smallest and oldest group, and are thought to have arrived in Malaysia between 8,000 and 10,000 years ago from the Andaman Islands. They mostly live in the north of the peninsula and are one of the last tribes to lead a truly nomadic life.

An Orang Asli village in the hills

A traditional building

Other Orang Asli are not recognisable as such at all, blending into the urban Kuala Lumpur scene and doing conventional jobs. Those on the road to the Cameron Highlands are most likely to be Semai, part of the Senoi group, who traditionally lived as shifting cultivators. Others, such as the Orang Laut, Orang Seletar and Mah Meri, live near the coast and gain their livelihoods mostly by fishing.

Whatever their diverse origins, the Orang Asli have suffered from neglect, poverty and the abuse of their human rights since before colonial times. In the 19th century they were subject to slave-raids, and even under the British were referred to as *sakai*, or debt-slaves.

With the advent of independence, the Orang Asli found that the land they had always considered their own was no longer under their control. This is still the situation today under the Aboriginal Peoples Act, which has taken away the right to self-determination for the majority of Orang Asli communities. While there have been considerable advances in terms of health, education and agricultural development, it was not until 2002 that the traditional land rights of the Orang Asli were legally recognised.

For more information on Malaysia's indigenous peoples, contact the **Centre for Orang Asli Concerns,** *PO Box 3052, 47590 Subang Jaya, Malaysia. www.coac.org.my*

A park ranger talks to an Orang Asli hunter collecting poison for his blowpipe darts

MELAKA

Malaysia's oldest town, Melaka (Malacca) has witnessed the sweep of history as rival colonial powers fought for possession and occupied it, each in turn leaving their mark. This heritage has left Melaka with a legacy of historical relics and monuments unparalleled elsewhere in the country.

Melaka was founded in 1400 by a Hindu nobleman, Prince Parameswara, who came from Sumatra. In 1405 Admiral Cheng Ho came as an envoy of the Ming dynasty and offered to provide protection against the Siamese to the north. Melaka soon prospered. The Chinese brought gold, silver, porcelain and silk; Indian traders brought textiles and brassware; the Siamese brought ivory; and Arabian merchants brought perfumes, pearls, incense and opium.

Tales of this wealthy seaport reached the Portuguese, who conquered it on 25 July 1551 under Admiral Afonso de Albuquerque. The Portuguese were overthrown by the Dutch in 1641 after a six-month-long siege. Then it was the turn of the British, who seized Melaka in 1795. In 1818 it was returned to the Dutch under treaty, but was restored to the British in 1824. In 1826 it became a Straits Settlement and, a year later, a Crown Colony along with Pinang and Singapore. During World War II it was under Japanese occupation. With Independence in 1957, the first local governor was appointed.

Over the centuries, successive communities brought with them their culture, religion and architecture. The result is that the streets of Melaka make up a multicultural tapestry of mosques, churches and other ancient buildings. The best way to see these is on a walking tour (*see pp44–5*); you can also get around town by trishaw.

Apart from daytime sightseeing (for which you should allow a couple of days), there isn't a great deal to do. Sound-and-light shows take place in the stadium on the Padang every evening. Melaka has several antique shops (*see p128*), and is one of just a handful of places where you can try Nyonya food (*see pp155–6*).

Baba Nyonya Heritage Museum

The Baba Nyonya Heritage is one of two museums devoted to Peranakan or Straits Chinese culture (*see pp20–21*); it is located in a real Peranakan house, with many of the furnishings and artefacts displayed as they would have been originally used. The other is the Peranakan Museum, Singapore (*see p106*). The interior of the house is almost palatial, extending some 30m (98ft) back from the street with several interior courtyards open to the skies to admit light and air. The museum is run by the same Peranakan family whose ancestors originally built it, and it is well worth a visit.

48–50 Jalan Tun Tan Cheng Lock. Tel: (06) 283 1273. Open: daily 10am–12.30pm & 2–4.30pm. Admission charge includes guided tour.

Bukit China

The history of Bukit China, the 'Chinese Hill', can be traced back to the earliest contacts between Imperial China and the Melaka Sultanate.
In 1405 the Imperial envoy, Admiral Cheng Ho, pitched his quarters here. And in 1459, when Sultan Mansur Shah married Princess Hang Li Poh, daughter of Emperor Yung Lo, he gave her the hill as a place of residence to accommodate her entourage of 500 handmaidens. Under the Portuguese, a monastery and chapel were built on top of the hill, but these were destroyed by the Achinese in 1629. Under Dutch rule, the hill was donated to the Chinese community for a burial ground, which it has remained to this day, with around 12,500 graves on its slopes – many dating back to the 17th century.
Jalan Hang Li Po.

Nyonya heritage in Melaka's Chinatown

Cheng Hoon Teng Temple

Melaka's oldest and most grandiose Chinese temple, Cheng Hoon Teng ('The Abode of Green Clouds') is dedicated to Kwan Yin, the Goddess of Mercy. Built between 1646 and 1704, craftsmen and materials were brought over from South China to decorate the temple: the result is a colourful fantasy of dragons and other mythical creatures on the eaves and ridges of the roof, while the interior of the main hall is resplendent with ornate woodcarvings and lacquerwork.

At the back of the main hall are the ancestral tablets of all the *Kapitans China* of Melaka, including that of Kapitan Lee Wei King, who founded the temple.
Jalan Tokong. Tel: (06) 282 9343. www.chenghoonteng.org.my. Open: daily 7am–7pm. Free admission.

Christ Church

In the heart of the town, Christ Church was built by the Dutch to commemorate the centenary of their occupation of Melaka. Started in 1741, it was completed in 1753 and the original, hand-carved wooden pews from that date are still used by worshippers today. The nave is supported by a series of 17 massive, 15m (49ft) long beams, each carved from a single tree.
Dutch Square. Tel: (06) 284 8804. Open: Mon–Sat 9am–5pm. Free admission.

Independence Memorial Hall

Formerly the Malacca Club, this handsome building now houses a

permanent exhibition illustrating the history of Malaysia from the 15th-century Malay Sultanate up to the struggle for independence. Outside stands the battered '57 Chevy used by the first prime minister-elect, Tunku Abdul Rahman, to campaign across the country.
Jalan Parameswara. Open: Tue–Thur, Sat & Sun 9am–6pm, Fri 9am–noon & 3–6pm. Free admission.

Masjid Kampung Kling

The Kampung Kling Mosque is an unusual structure. Instead of the usual dome, it has a pyramid-shaped roof of Sumatran design, and instead of the normal spire-type minaret it has a square-shaped pagoda.

Further cross-cultural influences can be seen inside, where Corinthian columns support the carved wooden ceiling. Both British and Portuguese tiles grace the interior of the main prayer hall, while the woodcarvings on the pulpit display Chinese and Hindu influences.
Jalan Tokong Emas. Tel: (06) 283 7416. Open: daily, except at prayer times. Free admission.

Mausoleum of Hang Jebat

One of the legendary heroes of the Malay Sultanate during the mid-15th century, Hang Jebat was a loyal warrior, whose life ended tragically when, on the orders of the Sultan, he was killed by one of his blood brothers, Hang Tuah, as a result of a convoluted series of intrigues of which, ironically, they were both innocent.
Jalan Kampung Kuli. Free admission.

Muzium Budaya (Cultural Museum)

This magnificent wooden building is a reconstruction of the 15th-century Sultanate's *istana* (palace). Built in 1985 using entirely traditional methods of construction – there are no nails in the whole building – the design is based on sketches from the *Sejarah Melayu* (Malay Annals). It houses the Melaka Cultural Museum, with tableaux depicting life at the Sultanate's Court, the epic duel between the warriors Hang Tuah and Hang Jebat, and an Islamic Gallery and Costume Gallery.
Jalan Istana, St Paul's Hill.
Tel: (06) 282 7464. Open: daily 9am–6pm. Admission charge.

Porta de Santiago

Porta de Santiago is the last remnant of the massive stone fortress known as A Famosa, which was built by Afonso de Albuquerque after he conquered Melaka in 1511. When the Dutch overthrew the Portuguese, A Famosa was badly damaged, but they renovated the fort and inscribed 'Anno 1670', together with the Dutch East India Company's coat of arms, on the gateway to mark their victory. With the arrival of the British, the order was signed to destroy the fort to prevent it falling back into Dutch hands. This task was nearly completed when Sir Stamford Raffles, visiting

Melaka in 1808, persuaded them to save the gateway.
Jalan Kota.

Stadthuys

This was the first building the Dutch erected after they took over Melaka in 1641. The Stadthuys (Town Hall) is a massive, solid structure with thick masonry walls and heavy wooden doors, designed to protect the governor and his staff, who had their offices here. In the early 1980s it was converted into the **Melaka Historical and Ethnographic Museum**, which houses Dutch and Portuguese relics, Malay and Chinese wedding costumes and other displays.
St Paul's Hill. Tel: (06) 284 1934. Open: Sat–Thur 9am–6pm, Fri 9am–noon & 2.45–6pm. Admission charge.

St Paul's Church

Now in ruins, this church was originally built by the Portuguese in 1521 and was known as Our Lady of the Hill. With the arrival of the Dutch, the church was renamed St Paul's. Once they had finished building Christ Church they no longer used St Paul's for worship but simply as a burial ground, and many of the huge old tombstones can still be seen. After his death, St Francis Xavier was initially buried here before his body was taken to its final resting place in Goa.
St Paul's Hill. Open: Mon–Sat 9am–5pm. Free admission.

The Muzium Budaya is a skilfully crafted replica of the Sultan's 15th-century palace

MELAKA RIVER

Although Melaka's harbour has long since silted up, shallow-draughted Indonesian cargo boats still unload at the quayside downtown. The cargoes (of mangrove poles and sacks of charcoal) may not be as exotic as in the past, but the magnificent wooden seagoing vessels evoke the ghosts of traders from earlier centuries. Boat trips on the river, which encompass the quay, the downtown area and a Malay *kampung* (village), leave from behind the Tourist Information Centre.
Tourist Information Centre *Jalan Kota, Melaka. Tel: (06) 283 6538. www.melaka.gov.my. Open: weekdays 8.45am–5pm, Sat 8am–12.45pm.*

Temple of Admiral Cheng Ho

Admiral Cheng Ho was the Imperial trade ambassador to Emperor Yung Lo during the Ming dynasty. Legend has it that on his way to visit Melaka his ship was holed, but that he was saved by a fish, known as a Sam Po, which blocked up the hole (hence the temple is also known as Sam Po Kong Temple).
Jalan Puteri Hang Li Poh. Tel: (06) 283 6538. Open: daily. Free admission.

Walk: Melaka

This walk covers all of the important historic sights of Melaka north and south of the river. The town's one-way system makes traffic fast and furious, so be careful when you step off the pavement.

Allow 2–3 hours.

Start from the Tourist Information Centre in Jalan Kota, near Dutch Square.

1 Dutch Square

Directly facing you in Dutch Square are several important buildings dating from the Dutch era, including Christ Church (*see p41*) and the Stadthuys (*see p43*). In the middle is the Teng Beng Swee Clock Tower and the Queen Victoria Jubilee Fountain.

Walk along Jalan Kota towards St Paul's Hill. Take the steps up to St Paul's Church (see p43), and descend the other side to the Porta de Santiago (see pp42–3). On your left is the Muzium Budaya (see p42).

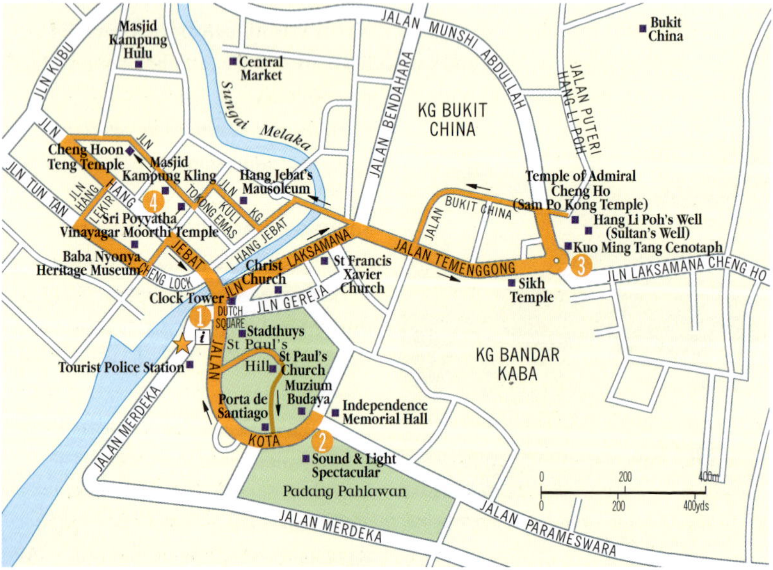

2 The Padang

In front of you is the Padang, an open space that is as significant to 20th-century history as Dutch Square is to the 19th century. Hidden away behind the souvenir stands is a green obelisk bearing the letter 'M' on all four sides (which stands for *merdaka*, meaning independence). It was on this spot that Independence was declared on 31 August 1957, at the same moment that an identical ceremony took place on the Padang in Kuala Lumpur. Fronting the Padang is the Independence Memorial Hall (*see pp41–2*).

Return to Dutch Square via Jalan Kota and enter Jalan Laksamana. Pass Christ Church and the twin-towered Church of St Francis Xavier, then take the second right, down Jalan Temenggong. At the roundabout, turn left and cross the road.

3 Princess Hang Li Poh's Well

Immediately in front of you is the Kuo Ming Tang Cenotaph, which commemorates some 1,000 Chinese civilians massacred during the Japanese occupation. Just past here on the right is the Temple of Admiral Cheng Ho (*see p43*). Next to it is Princess Hang Li Poh's Well (also known as the Sultan's Well), which was once the main source of drinking water for the town. In 1551 the Johor forces who were besieging Melaka poisoned the well, killing around 200 Portuguese. No doubt mindful of these stories, when the Dutch took Melaka they built a fortified wall around the well – the sentries' gunports can still be seen.

Turn right out of the temple, where steps lead up to Bukit China (see p41). Cross over the road and go down Jalan Puteri Hang Li Poh. Follow the road round and turn right into Jalan Temenggong, crossing the river at the end of the road. Take the first left, Lebuh Hang Jebat, and then the first right into Jalan Kampong Kuli (not signposted). Near the end of this road, on the right, is the Mausoleum of the 15th-century warrior, Hang Jebat.

Turn left at the end of the road and immediately right into Jalan Tokong Emas. Immediately on your left is the Sri Poyyatha Vinayagar Moorthi Temple and, past it, the Masjid Kampung Kling (see p42) on the corner of Jalan Lekiu.

4 Sri Poyyatha Vinayagar Moorthi Temple

This is the oldest Hindu temple in Melaka, built in 1781 and dedicated to Sri Vinayagar (Ganesh). On the central altar sits a carving of the deity, who has an elephant's head and four hands, made from Indian black stone.

Cross over into Jalan Tokong (Temple Street). Further up on the left-hand side after Masjid Kampung Kling is the Cheng Hoon Teng Temple (see p41). Follow the road round to the left, turn left on Jalan Hang Jebat and right into Jalan Hang Lekir. Turn left again on Jalan Tun Tan Cheng Lock, and you will soon find the Baba Nyonya Heritage Museum (see p40) on your left.

When leaving the heritage museum, turn left and then left again, then right on to Jalan Hang Jebat to the river bridge.

CENTRAL HIGHLANDS

Hill stations were an essential part of colonial life in the tropics, and it was common for the British, in particular, to establish residences high above sea-level where they could escape the desultory heat of their postings. In Malaysia the nearest mountains to Kuala Lumpur are in the Central Highlands, and the two main resorts here, Cameron Highlands and Bukit Fraser (Fraser's Hill), both date back to colonial times. Genting Highlands is a more recent development that holds little appeal for overseas visitors.

In the cooler climate of the highlands, mist and rain swathe the hillsides where pitcher plants, mosses and ferns flourish in the damp undergrowth of the upper montane forests. The altitude lends itself to the cultivation of tea, coffee, flowers and vegetables, and cooling breezes allow visitors to play golf or go walking without suffering from heat exhaustion. (For longer walking expeditions in the Central Highlands, with Orang Asli guides, *see p147.*)

Cameron Highlands

Malaysia's largest hill station, the Cameron Highlands consists of three townships at an altitude of just over 1,500m (4,920ft), surrounded by tea plantations, flower and vegetable nurseries and golf courses.

First discovered by a British surveyor, William Cameron, in 1885, the area was not developed as a hill station until 1926. Tourism has recently fuelled a construction boom, which experts say is leading to soil erosion, silting, landslides and flooding. The scars on the landscape are all too evident as you pass up through the townships.

The first town in the Highlands is **Ringlet**, an unattractive conurbation where few visitors bother to stop. **Tanah Rata** (13km/8 miles further on) is the main town, with a wide range of facilities including banks, restaurants and hotels. The last town is **Brinchang**, where hotels, shops and restaurants crowd in around a sloping town square.

The towns have none of the charm of Fraser's Hill, and the appeal of the Highlands lies mostly in walking in the surrounding hills (*see pp48–9*), playing golf or visiting tea plantations (*see pp50–51*) and the resort's many market gardens. Other notable sights include the **Sam Poh Temple** near Brinchang, a butterfly garden, and the atmospheric **Ye Olde Smokehouse** (*see p49 & p51*).

330km (205 miles) north of Kuala Lumpur. From Kuala Lumpur buses and trains run to Tapah on the Kuala Lumpur–Ipoh Road, from where taxis and buses operate regular services for the last 60km (37 miles). There are also long-distance, direct buses to/from Kuala Lumpur, Melaka and Butterworth. Self-drive takes around 4 hours from Kuala Lumpur, 2 hours from Ipoh.

Bukit Fraser (Fraser's Hill)

Set in the middle of the Central Range, Fraser's Hill is an attractive little hill resort reached after a spectacular drive up through the forest-clad mountain slopes from the Ipoh Road.

Named after a maverick Englishman, Louis James Fraser, who lived here at the turn of the 20th century (supposedly operating an opium and gambling den), it was developed as a hill station by the British from around 1910. They built a series of neat, greystone bungalows surrounded by roses, hollyhocks and geraniums, which still characterise Fraser's Hill today. The small township, with its colourful flower gardens and well-kept roads, makes a pleasant stopover for a day or two. At the centre of the resort is a nine-hole golf course; there are also facilities for tennis, swimming, squash, cycling and horse-riding. Nearby are the Jeriau Waterfalls (5km/3 miles from the centre).

100km (62 miles) north of Kuala Lumpur. Regular buses run from Kuala Lumpur's Pudu Raya bus station, with a change at Kuala Kubu Baharu. Self-drive takes about 2 hours from the capital.

Genting Highlands

A brash, modern resort with high-rise hotels, an artificial lake, golf club, miniature railway and cable-car rides, and Malaysia's only casino. It is popular at weekends and mostly patronised by residents of Kuala Lumpur, just an hour's drive away to the south.

www.genting.com.my.

Genting Highlands coach service from Pudu Raya bus station, Kuala Lumpur; eight services daily.

The Cameron Valley carpeted with tea

Walk: Cameron Highlands

This walk makes use of some of the more easily accessible jungle tracks around the resort areas. The starting point is Ye Olde Smokehouse (halfway between Tanah Rata and Brinchang), climbing gradually up to the summit of Gunung Berembun at 2,075m (6,808ft) before descending again to the Robinson Falls and looping around through Tanah Rata, past the Parit Falls and back to the Smokehouse. It is a fairly hard walk, with some steep sections, but for most of the way the tracks are spongy underfoot and easy going. Good walking shoes are essential.

Allow 3–4 hours.

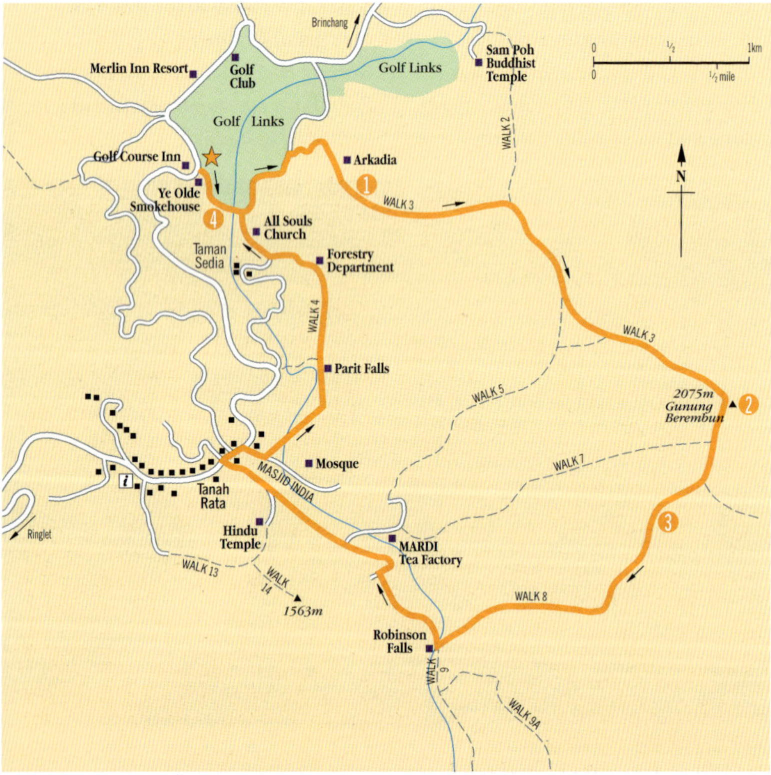

From the Smokehouse, follow the road past the red telephone box, skirting the golf course until you see a sign to 'Arkadia' and Jungle Walk 3 on your right. At the top of the metalled track, a sign indicates the path into the forest.

1 Forest World

You soon enter a Hobbit-like world, with the track winding along between banks covered in mosses, lichens and liverworts. Gnarled and withered tree trunks and limbs twist and turn in all directions, supporting numerous ferns, flowering orchids and other epiphytes.
Continue along Walk 3. After a further 20–25 minutes you will see a sign to the right for Walk 5: keep going up to the left on Walk 3.

2 Gunung Berembun

The path gets increasingly steep until finally you emerge among thickets of bamboo. From here on the going is level to the summit of Gunung Berembun, a few metres further on. The thick vegetation makes views from the top disappointing.
A short distance beyond the summit, Walk 7 is marked to the right: continue straight on towards Walk 8.

3 Siamangs and Butterflies

The track soon begins to descend. You may hear the booming double-note call of the siamang, a black-furred gibbon with the unusual characteristic of having two webbed toes. Even if you don't hear (or see) siamangs, it would be hard to miss the many beautiful butterflies flitting about the forest.
After descending for around an hour (the distance from the summit is 1.4km/nearly a mile), you will reach a concrete path: on your left are the Robinson Falls. Walk back up the concrete path to the road, from where it takes around 15 minutes to Tanah Rata. In Tanah Rata, turn right at the main road, then immediately right into Masjid India. After 200m (220 yards), a sign on your left indicates the path to the Parit Falls.

Crossing the bridge over the waterfall, turn left and follow Walk 4. The track here is flat for most of the way, a pleasant, easy section that skirts the edge of towering pine and eucalyptus plantations. After 1.6km (1 mile), you emerge on to the road again. Follow it to the main junction (do not take the first left turn) and turn left to return to the Smokehouse.

4 Ye Olde Smokehouse

You now deserve some refreshment, and what better place than an English country inn? As you sink into a deep leather armchair in front of a roaring log fire, tea with scones and strawberry jam is served. (*See p51.*)

The misty Cameron Highlands

Tea plantations

Thought to have originated somewhere in the mountainous Indo-China region, the tea plant (*Camellia sinensis*) is a hardy evergreen with fragrant white flowers. Left to grow naturally it would produce a tall, straggly bush, but this would make plucking on a commercial scale difficult, so bushes on plantations are carefully shaped and pruned for the first few years of their lives to produce a flat 'table top' to make the plucker's job easier. Once mature, the bushes are plucked every fortnight, with an experienced plucker able to harvest around 200kg (440 pounds) of leaves in a day. If well looked after, the bushes continue to provide good-quality tea leaves for up to 100 years.

Like the best wines, good-quality tea is also influenced in its flavour, bouquet and character by factors such as the climate, altitude and soil where it is grown. The rich, fertile soils, ample rain and sunshine, and cool temperatures of the Cameron Highlands provide the ideal conditions for tea-growing, and the region now accounts for 70 per cent of all the tea produced in Malaysia.

Baled up and trucked off to the factory, the natural tea leaves are put

Cameron Valley Tea Estate, Cameron Highlands

Tea bushes are picked about once every couple of weeks

through a variety of processes before they're ready for the teapot. Nowadays, the machinery is fully automated and computerised, rapidly subjecting the raw material to withering (to reduce the moisture content), rolling (to crush the leaf cells), fermentation (to give the tea aroma), drying (which stops further fermentation) and, finally, sorting. The last stage, packing, is something that no machine can do, but the fastest packers can fill up to 1,000 packets a day.

The largest tea plantation in the Cameron Highlands is the Boh Estate, established by John 'Archie' Russell, an English entrepreneur who persuaded the government to grant him a large tract of land in 1928 to see if tea cultivation could work in Malaysia. Today, spread over three different sites, the Boh Estates are the largest producers in the country, with some 1,200 hectares (2,965 acres) of mature tea plants carpeting the rolling hillsides in emerald green.

Other prestigious tea plantations include the Bharat Tea Estate and the Sungai Palas Tea Estate. Most of the plantations operate guided tours between 9am and 4.30pm (*www.cameronhighlands.com*).

Ye Olde Smokehouse *By the Golf Course, Cameron Highlands. Tel: (05) 491 1215. www.thesmokehouse.com.my/ch.htm. Open for lunch noon–2pm, tea all afternoon, dinner 6.30–9pm.*

NORTHWEST COAST

From the highlands down to the sea, the coastal plains of the northwest are dominated by endless rows of rubber and oil-palm trees undulating over the hillsides and valleys. After leaving Kuala Lumpur and passing through the state of Selangor you soon cross the border into Perak, one of the oldest states on the peninsula.

For centuries, **Perak** has been the centre of tin-mining in Malaysia – even the name (Perak means 'silver' in Malay) derives from the shining tin ore on which so many fortunes have been founded. Warring factions fought over the tin deposits until the British took control of the state in 1874. Mining on a large scale began in the mid-18th century, with the richest deposits being discovered towards the end of the century in the Kinta Valley, transforming the small market town of Ipoh into the tin capital of Malaysia.

Located about halfway between Kuala Lumpur and Pinang, **Ipoh** is the state capital of Perak. For the visitor, there are cave temples nearby and a magnificent mosque at **Kuala Kangsar** (50km/31 miles to the north), but otherwise Ipoh is largely a transit stop. To the southwest is the port of **Lumut**, home base for the Malaysian Royal Navy and the main departure point for the islands of Pulau Pangkor and Pangkor Laut.

Travelling northwards 164km (102 miles) from Ipoh you reach Butterworth, the gateway to **Pulau Pinang**. The island was first discovered by the hippy travellers of the 1960s and later became Malaysia's most famous international resort. Previously only accessible by air or ferry, it is now linked to the mainland by the 13.5km (8-mile) Pinang Bridge, one of the longest in the world.

Beyond Pinang are the states of Kedah and Perlis, with the islands of Pulau Langkawi offshore (reached from either Kuala Perlis or Kuala Kedah) right up by the Thai border.

Pulau Pangkor and Pangkor Laut

Overlooking the Selat Melaka (Straits of Malacca), Pulau Pangkor is a popular island with some fine beaches: the smaller and more exclusive island of Pangkor Laut is tucked away off the southwest tip of the main island.

Pangkor is an important centre for anchovy fishing, the main fishing villages being on the east coast. The beaches are on the west coast, the principal resort area being Pasir Bogak. North of Pasir Bogak there are several good beaches, such as Teluk Ketapang (where turtles nest during May, June and July), Teluk Nipah (a lovely beach from where you can rent canoes and paddle out to the islet of Pulau Gian), and Coral Bay. The island is crowded at weekends and during holidays – try to visit on a working day.

Pangkor is small enough to explore by bicycle (a circuit of the island takes around half a day) or motorbike, either of which can be rented. The busy boat-building yards and workshops on the east coast are worth a visit, and there are also a restored Dutch fort, rock inscriptions and a Chinese temple to enliven your tour around the pot-holed coast road.

Neighbouring Pangkor Laut is a gem of an island – 300 hectares (741 acres) covered in jungle and with only one hotel, the Pangkor Laut Resort, on the east coast. On the other side of the island from the resort – reached by a short jungle track – is Emerald Bay, which is indisputably one of the most beautiful beaches on the whole west coast of Malaysia. The horseshoe-shaped bay has clear water and a fine sandy beach surrounded by casuarinas and spiky pandanus palms. Behind the beach, magnificent hornbills swoop between the tree-tops – this is probably one of the best places in Malaysia for a guaranteed close look at these fabulous birds in the wild.

There is a regular ferry service from 6.45am–8.30pm from Lumut directly to either island, with smaller boats making the short crossing between the two from Pasir Bogak from 10.30am–7.30pm. There are buses between Lumut and Kuala Lumpur, Cameron Highlands, Ipoh and Butterworth (and long-distance taxis from the latter two). Teluk Dalam on Pulau Pangkor has an airport.

Fishing boat on a deserted beach, Pulau Pangkor

PULAU PINANG

The state of Pulau Pinang encompasses the island itself and a mainland coastal strip, Province Wellesley, with the port of Butterworth directly opposite the island. The capital of Pinang is Georgetown (*see* Walk, *pp60–61*), a thriving port that has many sights of historic interest. The first settlement on Pinang was founded in 1786 by Captain Francis Light, an adventurer working on behalf of the East India Company. Desperate for a station on the east side of the Indian Ocean to supply and protect their ships carrying precious cargoes of tea and opium from China, the British tricked the Sultan of Kedah by offering him protection from his enemies in return for Pinang. By the time the Sultan realised they had no intention of honouring their side of the bargain it was too late, and when he tried to retake Pinang he was easily defeated.

Georgetown

Light carved his capital out of the jungle and named it Georgetown in honour of King George IV. The colony soon prospered, with traders drawn from far and wide to the tax-free port. In 1826 Pinang joined together with Melaka and Singapore to form the Straits Settlements, although later it was eclipsed by Singapore as the centre of trade and commerce in the region. Pinang benefited enormously from the tin trade and, later, from the boom in rubber early in the 20th century. Georgetown today is a prosperous, cosmopolitan city. The population of 400,000 is mostly Chinese, and although the modern, 65-storey Komtar building towers above the downtown area it is in the intriguing shop-houses and crowded streets of Chinatown that the soul of the city lies. Most of the areas of interest are within 3sq km (1sq mile) and easily explored on foot. Bicycle rickshaws are a practical way of getting around the town. It is also worth hiring a car for the day to explore the island (*see pp62–3*).

Botanic gardens

The 30-hectare (74-acre) gardens nestle at the base of Bukit Bendera (Pinang Hill). The spacious lawns are surrounded by hardwood trees, fern rockeries, ponds, palm groves and flowering plants. If you have come for a picnic, be wary of the acquisitive common leaf monkeys that roam the grounds.

Off Waterfall Road, 8km (5 miles) from Georgetown. Tel: (04) 227 0428. http://jkb.penang.gov.my. Open: daily 5am–8pm. Free admission. Bus: 7 or taxi.

Clan piers

The clan piers are a series of wooden jetties projecting out over the harbour

PENANG OR PINANG?

The Malays called it Pulau Ka Satu, or Single Island. It appears as Pulau Pinang, or Betelnut Tree Island, on early navigational charts. Francis Light renamed it Prince of Wales' Island, in honour of the uncrowned George IV (hence also Georgetown). Pulau Penang was how it was marketed as a tourist destination in the 1970s. It has now reverted to the correct Malay spelling – Pulau Pinang.

with houses built on stilts around them. They are unusual because the Chinese fishing families who inhabit them live on separate jetties according to their clans, of which there are seven. *Pengkalan Weld Quay. Ten-minute walk south from the Clock Tower, Georgetown.*

Fort Cornwallis

When Captain Francis Light landed on this spot on 17 July 1786, it was no more than a sandy beach backed by solid jungle. Legend has it that Light fired a cannon full of silver dollars into the undergrowth in order to spur his men on to clear the jungle, and thus soon established camp. The first fort was made of wood, but Light persuaded the directors of the East India Company to rebuild it in stone at the beginning of the 19th century. They were reluctant to do so, despite the escalation of Anglo-French hostilities in the region, and in the end they were proved right, since never has a shot been fired in anger from its cannons.

The fort became the central focus of the growth of Pinang, even after it fell into decay. In 1977 it was declared a National Monument, and the area inside was landscaped to include a small park, a Police Museum, and a minute but interesting Memorial Gallery housed inside one of the old powder magazines, which contains old prints, documents and photographs. *Lebuh Light, Georgetown. Tel: (04) 261 0260. Open: daily 8.30am–7pm. Admission charge.*

Kapitan Kling Mosque

See p61.

Khoo Kongsi

A *kongsi* is a Chinese clan-house, the focus of the community for members of the same clan, which serves not only as a temple but as a meeting place and a venue for ceremonies. Members of the Khoo clan from Hokkien province in China started to build this clan-house in the 1890s. It took them eight years to complete, but soon afterwards it was gutted by a mysterious fire. Taking this as a sign that the opulence of the clan-house had offended the deities, they rebuilt it on a lesser scale. The original building must have been amazing because even its replacement is magnificent, covered in a profusion of colourful carvings representing scenes from Chinese legends. A separate hall contains the clan's ancestral tablets and in the large courtyard is a stage for opera. *18 Cannon Square, Jalan Acheh, Georgetown. Tel: (04) 261 4609. www.khookongsi.com.my. Open: weekdays 9am–5pm, Sat 9am–1pm. Free admission.*

Kuan Yin Temple

See p61.

Pinang Museum and Art Gallery

The ground floor of the museum holds an unusual collection of curiosities, memorabilia, maps and photographs. As well as a mock-up of an ornate Chinese bridal chamber, there are displays of jewel-encrusted *kris* (the

traditional Malay dagger), magnificent opium beds inlaid with mother-of-pearl, and early rickshaws. There is an art gallery on the first floor.
Lebuh Farquhar. Tel: (04) 261 3144. Open: Sat–Thur 9am–5pm. Closed: Fri. Admission charge.

Sri Mariamman Temple
See p61.

Batu Ferringhi Beach

Pinang's only major beach resort is a tourist magnet with numerous up-market hotels overlooking a 3km (2-mile) sandy strip on the north coast of the island. The beach offers a full range of watersports and activities such as parasailing, water-skiing and snorkelling, as well as trips to nearby islands. Under the shade of the casuarinas, reflexology and traditional acupressure massages are also popular. Behind the beach road is an abundance of seafood restaurants, bars, market stalls, photo-processing shops, money-changers and the like.

The sea at Batu Ferringhi has always been murky, a fact that prompted many visitors to avoid it altogether and stick to the hotel swimming pools. Their instincts were right, since a study by the Consumer's Association of Pinang found that seawater all around the Pinang coastline was heavily polluted with sewage – at Batu Ferringhi, bacteria levels at one time exceeded government guidelines by a factor of 13,000! Things are gradually improving, but it is safer to stick to the hotel pools.
14km (9 miles) from Georgetown. Bus: 93 or taxi.

Bukit Bendera (Pinang Hill)

Pinang Hill has long been the lungs of Georgetown, a cool retreat 830m (2,723ft) above sea level that is held in great affection by local residents, who have been coming up here by funicular railway for generations to relax and to walk the jungle paths and ridges in the hill complex. The natural vegetation of Pinang Hill is the last remnant of the rainforest that once covered the island, and is home to around 80 species of birds as well as a rich flora, including several endemic species.

The first funicular railway was built up the hillside in 1922, after which a hill resort developed with just a few bungalows, gardens and one hotel (the old Bellevue, which still exists). The only way up the hill is still by funicular, although now it is a modern, Swiss-built system. From the top, there are good views across Georgetown and towards the mainland.
The funicular runs from just near Ayer Itam, Mon–Fri 6.30am–9pm, Sat–Sun 6.30am–11.15pm. It takes 45 minutes to reach the top (with a change of cars half-way). Bus: 1 to Ayer Itam, then walk or Bus 8.

Butterfly Farm

This fabulous garden houses thousands of butterflies from over 50 species, many of them rare and very beautiful. At times, the air is so thick with butterflies fluttering around your head that it is unnerving. The butterflies are at their most active early in the morning. Next to the butterfly enclosure there is an **Insect Museum** with a well-presented collection of beautiful and bizarre moths and butterflies as well as the world's longest, heaviest and biggest insects. Even if insects give you the creepie-crawlies, this is an absorbing display.

Butterfly Farm, 830 Mk 2, Jalan Teluk Bahang. Tel: (04) 885 1253. www.butterfly-insect.com. Open: weekdays 9am–5.30pm, weekends & public holidays 9am–6pm. Admission charge (extra for cameras and videos).

The Kek Lok Si Buddhist Temple, Pinang

Kek Lok Si Temple

Work began on this enormous and ornate temple complex, the largest Buddhist temple in Pinang, in 1890 and took 70 years to complete. Expansion is still going on today, and the complex now includes a multistorey car park and a smart, air-conditioned vegetarian restaurant. The Great Pagoda Tower, seven storeys high, is renowned as an architectural oddity, since it has a Chinese base, a Thai middle section, and is topped off with a Burmese spiral dome tower. Above the temple on the hillside a gigantic statue of Kuan Yin presides over all.

Ayer Itam, 8km (5 miles) from Georgetown. Tel: (04) 828 3317. Open: daily 9am–6pm. Bus: 1 from Jalan Maxwell.

Snake Temple

See p63.

Wat Chayamangkalaram

The enormous, 32m (105ft) long reclining Buddha inside the temple was built during the celebrations to mark the 25th centenary of the birth of Buddha in 1958. Across the road is the equally interesting Dhammikarama Burmese Temple.

Jalan Burmah, 3km (2 miles) NW of Georgetown. Tel: (04) 261 6663. Open: daily 6am–5.30pm.

PULAU LANGKAWI

The northernmost resort island on Malaysia's west coast, Pulau Langkawi is the major of 104 islands that make up the Langkawi group, most of which are uninhabited. The approach by ferry is sublime. The hazy silhouettes of the islands gradually resolve themselves into a series of wooded hillsides and cliffs separated by a maze of inlets and bays, with hardly a building in sight. As the ferry enters Kuah harbour, the large number of yachts at anchor bears testimony to the delights of cruising in the archipelago.

Langkawi has always been considered 'an island apart', relatively unspoiled and traditional in outlook. The majority of the 50,000 population are Malays, and fishing and rice-farming are still the mainstays of the economy. The island has recently been targeted

CLAN-HOUSES

The Khoo Kongsi is one of many 'clan-houses' built by clan associations of Chinese immigrants in the 19th century.

Governed by a body of elders, these associations provided support to people who spoke the same dialect or came from nearby villages. They helped welcome newcomers, settled disputes between members, and helped in times of sickness and death. Most importantly, they assured clan members of a proper ceremonial burial, without which, according to Chinese belief, the spirits of the dead cannot rest in peace.

The *kongsi* was the focal point of the community, housing not only the ancestral table but also a hall of fame honouring prominent clansmen.

Though not as important as they used to be, the *kongsi* are still active in ancestor-worship ceremonies and gatherings to celebrate achievements by clan members.

for tourist development, and although there has been an increase in the number of hotels under construction, much of it remains untouched, with wonderful landscapes of emerald-green *padi*-fields on the flatlands leading off to forest-clad mountain peaks swirling with clouds.

The main town of Kuah is a duty-free port, with plenty of shops and seafood restaurants. Most of the island's beach accommodation is at Pantai Cenang, with some facilities also available at Pantai Kok. The island does not have a vast number of tourist sights, but it makes up for this in the richness of the myths and legends that surround those it does have. All the places of interest can easily be seen on a day tour (*see pp64–5*). Island-hopping excursions are popular (particularly to Pulau Dayang Bunting, the Island of the Pregnant Maiden, and the wildlife sanctuary on Pulau Singa Besar), and scuba-diving trips to the Pulau Payar Marine Park can also be arranged (*see p120*).

MAS and Air Asia operate direct daily flights from Kuala Lumpur. Silk Air operates ten flights a week to Langkawi International Airport at Padang Matsirat (1 hour) from Singapore. Regular ferries run from either Kuala Perlis (45 minutes) or Kuala Kedah (1 hour). There are also express ferry services to Pinang (daily) and Satun in Thailand (Mon & Wed).

The domes of the Kapitan Kling Mosque, Georgetown, Pulau Pinang

Walk: Georgetown

This walk crisscrosses through the heart of Georgetown, taking in some of the most interesting buildings as well as the sights and sounds of Chinatown. The walk starts and finishes at the Clock Tower next to Fort Cornwallis.

Allow 2–3 hours.

From the Clock Tower, walk down Lebuh Light, past Fort Cornwallis (see p55), and take the third turning on the left, Jalan Masjid Kapitan Kling. At the junction with Lebuh Farquhar, St George's Church is on your right.

1 St George's Church

This splendid, classically proportioned church was built in 1818 by convict labour and is one of the oldest landmarks in Pinang. In 1941 it was bombed by the Japanese, and stood unused without a roof until it was finally rebuilt in 1948. The small pavilion in front of the church is a memorial to Captain Francis Light.

Further down Jalan Masjid Kapitan Kling is the Kuan Yin Temple.

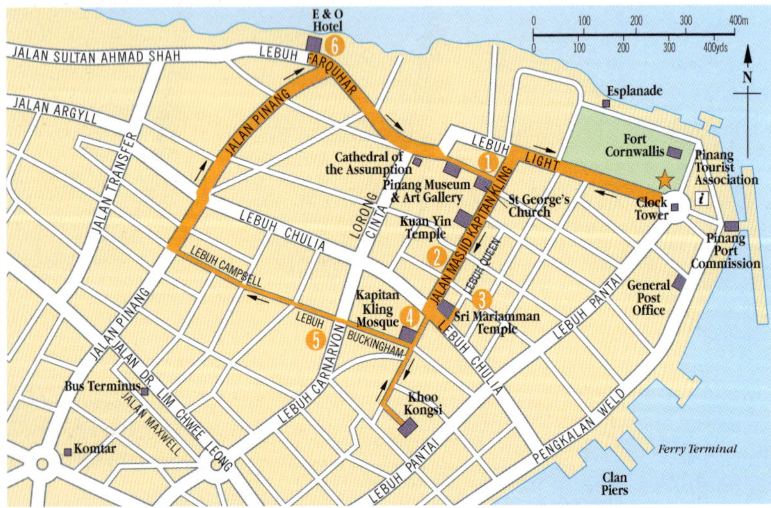

2 Kuan Yin Temple

The Kuan Yin (Goddess of Mercy) Temple is one of the most popular, with a stream of devout people paying their respects to Kuan Yin. Thought to have been built around 1800, it is the oldest Chinese temple in Pinang.

Continue down Jalan Masjid Kapitan Kling, then turn left into Lebuh Chulia and left again into Lebuh Queen to reach the front of the Sri Mariamman Temple.

3 Sri Mariamman Temple

The Sri Mariamman is the earliest Hindu temple on the island, built in 1883. The interior holds the statues of several deities, among them that of the richly decorated Lord Subramaniam, which leads the chariot procession during the Thaipusam Festival (*see pp26–7*).

Retrace your steps to the Jalan Masjid Kapitan Kling junction and cross over to explore the Kapitan Kling Mosque.

4 Kapitan Kling Mosque

Completing this quartet of Pinang's oldest places of worship, the Kapitan Kling Mosque is named after the headman (the *Kapitan*) of the South Indian Kling community, who first arrived in Pulau Pinang as *sepoys* (Indian mercenaries) with Captain Francis Light.

Continue down Jalan Masjid Kapitan Kling until the road begins to narrow. Halfway down the row of neat houses on your left a sign reads 'Leong San Tong Khoo Kongsi', which is the entrance to the courtyard of the ornately decorated Khoo Kongsi (see p55). Retrace your steps and turn left down Lebuh Buckingham.

5 Lebuh Buckingham

Wander down Lebuh Buckingham and the neighbouring streets to savour the hustle and bustle of Malaysia's largest Chinese community. Bicycle repair shops, sign-makers, and fabric and shoe shops vie for space with restaurants advertising 'Famous Hainan Chicken Rice' and street-stalls with piles of salted duck eggs and other exotica. In the air-conditioned calm of the many goldsmiths' shops, phalanxes of sales assistants sit aloof from the clamour out in the surrounding streets, poised behind their glittering display cases.

Turn right on Jalan Pinang and continue until you come to the E & O Hotel on Lebuh Farquhar.

6 E & O Hotel

Founded by the Sarkie Brothers before they went on to build Raffles in Singapore, the E & O (Eastern & Oriental) is an old colonial landmark in the city and still retains a delightful atmosphere. Dance parties in the Ballroom and Curry Tiffin on Sunday afternoons echo the bygone days.

Turn left out of the E & O, follow Lebuh Farquhar, and cross the road near the cathedral on your right. Shortly thereafter is the Pinang Museum and Art Gallery (see pp55–6). Turn right out of the museum, left again on Jalan Masjid Kapitan Kling and right on Lebuh Light to return to the Clock Tower.

Tour: Pulau Pinang

This 70km (43$^{1}/_{2}$-mile), circular route covers most of the sights outside of Georgetown. Driving on Pinang presents few problems, although Sundays should be avoided since most of the places of interest and the roads are packed with local residents on family outings. If you are staying at Batu Ferringhi you can avoid driving into Georgetown. The tour can also be done in part by public transport with several changes of bus.

Allow most of the day.

From Georgetown follow the signs to Batu Ferringhi, which is 14km (9 miles) along the winding, northern coast road. From the beach, continue westwards to the fishing village of Teluk Bahang, where the road leaves the coast and heads inland. Turn left at the roundabout and after 1km (2/3 mile) you will come to the Butterfly Farm (see pp56–7) and, just next to it, the Forest Recreation Park.

1 Forest Recreation Park

The park covers 10 hectares (25 acres), with some pleasant walks through its wooded slopes. A museum displays traditional uses of forest products (such as musical instruments and rattan craftwork) as well as modern industries such as plywood and furniture manufacture.
Forest Recreation Park open: daily 7am–7pm. Free admission.
Museum open: daily 9am–5pm. Admission charge.

Turn left out of the Forest Park. The road winds uphill for 11km (7 miles), passing the Titi Kerawang waterfall just after the summit.

2 Traditional *kampungs*

As the road drops down the other side of the hill there are extensive views of the rice paddies stretching across to the western coast of the island. Once down on the plains, you pass through small *kampungs* where the pace of life has changed little, with traditional Malay houses elevated on stilts to keep the damp and insects at bay.

Follow the signs to the town of Balik Pulau, and from here to Bayan Lepas (airport). Approximately 2km (1¼ miles) after the airport is the Snake Temple, but with no signpost it is easily missed.

3 Snake Temple

As you enter the Snake Temple, a sign requests mediums not to fall into a trance in the temple, 'to avoid causing inconvenience to worshippers and visitors'. Whether this is because they are hypnotised by the snakes or vice versa is not clear, but the snakes themselves – coiled around the altars and lounging in trees in the courtyard – exert a magnetic fascination. Around 50 or so pit vipers have taken up residence here, and their numbers are said to increase around the birthday of Chor Soo Kong, to whom the temple is dedicated. Some have been de-fanged for tourist photographs. The rest should not be approached.
Open: daily 7am–7pm. Free admission.

Continue down the dual carriageway and take the first left exit, signed Bukit Bendera or Ayer Itam. On entering the town of Ayer Itam, follow the one-way system to the left of the market and take the first left to Kek Lok Si Temple (see p58). Now follow signs to the left for Bukit Bendera (Pinang Hill, see p56). Heading towards Georgetown, follow the signs for Batu Ferringhi or downtown.

Tour: Pulau Langkawi

Starting at Pantai Cenang, this tour encompasses all the sights of interest and the best beaches on the island. There are excellent, well-signposted roads on the island and very little traffic. Scooters are readily available and some resorts also have jeeps for hire.

Allow 3–5 hours.

Take the road that skirts the end of the airport runway. Just after the village of Kuala Teriang turn left to Pantai Kok.

1 Pantai Kok

The road winds around the unspoiled forested headland of Tanjung Belikit down to Pantai Kok, one of the better swimming beaches on the island. This beautiful bay is framed to the north by the limestone peaks at Tanjung Belua.

Continue to the end of the bay and turn right down a dirt track at the end of the beach, signposted Telaga Tujuh (Seven

Wells). Continue for 1.5km (1 mile) until you reach a car park and refreshment stalls, then continue on foot up to the falls.

2 Telaga Tujuh

Cascading down a massive rock face, the first waterfall and the rock-pools beneath it are reached via a short track off to the left. It is well worth continuing up to the top (a steep, 10-minute hike), where you can cool off in more rock-pools, with a fabulous view back down to the beach.

Retrace your route and turn left at Pantai Kok. Continue past Pasir Hitam to the roundabout and turn left to Pantai Rhu.

3 Pantai Rhu

This is a peaceful beach overlooking the crags of Langkawi's northernmost promontory. The islets in the bay (Pulau Kelam Baya and Pulau Cabang) can be reached on foot at low tide, or by canoe (which you can rent on the beach). From here there are boat trips which go round the cape to Gua Cerita, the Cave of Legends, whose walls have been inscribed with Koranic texts.

Drive back to the roundabout and turn left, shortly after which you will come to Telaga Air Hangat.

4 Telaga Air Hangat

Legend has it that two powerful families fell out over the marriage proposed between their offspring. In the ensuing fracas, pots and pans were flung about, with the gravy dish landing at Kuah (which means gravy), a pot landing at Belanga Pecah (broken pot) and the pans of boiling water landing here, at Telaga Air Panas (hot-water springs). The three original hot springs, previously a rather uninspiring attraction, have now been transformed into the centrepiece of Telaga Air Hangat, an excellent cultural centre. The springs themselves now well up through a three-tiered fountain and flow through the gardens to a 6m (20ft) long, free-standing mural depicting the story of the feuding families.

The centre hosts a wide range of activities, including Malay folk and classical dances.

Continue down the same road for 16km (10 miles) to Kuah. Turn right and follow the signs for Makam Mahsuri.

5 Makam Mahsuri (Mahsuri's Tomb)

Mahsuri's marble tomb is set in a white-walled garden. The subject of one of Langkawi's most enduring legends, Mahsuri was a beautiful princess who was wrongly accused of adultery.

A soldier was ordered to kill her by plunging a *kris* (Malay dagger) into her heart, and as he did so her innocence was proven by the white blood that flowed from the wound. As she lay dying, Mahsuri laid a curse on the island that it would not prosper for seven generations.

Return back down the road and turn right at the junction, following the signs for the Field of Burnt Rice and then on back to Pantai Cenang.

EAST COAST

In contrast to the energetic, crowded cities and busy highways and towns on the west coast, the east coast has a more relaxed, easy-going atmosphere. Here, the enduring image is of crescent-shaped fishing boats hauled up on the beach, in front of quiet *kampungs* (villages) hidden away among the coconut groves. The reason the east coast has managed to retain its traditional character is because until recently it was relatively inaccessible. The impenetrable jungles of the central mountains effectively cut off the east from the west.

Although the lifestyle has remained practically unchanged, there are now good transport links to the rest of the country. The east-coast highway runs for 730km (454 miles) from north to south, and the central highway links Kuantan with Kuala Lumpur, crossing the middle of the peninsula. The east–west highway carves its way through the mountains near the Thai border, linking Kota Bharu with the west coast.

The northernmost state on this coast is **Kelantan**, the heartland of Malay culture. The state capital, Kota Bharu, is just a few kilometres from the Thai border. Further south, the state of **Terengganu** has miles of sandy beaches along the coastline, with the islands in the Perhentian group offshore to the north and the famous turtle-nesting beaches at Rantau Abang to the south of the capital, Kuala Terengganu. Beyond here is **Pahang**, with well-known resorts such as Cerating and Teluk Cempedak (Kuantan) on the coast. Inland, jungle encompasses the peninsula's biggest National Park, Taman Negara (*see p118*), and there are the mysterious lakes at Tasik Cini. Finally, there is **Johor**, jumping-off point for popular islands such as Pulau Tioman.

Most destinations on this coast are linked by an express bus network (*see p179*); driving down the coast is also an option.

Beserah

This small fishing village north of Kuantan is a major centre for *ikan bilis* (anchovy) fishing. Its main appeal for tourists is the rather unusual method of hauling the day's catch up the beach at midday using water-buffalo carts. Beserah is also well known for batik and other cottage handicrafts.
10km (6 miles) from Kuantan.

Cerating

The home of Asia's first Club Med (which covers three of the best beaches along here), Cerating has a wide range of budget chalets at Pantai Cerating, 2km (1¼ miles) north of the main village. Cerating is a centre for handicrafts (batik courses are available) and there are cultural performances in season.
47km (29 miles) north of Kuantan.

Kota Bharu

The capital of Kelantan, set on the banks of the Kelantan River, is a leading centre for traditional arts and crafts. Cultural performances at the **Gelanggang Seni (Kelantan Cultural Centre)** are a major attraction. Most of the historic sights are located around Merdeka Square. At the eastern end of the square is the old royal palace, the **Istana Balai Besar** (Palace with the Large Audience Hall); built in 1844, it houses some beautiful woodcarvings (entry requires special permission). Beside it stands the smaller **Istana Jahar**, completed in 1889, which now houses the **Museum of Royal Traditions and Customs**. Just past here is the State Mosque and the State Religious Council Building. Also in Merdeka Square is the **Handicraft Village and Craft Museum**.

A short walk from Merdeka Square is the three-storey Central Market, where a profusion of tropical produce is displayed over the vast central floor. Stalls on the other two floors specialise in spices, dried foods, batik and basketware. There is also an excellent *pasar malam* (night market) with a wide range of tasty Malay foods.

Docked fishing boat, Kuantan

Other sights in the vicinity include a massive, 40m (131ft) long reclining Buddha at **Wat Phothivihan** (15km/ 9 miles to the north) and **Pantai Cahaya Bulan** (the Beach of the Shining Moon) 10km (6 miles) to the north. Though the beach is about average, it has a number of batik, songket-weaving and kite-making workshops on the road leading to it (*see p129*).

Gelanggang Seni: performances daily Feb–Oct. Tel: (09) 743 7373 for information.

Royal Museum open: Sat–Thur 8.30am–4.45pm. Closed: Fri.

MAS flies to Kota Bharu from Kuala Lumpur and Pinang. Air Asia flies from Kuala Lumpur four times daily. Express buses link Kota Bharu with the west coast, Kuala Lumpur, most towns on the east coast and Thailand.

Kuala Terengganu

Situated at the mouth of the Terengganu River, Kuala Terengganu has been transformed by oil revenues into a busy modern town that holds little of interest for visitors. Stroll down Jalan Bandar, a narrow, curving thoroughfare lined with old Chinese shop-houses.

MAS has flights to Kuala Lumpur. Air Asia flies from Kuala Lumpur three times daily. Buses connect north and south along the coast.

Kuantan

State capital of Pahang, Kuantan is a modern city and an important transport hub. Most people stop here awhile on the way to the beach at Teluk Cempedak (*see p71*).

MAS has flights to Kuala Lumpur. Air Asia flies from Kuala Lumpur once a day. Buses connect Kuantan to Singapore, Kuala Lumpur and coastal resorts.

Marang

A picturesque fishing village on the mouth of the Marang River with a laid-back atmosphere that appeals to travellers stopping here on their way out to Pulau Kapas. Guesthouses near the beach cater for people waiting for a ride to the island.

15km (9 miles) south of Kuala Terengganu, 45 minutes by bus.

Pulau Kapas

One of the most easily accessible islands, just half an hour by speedboat from Marang, Pulau Kapas has pretty, unspoilt beaches and reefs. There are huts and chalets on the main beach (camping is possible).

6km (4 miles) offshore from Marang.

Pulau Perhentian

The fishing port of Kuala Besut is the jumping-off point for the islands in the Perhentian group, notably Pulau Perhentian Besar and Pulau Perhentian Kecil. The islands have long been a stop-over point for migratory birds as well as fishermen (hence the name, Perhentian, meaning 'stop'). The larger of the two is Perhentian Besar, which is separated from its smaller sister island by a narrow channel. Most of the accommodation is on Perhentian Besar, but small boats ply between the two. Both islands are delightfully unspoilt with excellent beaches, shallow reefs and (on Perhentian Besar) jungle trails.

20km (12 miles) offshore from Kuala Besut (1½–2 hours by boat).

Pulau Rawa

The best-known resort island offshore from Mersing after Pulau Tioman, Pulau Rawa is tiny by comparison and has just one chalet resort hidden away behind the coco-palms on the beach. It has good beaches, though the coral is badly damaged, but tends to be crowded at weekends owing to its proximity to Mersing. Facilities available include fishing, snorkelling and scuba diving.

16km (10 miles) from Mersing, 1½ hours by boat.

Rawa Island Safaris Resort, Tourist Centre, Jalan Abu Bakar, Mersing. Tel: (07) 799 1204. www.rawa.com.my

Pulau Redang

One of the more remote east-coast islands, Pulau Redang has long been popular with scuba divers, thanks to the excellent condition of the reefs and the abundant marine life that surrounds it. It was gazetted as a marine park in 1985. The Berjaya Redang Golf and Country Resort has changed the island's character somewhat.

45km (28 miles) from Kuala Terengganu, 3–4 hours by boat.

A beach barbecue gets underway on Pulau Tioman

Pulau Tenggol

The small rocky island of Pulau Tenggol is famous for its beautiful reefs, rocky cliffs, caves and a lovely white-sand beach on the western side. A small resort with just 20 Malay-style chalets, the Tenggol Island Resort, has opened, offering scuba diving and watersports facilities.
For bookings at the Tenggol Island Resort, tel: (09) 848 4862. www.tenggolisland.com

Pulau Tioman

The largest island on the east coast, Tioman is also one of the most popular. It is an intriguing island in more than one respect. Owing to its isolation from the mainland it has developed several subspecies of flora and fauna: as much as 25 per cent of the plant life is thought to be unique to the island, and separate subspecies of squirrels, butterflies, insects and small cats have evolved here. There are relatively large populations of mouse deer and lizards, as well as bats. The island's single primate, the long-tailed macaque, can be seen roaming the forest fringes near the sea.

Tioman's rich natural history is complemented by an equally absorbing maritime history. Thanks to abundant fresh water supplies and its two 1,000m (3,281ft) high peaks – easily visible to seafarers – Tioman became an important trading post and storm shelter for ships engaged in the spice trade. It was first mentioned in *Tales from China and India* (an early Arabic book upon which the *Tales of Sinbad* was based). In the 1950s, Tioman achieved fame as the setting for the Hollywood musical *South Pacific.*

The island's main village is Kampung Tekek. Over the headland to the south there is a long beach occupied by the Berjaya Tioman Beach Resort, the most exclusive place to stay on Pulau Tioman; to the north there are several beaches with accommodation.

In addition to snorkelling or lazing on the beach, a popular activity is to trek across the central ridge to Juara Bay on the other coast, which will take about three hours. If you don't want to walk back you can get a lift on the round-island Sea Bus service (in season only).
There are direct flights with Berjaya Air from Tioman's airport to Kuala Lumpur and Singapore. From Mersing, boats range from slow fishing boats (3–4 hours) to express launches (2 hours). A new ferry service now links Tioman and Singapore (4½-hour journey, daily except Wed). Buses connect Mersing with Johor Bahru, Singapore and Kuala Lumpur.

Rantau Abang

Although it is by no means the only place in Malaysia where turtles nest, Rantau Abang is by far the most famous, and for this reason has drawn thousands of visitors over the years to watch this compelling sight. Seven different species of turtle nest along this section of coast, but for most people the star attraction is the giant leatherback, the largest of all sea turtles. Rantau Abang is one of their prime nesting locations.

In the past, considerable disturbance has been caused to the turtles on this beach, with people riding on them after they had nested and having beach parties – with bonfires and radios – during the nesting season. Thankfully, all these activities have now been stopped, and visitors' conduct during turtle nesting is more closely controlled. The beach is divided up into sanctuary areas and those areas where access is allowed. No lights, fires, noise or egg collecting are permitted, and the turtles must have started laying before you can approach them.

Tasik Chini (the Lotus Lake), west of Kuantan

LEATHERBACK TURTLES

The leatherback, which can weigh up to 900kg (1,984 pounds), is the largest turtle in the world. Unlike other marine turtles, it does not have a hard shell but a leathery carapace with seven long ridges. Deeply notched upper jaws help it catch its favourite food – jellyfish. Regular divers down to 400m (1,310ft) or more, the deepest recorded touched 1,200m (3,937ft)!

Like all marine turtles, leatherbacks come ashore only to lay eggs (four to six times during the season). After dragging herself up the beach, the female excavates an egg chamber with her flippers, into which she deposits between 50 to 200 white, soft-shelled eggs. After covering up the hole, she lumbers back down the beach. Two months later, the young hatchlings emerge and make their way down to the sea to begin their perilous lives, with the chances of survival to adulthood being only one in 1000.

The season usually runs from June to September, with the peak during August. The optimum viewing time is at high tides or on a full moon – at night, of course.

There are numerous small chalets and huts where you can stay, and you will generally be called out if turtles are seen starting up the beach to lay. The **Turtle Information Centre** is well worth a visit beforehand.

58km (36 miles) south of Kuala Terengganu, 160km (100 miles) north of Kuantan.

Rantau Abang Turtle Information Centre. Tel: (09) 844 1533. Open: Sat–Thur 9am–11pm, Fri 9am–noon &

3–11pm (shorter times out of season). Buses run to Dungun hourly, from where there are services to Kuantan, Mersing and Kuala Lumpur.

Tasik Chini (the Lotus Lake)

Malaysia's second-largest natural lake, Tasik Chini is hidden away in the wilds of Pahang, 100km (62 miles) southwest of Kuantan. During the flowering season (June–Sept) the surfaces of a dozen interconnecting lakes are carpeted in the lovely pink and white blossoms of the lotus flower which gives Tasik Chini its name.

Getting to Lake Chini is half the adventure, and there are two ways of doing this. The classic approach is by boat, in which case you turn off the Kuantan–Kuala Lumpur highway towards Kuantan and hire a motorised longboat at the jetty. After crossing the fast-flowing Pahang River, the boat enters the jungle up the Sungai Chini (Chini River). This is a beautiful journey, as the boat follows the tributary to the lake: kingfishers, butterflies and dragonflies scoot over the water, while monkeys leap from tree-top to tree-top above. Twisted and gnarled lianas hang in great loops over the water and tree branches are blanketed with enormous and luxuriant bird's-nest ferns.

The other way to reach the lake is to drive down the Kuantan–Segamat highway, following the signs from the Chini village junction: the last part of the journey is along a bumpy track through oil-palm plantations, until finally the Lake Chini Resort appears among the trees.

In front of the resort there is a jetty where boats can be hired for trips around the lakes. Chalet, dormitory and camping accommodation are provided in a pleasantly low-key resort which organises numerous jungle activities.

Lake Chini Resort: c/o Lembaga Kemajuan Pahang Tenggara, Wisma Sultan Ahmad Shah, 26700 Muadzam Shah, Pahang, Darul Makmur. Tel: (09) 477 8000. Email: tasikchini@hotmail.com.

Malaysian Overland Adventures: Lot 1.23, 1st Floor, Bangunan Angkasaraya, Jalan Ampang, 50450 Kuala Lumpur. Tel: (03) 241 3569. Fax: (03) 241 4030.

Teluk Cempedak (Kuantan)

Five kilometres (3 miles) outside Kuantan, Teluk Cempedak is a sizeable beach with good swimming and a wide range of accommodation and watersports facilities. Some development is taking place, but a few minutes' walk around the headland to the north will bring you to an untouched, natural beach where eagles ride the thermals above the headland and monkeys from the jungle behind roam the sands. Teluk Cempedak has a good selection of seafood restaurants and food stalls on the beachfront.

MAS has flights to Kuala Lumpur. Air Asia has a daily flight to Kuala Lumpur. Buses connect Kuantan to Singapore, Kuala Lumpur and coastal resorts. From Kuantan, Teluk Cempedak is reached by bus or taxi.

Coral reefs

A thriving coral reef is a glorious sight, a magical kaleidoscope of beautiful fish and colourful life forms. Second only to rainforests in the number of animals and plants that they support, it is little wonder that reefs captivate the imagination of divers and snorkellers, compelling them to return again and again to experience this dazzling and intricate environment.

Coral reefs have existed for around 450 million years in one form or another, making them probably the oldest ecosystems on the planet. Although corals look like plants, coral reefs are in fact built by a tiny animal, the coral polyp. This remarkable creature is responsible for building the largest structures made by life on earth. This ability is even more extraordinary in that it is achieved in shallow, tropical waters where the nutrients essential for growth are virtually nonexistent. The polyp is able to do this thanks to the symbiotic relationship it has with tiny plants called zooxanthellae that live within its tissues. The zooxanthellae convert carbon dioxide by photosynthesis into oxygen and carbohydrates, which the polyp uses to build its stony, limestone skeleton – which in turn builds up to form a reef.

A diver surrounded by a flurry of butterfly fish

Anyone seeing a coral reef for the first time is likely to find it a bewildering and mysterious place, teeming with life of every description in what seems to be a random explosion of exuberance and colour. But beneath the apparent chaos there are complex patterns of behaviour that allow the vast array of reef creatures to share this habitat and thrive. Some fish, such as cardinalfish, squirrelfish and soldierfish, only feed at night. As they disappear into nooks and crannies at daylight, others emerge to take over the niches they have vacated. The gaudy parrotfish

The reefs of Malaysia are home to a teeming array of iridescent fish and colourful corals

(which spends the night wrapped in a protective layer of mucus that renders it undetectable to predators) emerges to nibble away on corals; damselfish take up their places on patches of seaweed, which they 'farm', chasing away other herbivores; other fish – such as fusiliers or the glittering members of the Chromis family – feed on passing plankton. Others, the triggerfish and pufferfish, for example, specialise in eating sea-urchins. As the day dawns, the main reef predators like sharks and barracuda cruise in from the open ocean to hunt on the reef walls and channels.

For aeons, reefs have provided coastal communities in the tropics with a bountiful harvest of food as well as products such as jewellery, medicines and building materials. Until recently, coral reefs were able to withstand this harvest, but they are now under threat from a wider range of human activities – coastal development, over-fishing, sewage pollution and damage by tourists. The need to protect this fabulous and fragile ecosystem has never been greater.

A red-tooth triggerfish

SARAWAK

Sarawak is the largest state in Malaysia, stretching about 700km (435 miles) along the northwest coast of Borneo and flanked by Sabah, Brunei and the Indonesian province of Kalimantan. The economy is mostly dependent on natural resources such as oil, gas, pepper and, of course, timber.

Around 3 million people visit Sarawak every year, most of them drawn by the forests, national parks, caves and the fascinating diversity of peoples and tribal culture.

While oil and timber wealth may have transformed a few boom towns, many of the tribes still follow their traditional lifestyles (with the exception, naturally, of head-hunting) and live in longhouses, with the entire community under one roof. For many visitors, an overnight stay in a longhouse is the highlight of their trip.

There are few good roads in Sarawak so transport is mostly by river-boat or aeroplane: internal MAS flights (and flights to Sabah) are good value and save days of arduous travelling.

Kuching

When James Brooke became Rajah of Sarawak in 1841, he chose Kuching as his base. Located on the banks of the Sarawak River, 32km (20 miles) inland from the sea, this is a delightful city and the main springboard for adventures in Sarawak. It has several first-class hotels, a handful of interesting sights, and is one of the best places to buy tribal arts and crafts (*see p129*).

Astana

Charles Brooke, nephew of James, built this palace when he became Rajah in 1870. Brooding on the opposite side of the river from the Kuching, it is not open to the public, but you can jump on one of the small *tambangs* or river-taxis, which ply backwards and forwards to the other bank, for a closer look.

The riverfront at Kuching

Sarawak

Fort Margherita

Now a Police Museum, the fort was built by Charles Brooke to protect Kuching from pirates and named after his wife. *Downstream from the Astana, accessible by* tambang. *Tel: (082) 440 811. Open: Tue–Sun 10am–6pm. Closed: Mon. Free admission.*

Pasar Minggu (Sunday Market)

This is an incredible market with an amazing variety of plants and fruits harvested by the Bidayuh people (Land Dyaks). They come in with their produce on Friday nights and sleep by their stalls for the weekend, trimming up neat, symmetrical displays of curious roots and fruits as well as more familiar items such as whole honeycombs or small, very fierce chillies. Other Bidayuh whittle away at bamboo hearts or sell whole bamboos for cooking rice in (known as *pulut*, it is served sliced into sections). It is open on Saturday night as well, but the busiest day is Sunday. *Jalan Satok (from the town centre, walk down Jala P Ramlee and turn right at the roundabout).*

Sarawak Museum

Well worth a visit for the extensive ethnographic sections in both the older half (founded in 1891) and the new section (opened in 1983). Other displays focus on the animals and birds of the Borneo jungle, the marine life, and the cats – in deference to the name of the capital of Sarawak (*kuching* means 'cat' in Malay). *Jalan Tun Haji Openg. Five-minute walk from the town centre. Tel: (082) 244 232. www.museum.sarawak.gov.my. Open: daily 9am–4.30pm. Free admission.*

Bako National Park

Covering the entire northern section of the jagged Muara Tebas peninsula, Bako National Park is just two hours away from Kuching and is one of the most easily accessible wilderness areas in Sarawak. The country's oldest national park, it was chosen because of the enormous variety of flora and bird life found here: the diversity of plant life is unique, with many different types of vegetation and habitat. In addition, the coastline is spectacular, with small bays, beaches and coves backed by tall sandstone cliffs, and sea arches weathered into honeycomb patterns.

The park headquarters and visitors' accommodation is located behind the beach at Telok Assam, where there is a well laid-out Interpretative Centre. Within the park grounds are long-tailed macaques, silver-leaf monkeys and the strange bearded pig that saunters around the compound. Throughout the park there are over 30km (19 miles) of well-maintained trails, divided into 16 different routes (*see pp80–81*). Perhaps not the most spectacular of Sarawak's parks, it is, however, well managed and easily accessible, containing much that can be quietly enjoyed and appreciated.

37km (23 miles) from Kuching. Bus 6 from the marketplace goes to Kampung Bako, from where you have to catch a boat. Accommodation available in the park ranges from camping to hostel beds, rooms or rest houses. Permits must be obtained in advance from the Sarawak National Parks Booking Office, Tourist Information Centre, Main Bazaar, Kuching 93000. Tel: (082) 248 088.

Orchids at the Bako National Park

Gunung Mulu National Park

Sarawak's largest national park covers 529sq km (204sq miles) of mixed peat swamp and dipterocarp and montane forests. It is rich in plant and bird life (including eight species of hornbill), but the most compelling attractions are the massive caves, notably the Deer Cave (which is said to have the largest cave passage in the world), Clearwater Cave (which is criss-crossed with underground rivers), Wind Cave and Lang Cave.

Further caverns are being explored and opened to the public. On the other side of Gunung Mulu (a three-day trek around the mountain) are spectacular, 45m (148ft) high limestone pinnacles.

150km (93 miles) southeast of Miri. Flights from Miri land just outside the park. Accommodation is best booked in advance through the Miri Visitor Information Centre: Lot 452, Jalan Melayu. Tel: 085 434 181.

Email: stb@sarawaktourism.com. Permits for trekking can be obtained at the Park Headquarters, and further information can be found at www.mulupark.com

Iban longhouses

Each tribe has its own variation on the longhouse. Several variations of these can be seen at the Sarawak Cultural Village (*see p78*), but essentially they all embody the same principle, which is of several families living under one roof with their individual rooms leading off from a communal, enclosed veranda.

The most accessible longhouses to visit are those of the Iban, since they nearly always settle on the banks of navigable rivers. From the boat jetty, steps lead up the river bank to a central garden with strips of land allocated to each family. Corn, beans and pumpkins share garden space with fishing nets hung out to dry, boats under repair, and foraging chickens and pigs. Around the garden are the longhouses themselves, raised off the ground on stilts.

Longhouse visits on the Skrang River can be organised through travel agents in Kuching. There are fewer organised tours on the Rajang River, so you will either have to go it alone or try to hire a freelance tour guide. The latter is the best option, since unless you speak Iban you will need a guide to translate, as well as to advise you on how to behave with your hosts and to make arrangements for hiring a boat and organising food and gifts to take with you.

Once at the longhouse, you will stay in the family room of the *Tuai Rumah* (chief) and, after eating, the whole community will gather on the veranda for singing and dancing with plenty of *tuak* (rice wine) to make the party go. This is not a goldfish-bowl show for your benefit, since you will be expected to participate actively – usually resulting in much hilarity all round. In this respect, the larger the group you travel with the better, since the Iban will be disappointed if performances fizzle out early because your talents (musical or otherwise) have been exhausted.

Although many longhouses now have tin roofs and electricity, there may not be any toilet facilities and you will have to wash in the river, as they do, so you should be prepared to rough it.

Melanau longhouse, Sarawak

Kampung Budaya Sarawak (Sarawak Cultural Village)

Designed as a 'living museum' of Sarawak's rich cultural heritage, this award-winning project is set in 7 hectares (17 acres) of landscaped grounds at the foot of Gunung Santubong, behind Damai Beach. Scattered around an artificial lake are seven different ethnic dwellings, with typical longhouses of the Bidayuh, Iban and Orang-Ulu, a Melanau 'Rumah Tinggi' (a massive communal house on stilts), Penan huts, a Malay home and a Chinese farmhouse.

Upon entering, guides welcome you and cheerfully chat about the lifestyles and customs of their various tribes. There is something going on in each dwelling whether it be a handicraft demonstration, preparing ethnic foods, blow-pipe making, drumming or traditional games. Twice daily there is a highly entertaining dance show.

It sounds contrived and the entrance price is steep, but it is extremely informative and well organised, and there is plenty to occupy at least half a day. There is a restaurant and handicraft shop.

Kampung Budaya Sarawak, Pantai Damai, PO Box 2632, 93752 Sarawak. Tel: (082) 846 411. www.scv.com.my. Open: daily 9am–5.15pm. Admission charge. A shuttle bus from the Holiday Inn and Riverside Majestic, Kuching, stops at the gates.

Miri

A boom oil town near the border with Brunei, Miri is a useful transit point for permits for the Niah Caves or Gunung Mulu from the National Parks Office. Dull in the daytime, it is enlivened by numerous seedy bars – and some excellent seafood restaurants – in the evenings, when Bruneians cross the border to join in the fun.

Frequent MAS and Air Asia flights to Kuching, Kota Kinabalu and Johor Bahru, with connections through to Kuala Lumpur.

Niah Caves

'The cave deposits of this part of Borneo are wholly without interest except to local naturalists,' wrote the explorer A Hart Everett in 1879. He was mistaken, but it was not until nearly 80 years later that it became clear just how spectacularly wrong Everett had been. Excavations at Niah revolutionised prevailing theories on the distribution of early humankind across the globe. In 1957 the Curator of Sarawak Museum, Tom Harrisson, discovered a skull and other artefacts dating back to 37,500 BC, drawing worldwide attention to the caves and conclusively disproving the idea that early *Homo sapiens* had originated in Europe. Some of these finds are on display in the Sarawak Museum in Kuching. The famous skull can be seen at the Niah Park Headquarters.

The cave system lies underneath the limestone massif of Gunung Subis, in the centre of what is now the Niah

National Park. The crucial evidence was unearthed in the west mouth of the Great Cave (where the archaeological workings can still be seen), an awesome natural cathedral over 60m (197ft) high and around 245m (804 ft) wide, which is among the largest caves in the world. The magnitude of the cave, heightened by the sense of scale given to it by a handful of old buildings at its entrance, is overwhelming.

The caves are also still one of the major centres in Sarawak for a trade that is itself centuries old, the collecting of swifts' nests to make the highly prized bird's-nest soup.

The park headquarters is at Pangkalan Lubang, which is reached by a short boat ride from Batu Niah village. Buses or shared taxis run from Miri and Bintulu to Batu Niah. The caves are 4km (2½ miles) away along a plankwalk from the park HQ. Accommodation should be booked in advance through the Miri Visitor Information Centre: Lot 452, Jalan Melayu. Tel: (085) 434 181. Email: stb@sarawaktourism.com

Pantai Damai (Damai Beach)

The nearest coastal resort to Kuching, Damai has a reasonable beach, good views of Gunung Santubong (Mount Santubong) and a comfortable hotel.

35km (22 miles) north of Kuching. Damai Beach Resort, PO Box 2870, 93756 Kuching. Tel: (082) 846 999. Shuttle bus from the Holiday Inn all day.

Sibu

The second town of Sarawak and the main port on the Rajang River, Sibu is 60km (37 miles) from the coast. You can travel from here further upstream to Song or Kapit and then branch off into tributaries of the Rajang to visit Iban longhouses. From the top of the Chinese temple on the waterfront in Sibu there is a bird's-eye view of river traffic, including the log barges being towed downstream to the sawmills. Directly beneath the temple is the quay where the passenger boats berth. These extraordinary, fuselage-shaped speedboats that churn up and down the river from jetty to jetty all day are the chief means of transport on the river.

An exhibit of Iban weaving at the Sarawak Cultural Village

Walk: Bako National Park

This relatively easy walk mostly follows the Lintang Trail, which loops around behind the park headquarters and encompasses most of the different types of habitat to be seen at Bako. If you leave in the early afternoon you will arrive at Telok Delima, near the end of the walk, at the right time of day to try to see proboscis monkeys.

Allow 3–4 hours.

Starting from the park headquarters, cross the boardwalk through the mangroves and ascend the hill to the plateau. After a 10-minute climb you will come out in the kerangas *scrub.*

1 Ant-plants

Kerangas is an Iban word meaning 'land where rice cannot be grown'; because of the poor soil conditions there are few large trees and many plants have adapted ingenious mechanisms in order to make the most of the harsh environment. One such is the amazing ant-plant, of which there are four common species on the plateau.
The ants and the plants coexist in a symbiotic (mutually beneficial) relationship: the ants live inside the plant, and the debris they deposit contains nutrients that are in short supply in the soil.
At the junction with the Tanjor Trail, turn right. Shortly afterwards, the track slopes gently up through typical kerangas *pole forest.*

2 Kerangas pole forest

Such forest is characterised by dense strands of saplings and enormous Nibong bamboos, with sunlight dappling the spreading leaves of wild sago palms.
Follow the signpost on your left to the Bukit Tambi lookout.

3 Bukit Tambi lookout

From this vantage point there are magnificent views of Mount Santubong and Pulau Lekei. To the left, some of Kuching's buildings can be seen.
Continue along the Lintang Trail, following the red way-marks until you come to the junction with the Ulu Serait path. Turn left down here for a short way.

4 Carnivorous plants

This section of track is a good place to look for some of the rarer species of the pitcher plant. The leaves on these carnivorous plants have been modified to form a hollow tube containing a liquid into which insects fall. It is from this liquid that they are then digested. Other carnivorous plants include bladderworts and sundews.

Continue down the Lintang Trail. Eventually you will emerge at a lookout point above Telok Delima, from where the track descends more steeply, with wooden steps skirting huge, lichen-covered boulders.

5 Proboscis monkeys

Telok Delima is one of the best places to see the park's extraordinary-looking proboscis monkeys. As you descend, you will hear them hooting in the tree-tops. The males, with their huge, pendulous noses and large pot-bellies, look remarkably human. Females have a shorter, stubbier nose. Found only in Borneo and two small islands off its northeast coast, the species is restricted to mangroves and the river-bank and peat-swamp forests of the central lowlands. Habitat destruction is the greatest threat to their survival, and of the 1,000 still extant, 150 live here.

Continue on past Telok Delima to return to the park headquarters.

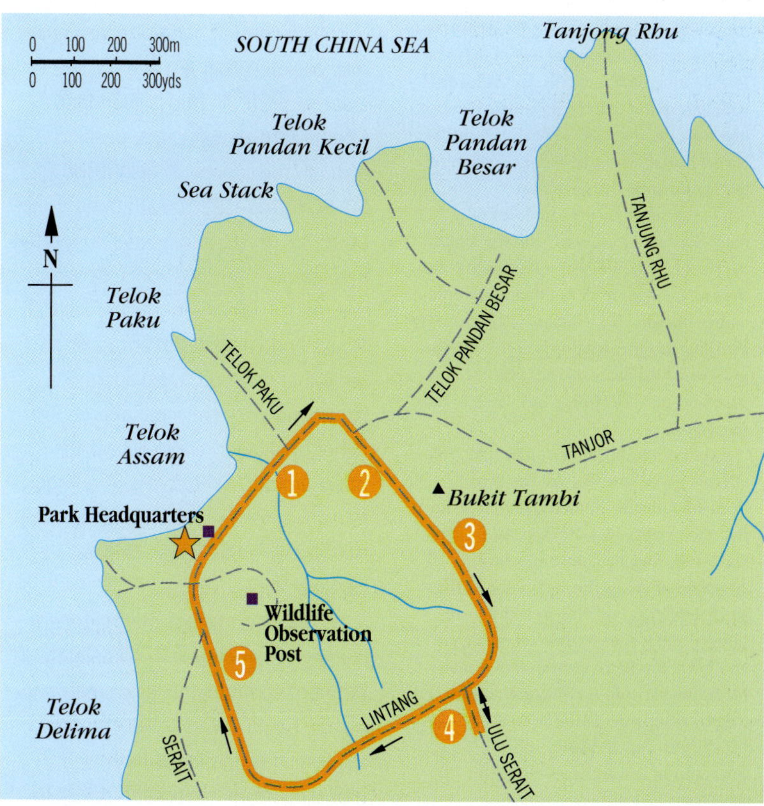

Rainforests

Most people tend to think of tropical rainforest simply as 'jungle', a steamy, impenetrable mass of vegetation containing enormous trees that somehow play a role in reducing the greenhouse effect. In fact, there are several kinds of rainforest, each with its own plant and animal communities, and each recognisable as a distinct ecosystem shaped by variations in soil, rainfall, altitude and human impacts.

Lowland rainforest is one of the most productive and biologically diverse habitats on the planet, home to more than half of all species in existence. Several hundred tree species may coexist within a space the size of a soccer pitch; the most abundant trees are the dipterocarps, pushing through the canopy to heights of 50–80m (164–262ft), with huge trunks up to 2m (6½ft) in diameter supported by enormous buttress roots. Beneath the canopy, lianas cling to the vertical trunks and epiphytes (plants such as ferns that grow on trees) abound. At ground level, the vegetation is less dense, making it relatively easy to move around in the forest. The largest remaining tract of lowland rainforest in Malaysia is in the Taman Negara National Park.

At higher altitudes, the rainforest changes character, with completely different communities of animals and plants. Up to 750m (2,460ft) above sea level it is known as lower montane (from 'mountain') forest,

LOGGING

Malaysia is the biggest exporter of tropical hardwoods in the world. In many parts of the country you will witness the destruction that has caused such an outcry in the West. In the Cameron Highlands, trucks loaded with logs roar down the mountain roads at night; on the rivers of Sarawak, streams of barges loaded with tree-trunks are hauled by tugs down to the sawmills.

One of the problems with forestry management in Malaysia is enforcement of the laws, with insufficient resources to police the vast areas of forest. Another is corruption, with politicians able to amass vast fortunes by awarding lucrative logging licences. To this must be added the disastrous practice of slash-and-burn clearing, which leads to huge forest fires.

Sarawak's rural communities have been affected by these activities. The Penan, Borneo's nomadic hunter-gatherers, claim that their rights are not respected by the State or by logging companies, and complain of illness through polluted rivers, game depletion resulting in widespread hunger, and loss of traditional medicines and forest products. Protests and timber blockades between native communities and logging companies are common. These are usually peaceful; however, police intervention is sometimes required.

The rainforests of Malaysia are home to myriad plant species

above 1,500m (4,920ft) as upper montane forest. The forest giants are less common at higher altitudes, with few trees reaching above 10m (33ft) in height. Temperate species such as oaks and heather predominate, and mosses and lichens thrive in the moist, cool air. These types of rainforest (sometimes also called 'cloud forests') can be found in the Central Highlands on the peninsula and on the slopes of Gunung Kinabalu in Sabah.

Where the virgin rainforest has been cleared by logging or for agriculture, a host of secondary species spring up to fill the vacant niches. Fishtail palms, resam ferns and other light-dependent species coat the forest floor. In the short term, animals and birds are driven out, but as the original plant communities regenerate, some wildlife gradually returns.

Plants crowd together in this dynamic ecosystem

SABAH

Sabah is the second-largest state in Malaysia after Sarawak and occupies the northeast sector of the island of Borneo. Whereas Sarawak is dominated by rivers, Sabah is synonymous with mountains – in particular, the towering massif of Gunung (Mount) Kinabalu, which at 4,101m (13,455ft) is the highest mountain between Papua New Guinea and the Himalayas. The surrounding national park is a treasure-house of plant and animal communities, an oasis of biological splendour in one of the largest remaining tracts of rainforest left in the country.

Other popular attractions include the world's largest orang-utan sanctuary at Sepilok, colourful tamus or tribal markets, and offshore islands ringed with coral reefs such as those in the Tunku Abdul Rahman National Park and Pulau Sipadan in the Celebes Sea – for scuba-divers the jewel in Malaysia's crown.

During the 17th and 18th centuries, when the European powers fought over the great seaports of Peninsular Malaysia, the island of Borneo remained relatively isolated. Most trading ships avoided this mysterious land, from whence came tales of rapacious pirates and head-hunting tribes lurking in the impenetrable jungle. Most of the land was nominally under the control of the Sultan of Brunei.

In the late 19th century an Englishman called Alfred Dent signed a lease with the Sultan of Brunei and the Sultan of Sulu (who ruled in the northeast of the country) and gained control of North Borneo. In 1881 Dent formed the British North Borneo Company, but they were not as successful as the white rajahs in neighbouring Sarawak at governing the populace. In 1895 the introduction of new taxes led to the famous Mat Salleh Rebellion, led by the charismatic figure of Mat Salleh, who was believed to be in possession of supernatural powers. The rebellion was not put down until 1905, although Mat Salleh himself was killed in 1900. Today, he is one of Sabah's best-known national heroes.

After World War II, both Sabah and Sarawak were handed over to the British government and became Crown Colonies. In 1963 they were merged into the Federation of Malaysia.

As you will find elsewhere in Malaysia, Sabah is a melting pot of people and cultures. The population of just over 1.5 million encompasses over

Rare proboscis monkeys near Sepilok, Sabah

Sabah

30 different tribes and races speaking some 100 different dialects, all with their own unique traditions, customs, festivals and culture.

The largest indigenous group are the Kadazan/Dusuns, who comprise around 30 per cent of the population and live mostly on the west coast. Traditionally they were the main rice producers in the country, although many now work outside agriculture. The second-largest group are the Bajau, who were once fearless sailors and wanderers. Now, most Bajau are settled on the land and renowned for their skills in horsemanship as well as in rearing livestock. Many Bajau Laut ('Sea Bajau', also called Sea Gypsies) still live on or near the water, in stilt villages or in boats known as *lipa-lipa*. The third main group are the Murut, who are mostly from the southwest and the interior. Their livelihood traditionally depended on hunting and shifting cultivation.

Travelling around Sabah presents few problems, with frequent and reliable minibuses linking towns and cities. Although some roads are still potholed and bumpy, most have been upgraded. If you want to save time, MAS and Air Asia operate a number of regular flights that are good value for money.

Gomantong Caves

These huge limestone caves, 32km (20 miles) from Sandakan, are home to around a million swiftlets. Locals collect the nests using the same, centuries-old techniques as they do at the Niah Caves in Sarawak (*see pp78–9*). The trip to the caves involves a boat-ride across the bay from Sandakan and then 16km (10 miles) by four-wheel drive through the forest.

Two-day expeditions to the Gomantong Caves and wildlife watching on the Kinabatangan River are organised by Wildlife Expeditions, Room 903, 9th Floor, Wisma Khoo Siak Chiew, Sandakan (tel: (089) 219 616; www.wildlife-expeditions.com).

The gigantic Gomantong Caves with ladders stretching to the ceiling used by bird's nest collectors

Kinabalu National Park

The Kinabalu National Park is one of Sabah's major attractions. Climbers are drawn to the towering peaks of Gunung Kinabalu (Mount Kinabalu), but there is more to Kinabalu than simply the challenge of climbing the mountain, since within the huge expanse of the park (which covers over 750sq km/290sq miles) a great variety of habitats can be found.

Within this protected environment a rich and diverse flora flourishes. One of the most famous species for which Kinabalu is known is the parasitic *Rafflesia*, the world's largest flower, with red blooms that can measure 1m (3ft) wide. Over 1,000 species of orchid can be found within the park, as well as over 20 varieties of rhododendron and a dozen different kinds of carnivorous pitcher plants (*Nepenthes*). Over half the plants growing above 900m (2,950ft) are found nowhere else in the world.

Despite claims that Kinabalu is an 'easy climb', the ascent to the summit takes two days and is a demanding haul even for those who are fit. If you intend to make the ascent, a comprehensive booklet, *Guide to the Summit Trail*, is available at the park shop. If you don't have the time to reach the summit there are well-marked trails around the park headquarters (*see pp92–3*).

Within the park there is a wide range of accommodation, two canteens and a shop selling necessities.

Overnight accommodation must be booked in advance through the Sabah Parks Office, Lot 1–3, Block K, Sinsuran Complex, Kota Kinabalu (tel: (088) 211 881/212 719; www.sabahparks.org.my).

Park headquarters is 60km (37 miles) from Kota Kinabalu, 2 hours by bus.

Kota Belud

This small town to the northeast of Kota Kinabalu is well worth visiting on Sunday mornings for the weekly *tamu* (market), where tribal peoples bring their produce to sell and Bajau 'cowboys' auction their horses and buffaloes. Although colourful enough on a normal Sunday, the best time to visit Kota Belud is at the annual Tamu Besar (*see p23*).

Minibuses from Kota Kinabalu take 1½ hours. The tamu *is a short distance outside Kota Belud.*

Kota Kinabalu

The state capital of Sabah is a relatively new city – the town was almost totally destroyed during World War II – and although its tree-lined avenues are pleasant enough, it has none of the historical resonances of Kuching. Apart from the State Mosque, whose gold dome glistens against a backdrop of jungle-clad hills, the main tourist attraction is the **Sabah State Museum**, which houses ceramics and craftwork from Bajau, Murut, Kadazan/Dusun and Rungus peoples. The mock-ups of tribal longhouses in the museum grounds are also well worth a look.

For most people Kota Kinabalu is a transit stop before heading out to explore points north and east. Day trips from here can be made to the Tunku Abdul Rahman Park (*see pp90–91*) and Kota Belud.

Sabah State Museum, Jalan Mat Salleh. Tel: (088) 253 199. www.mzm.sabah.gov.my. Open: Sat–Thur 9am–5pm. Closed: Fri. Free admission.

The Sabah State Mosque at Kota Kinabalu has a commanding presence in the capital city

Poring Hot Springs

Part of the Kinabalu National Park, the hot springs are an hour or so away from park headquarters. The sulphurous water steams into a series of old-fashioned tubs where you can soothe your aching muscles after climbing the mountain.

A short walk further up the hill there is a terrific **Canopy Tree Walk** that sways between the tree-tops and provides a great view of the forest at canopy level. Despite the fact that it is netted and quite safe, the 200m (656ft) long walkway can still induce vertigo as you look down to the forest floor some 50m (164ft) below ('scary but great fun' was a typical comment in the visitors' book at the last tree).

19km (12 miles) north of Ranau, reached by minibus or taxi. Tel: (088) 243 629 (for accommodation). Open: daily 7am–6pm. Admission charge.

Canopy Tree Walk. Open: 10.30am–4pm. Admission charge. There are hostels and chalets for overnight stays – book through the Sabah Parks Office (see p86).

Pulau Sipadan

As the boat from Semporna approaches Pulau Sipadan across the Celebes Sea, it looks no different from any other tropical island – a small blob in the ocean surrounded by white coral-sand beaches and topped off by jungle vegetation. Sipadan, however, is not just any old island. It is the only deep-water oceanic island in Malaysia and sits on top of a massive limestone sea-mountain that extends some 600m (1,969ft) down to the sea bed. A magnificent reef ecosystem has developed on the sheer walls of this sea-mountain, and it is a magnet for divers from all over the world.

Accommodation on the island is basic, as befits a resort where the majority of visitors are inclined to spend most of the day underwater. There are three dive lodges on the island, the longest-established of which is the Sipadan Dive Lodge operated by Borneo Divers. For non-diving partners the 12-hectare (30-acre) island has a few short jungle trails to explore (the island is also an important bird-nesting site), but apart from that there is nothing to do except relax.

The diving is exceptional. Just a stone's throw from the beach bar, the pale aquamarine waters over the sandy sea bed change abruptly to hues of deep blue, indicating the beginning of the massive coral drop-off. Underwater, the reef is a profusion of sea-fans, black coral, soft corals and iridescent hard corals inhabited by shoals of fusiliers, parrotfish, grouper, sweetlips and other colourful fish.

Because of its position in mid-ocean, Sipadan also has large numbers of pelagic (open-water) species cruising the reefs, with schools of manta rays, barracuda and hammerhead sharks frequently seen in currents on the reef headlands. There are so many turtles here (hundreds, possibly thousands, live around Sipadan) that once underwater you can hardly turn around without seeing them snoozing under reef ledges, scooting off into the deep blue, feeding on the reef or floundering around on the surface as they mate.

Turtles nest on the beach all year round (the peak season is from August to October) and most nights there is a guided walk with a ranger to watch them (walking on your own at night around the island is prohibited).

Pulau Sipadan is 1½ hours by speedboat from Semporna. Dive packages are available, usually for 5 days, typically including transfers from Kota Kinabalu, accommodation, food, three boat-dives per day and unlimited beach diving.
Borneo Divers. 9th Floor, Menara Jubili, 53 Jalan Gaya, Kota Kinabalu. Tel: (088) 222 226. www.borneodivers.info.
Pulau Sipadan Resort. 484 Bandar Sabindo, Block P, PO Box 61120. Tawau. Tel: (089) 765 200. www.sipadan-resort.com.
Sandakan Office, Ground Floor, Lot 38 & 39, Mile 6, Bandar Tyng. Tel: (089) 673 999.

Sandakan

Sandakan was the capital of Sabah from 1884 until it was demolished by Allied bombing at the end of World War II, after which the capital was transferred to Kota Kinabalu. This compact, modern city holds few sights of its own, but is the main gateway in eastern Sabah for nearby attractions, such as the Sepilok Orang-Utan Sanctuary, the Gomantong Caves and the Turtle Islands National Park.

Frequent MAS and Air Asia flights link Sandakan with Kota Kinabalu (40 minutes). Long-distance minibuses

Puu Jih Shih Temple, Sandakan

take around 8 hours to cover the 386km (240 miles) to the capital.

Semporna

This small town on the southeastern tip of Sabah is the departure point for Sipadan Island. It has a lively waterfront market, and boats can be hired to visit the nearby stilt village of the Bajau Laut, Sabah's renowned 'sea gypsies'. Tourist facilities are virtually non-existent, and excursions are costly. *MAS flies to nearby Tawau and there are frequent minibuses from Tawau. The comfortable Dragon Inn stands on stilts over the water.*

Sepilok Orang-utan Sanctuary

The Sepilok Orang-utan Sanctuary was established in 1964 to re-train young orang-utans, captured illegally for the wildlife trade, to fend for themselves and re-adapt to natural ways. The sanctuary now primarily handles orphaned orang-utans brought in from logging camps. The young apes have to be taught survival skills by the wildlife rangers before being taken to the forest where their new life begins, but they are still fed twice daily while learning to forage for themselves.

Feeding times (10am & 2.30pm daily at Platform A) are the high point of the day and are a great magnet for tourists and photographers.

Further into the forest (half-an-hour's walk from Platform A) is the second feeding station, Platform B, where some orang-utans still turn up for a supplementary feed. Rangers leave the Education Centre at 11am for this trek.

The sanctuary is just a small part of the 4,000-hectare (9,884-acre) Sepilok Forest Reserve, which is home to a wide range of wildlife including Bornean gibbons, proboscis monkeys, Malaysian sun bears, barking deer and pangolins. *24km (15 miles) from Sandakan, 11km (7 miles) from Sandakan airport. Open: daily, 8am–noon, 2–4pm. Further details from Sabah Parks Office (see p86). Admission charge. Buses (marked 'Sepilok Batu 14') depart from Sandakan at 9.20am, 11.20am, 1pm & 3pm; journey time 45 minutes. The timing for watching the feeding is inconvenient, and it is better to take a shared taxi if possible. It is feasible to visit Sepilok for the day from Kota Kinabalu, using an MAS return flight.*

Tunku Abdul Rahman Park

The five islands in the Tunku Abdul Rahman Park are easily reached from Kota Kinabalu for day trips or overnight stays. The islands have good beaches, coral reefs for snorkelling and diving, and unpolluted water.

The largest island is **Pulau Gaya**, covering 1,500 hectares (3,707 acres), with one of the best beaches at Bulijong Bay (also known as Police Bay). The island has 20km (12 miles) of walking trails through the forests and mangroves, and is home to monkeys, pangolins and bearded pigs. Outside the park boundary there is a huge stilt village.

The second-largest island is **Pulau Manukan**, the location of the park headquarters, which has been redeveloped with chalets, a swimming pool, restaurant and bar. Watersports available include water-skiing, windsurfing and dinghy-sailing.

The most heavily visited of the islands is **Pulau Sapi**, off the southwest tip of Pulau Gaya. There are camping and picnic facilities. **Pulau Mamutik** is the smallest island in the park, and is also popular with day-trippers on weekends and holidays. **Pulau Sulug**, the most remote of the islands, is the least visited and as yet has no facilities.

Boats to the islands leave from the quay behind the Hyatt Hotel in Kota Kinabalu. Accommodation or camping must be booked in advance through the Sabah Parks Office, Lot 1–3, Block K, Sinsuran Complex, Kota Kinabalu (tel: (088) 211 881/ 212 719; www.sabahparks.org.my).

Turtle Islands National Park

These islands are an important turtle-nesting location and have been a marine park since 1977. The main islands are Pulau Selingan, Pulau Gulisan and Pulau Bakungan Kecil; green turtles predominantly nest on Pulau Selingan, while hawksbills are more common on Pulau Gulisan. The main nesting season is August to October, and you can stay in the Sabah Parks Chalets on Pulau Selingan to watch the turtles at night.

40km (25 miles) from Sandakan, 3 hours by boat. Permits and accommodation bookings through the Sabah Parks Office (see p86).

An inhabitant of the Sepilok Orang-utan Sanctuary

Walk: Mount Kinabalu National Park

This walk links up the Kiau View Trail with parts of the Silau-Silau and Mempening trails to make a circuit around the central park area. It is an easy walk, and the starting point is the reception area at the park entrance.

Allow 2½ hours.

Pass under the entrance archway and take the track marked Kiau View Trail.

1 Kiau View Trail

The trail climbs fairly steeply beside a moss- and fern-covered bank for the first 10 minutes before levelling off near the first shelter. As you walk along the ridge, the dense woodland on either side displays a glorious profusion of mosses, ferns and bamboo. Since this is one of the least-used trails, there is a good chance of seeing birdlife, such as scarlet sunbirds, grey drongos, laughing thrushes and Malaysian treepies.

The trail winds gently up the eastern end of the ridge until you reach the second shelter, after which it is more or less level going.

2 Orchids

Along the track, cobwebs by the hundreds festoon the wayside plants. Hidden away on the forest floor are orchids such as the yellow-flowered *Spathoglottis*, the small *Spiranthes* and the bamboo orchid, *Arundin.*

After about 1 hour, you will reach the last lookout point, and immediately afterwards the track descends to the metalled Power Station Road. Turn left and then right on to the Silau-Silau Trail.

3 Silau-Silau Trail

The path follows the course of the Dewan Kinabalu. Look out for frogs along the banks (some 45 species inhabit Kinabalu), or the bizarre Borneo sucker-fish (*Gastromyzon borneensis*), which has developed a means of clinging to rocks so that it can graze on the algae found there. There are also thousands of species of insects in the park; one of the easiest to spot is the black and orange trilobite beetle, which chews its way slowly over decaying logs.

Turn left at the next junction and follow the signs up to Bukit Tupai shelter, turning right on the Mempening Trail.

4 Mempening Trail

On a clear day there are spectacular views of the summit of Mount

Kinabalu. Temperate species such as oaks proliferate, with ferns such as the broad-leaved *dipteris* covering the ground beneath them. One unusual tree that is common here is *tristania*, easily identified by its peeling bark.

Continue until you reach Bukit Burung shelter, and then descend. Once you reach the stream turn right, then left across the wooden bridge, and right at the road. Follow the road up past the Sports Centre until you reach the Mountain Garden.

5 Mountain Garden

This very beautiful and well-kept little garden contains over 3,000 orchids (representing some 500 species) and 4,000 other plants.

Open: Mon–Fri 7.30am–4.30pm, Sat 8am–5pm, Sun & public holidays 9am–4pm. Free admission.

In front of the Mountain Garden is the administration building, with a road leading back to the park entrance.

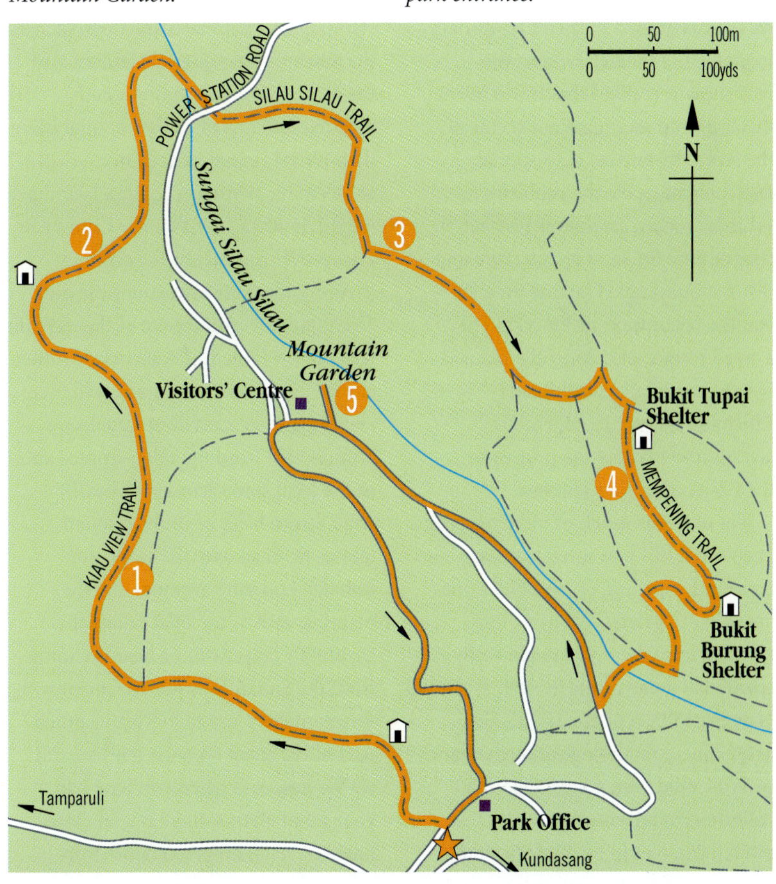

Singapore

For many visitors Singapore is synonymous with gleaming skyscrapers and endless shopping malls. They have a vision of a modern and efficient city of air-conditioned concrete and glass buildings. Is this really all there is to Singapore? Two decades ago the answer might have been 'yes'. While economists praised the achievement that has made Singapore the wealthiest country in Southeast Asia, visitors went elsewhere in search of the authentic Orient.

As visitors elected to spend fewer days in Singapore than elsewhere, the government realised that it was losing income from an important sector of the economy and set up a special task force to tackle the problem. Its solution was an ambitious restoration programme for local architecture and historic buildings. The first project was the restoration of Emerald Hill, a small terrace of colourfully painted houses just off Orchard Road. Emerald Hill was an enormous success and became the prototype for a host of similar schemes.

Not only has much of old Singapore been saved but new attractions are constantly opening up and older ones are being upgraded. Many of these are theme parks where you could easily spend half a day or more, such as the old Haw Par Villa, reopened in 1985 as a Chinese mythological theme park, or Wild Wild Wet, a hugely popular collection of adventurous water attractions. Not to be outdone, long-standing and popular attractions such as the Singapore Zoological Gardens and the Jurong Bird Park have recently invested millions of dollars in upgrading their already excellent facilities. Underwater World on Sentosa Island is one of Southeast Asia's largest and most impressive tropical sea-life centres.

Alongside these attractions the old cosmopolitan atmosphere of the city still remains. In Little India, sari-clad women cluster over display cases of gold jewellery, while next door tantalising aromas waft from the open-fronted shop of the local spice-grinder. In nearby Arab Street, bales of multicoloured fabrics from all over the world are unloaded on the pavement and the plaintive wail of the *bilal* calling the faithful to prayer can be heard echoing from the Sultan Mosque. In Chinatown, fortune-tellers and tailors are as much part of the street scene as temples and tea-houses. And when you have had your fill of all this, there is a fabulous range of restaurants to choose from,

Singapore Island

covering the whole spectrum from colonial elegance to noisy jazz cafés.

Arab Street

In the 19th century, merchants and traders from Malaya, Java, India and Arabia created a bustling community centred around Arab Street and the nearby **Sultan Mosque** on North Bridge Road. Arab Street is now the main centre for the textile trade, with Javanese batiks, Thai and French silks, sarongs, lace, brocades and colourful cottons piled to the ceilings in the shops down either side of the road. Leather-ware and basketware shops also line the covered walkways, while nearby restaurants turn out tasty *murtabak* (savoury pancakes) and other snacks.

Bussorah Street, leading down from the Sultan Mosque, has become a pedestrian zone with more shops; many of the old houses surrounding Arab Street are being restored as part of the Kampung Glam Conservation Area. Nearby on Beach Road is the **Hajjah Fatimah Mosque**, somewhat less grandiose than the Sultan Mosque, built by a Malay woman called Hajjah Fatimah in honour of her late husband.
Both mosques can be visited outside of prayer times. MRT: Bugis. Bus: 2, 7, 12, 32, 33, 51, 61, 62, 63, 125, 130, 145, 197, 520, 851 & 960.

Armenian Apostolic Church of St Gregory (1835)

Considered to be one of the finest works of the colonial architect George Coleman (who also designed Parliament House and the Supreme Court), the Church of St Gregory was commissioned by Singapore's once-thriving Armenian community – refugees from Turkey. In the graveyard are the weather-beaten tombs of many of the Armenian settlers, including that of Agnes Joaquim, after whom Singapore's national orchid, the *Vanda* 'Miss Joaquim', is named. The oldest surviving church in the country, St Gregory's is now a national monument and no longer used as a place of worship.
Hill Street, below Fort Canning. MRT: City Hall. Bus: 2, 12, 32, 33, 51, 103, 124, 147, 174, 190, 197 & 851.

SINGAPORE – THE GARDEN CITY

One of the first things you notice in Singapore is the tropical greenery which flourishes everywhere, disguising concrete bridges and brightening up the roadside verges. This is not simply nature taking over, but part of a concerted strategy that began in the 1960s to turn Singapore into a Garden City. In the early days, the plan was limited to roadside tree-planting and creating parks. In the 1970s and 80s, the scheme developed further with the introduction of fruit trees, ferns, vines and more colourful and fragrant plants. In the 1990s, the concept grew to include a network of walkways, cycleways and canal-side paths, which were developed to link together reserves, residential areas and parks.

Even in the tropical humidity, this luxuriance means that today Singapore has become one of the most enjoyable cities in Asia to visit.

Singapore city

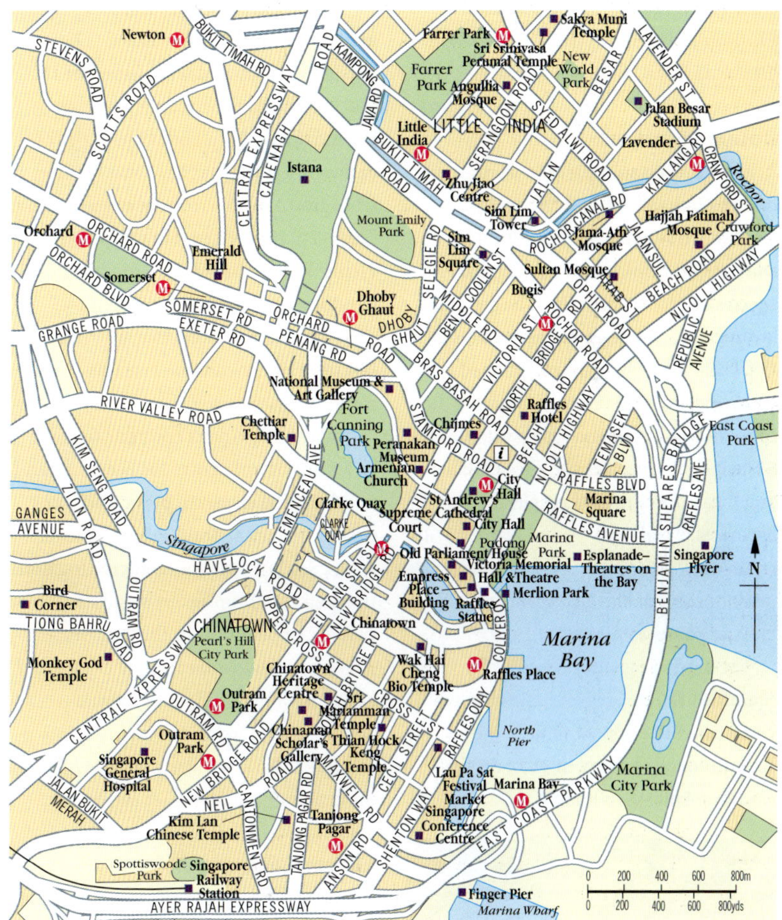

Bird Corner

Every Sunday morning, from 8am onwards, bird enthusiasts congregate in this small outdoor area for a friendly singing competition between their feathered charges. In their bamboo cages suspended on a grid above the café, melodious *merboks* and *sharmas* trill away while their owners compare diets and handling techniques. Every so often the owners move their birds around, hoping that proximity to a different neighbour will produce sweeter sounds. Some of the bamboo cages, which are decorated with porcelain or jade ornaments, are over 80 years old.

Block 4A Boon Tiong Road, Tiong Bahru Road. MRT: Either Tiong Bahru or Outram Park. Bus: 5, 16, 33, 63, 123, 195 & 851.

Botanic Gardens

Just a short distance past the northern end of Orchard Road, the attractively landscaped Botanic Gardens contain some 2,000 tropical and subtropical species of plants and trees. The grounds are popular with joggers and walkers at the weekends, with well-maintained paths meandering between lakes, gazebos, fountains and rose and fern gardens. The 52-hectare (128-acre) site also includes a small patch of primary jungle and the spectacular National Orchid Garden with over 60,000 specimens. A 'reverse greenhouse' enables alpine and cold-climate plants to flourish.

The garden's genesis lies with Sir Stamford Raffles, a keen naturalist, who established the first 'Botanical and Experimental Garden' in 1822 on Fort Canning Hill (then known as Government Hill) with the aim of introducing crops yielding spices, timber and raw materials to the island. The present gardens were established in 1859 and continued their role in fostering potentially useful plants. One of their earliest successes was the introduction from Brazil in 1877 of rubber trees, using seeds sent out by London's Kew Gardens. Henry Ridley, one of the early directors, conducted a relentless campaign to convince local planters to grow rubber, but once the pneumatic tyre was invented his perseverance paid off.

The Sultan Mosque, established by Arab traders

Today, the gardens continue to serve as an important centre for botanical and horticultural research, particularly in orchid breeding. Trail leaflets indicate where some of the more interesting and unusual or economically significant plants can be found in the gardens.

Main gate, junction of Cluny & Holland roads, another on Tyersall Avenue (opposite the Orchid Garden).
Tel: 6471 7361. www.sbg.org.sg. Open: daily 5am–midnight. Free admission. SBS bus: 7, 105, 106, 123 & 174 from Orchard Boulevard.

Bukit Timah Nature Reserve

This 81-hectare (200-acre) reserve is all that remains of the rainforests that once covered the island. It encompasses Singapore's biggest hill, Bukit Timah, a granite outcrop 163m (535ft) high, which affords good views. From the Visitor Centre, well-marked trails branch off and thread their way around the hillsides (*see pp112–13*).

Just off Upper Bukit Timah Road, at the end of Hindhede Drive (12km/7 miles from Orchard Road). Tel: 6468 5736. www.nparks.gov.sg. Open: daily 8.30am–6pm. Free admission. MRT: Newton, then bus 170 or 182.

Changi Prison Chapel and Museum

Situated in the grounds of the current Changi Prison, the museum is a moving testimony to the lives of the Allied POWs who were incarcerated here during the Japanese occupation of Singapore.

Changi Prison, 1000 Upper Changi Road North. Tel: 6214 2451. www.changimuseum.com. Open: Mon–Sat 9.30am–5pm. Free admission. MRT: Tanah Merah, then SBS bus 2. Bus: 2 & 29.

Chettiar Temple

Dedicated to the six-headed Hindu deity Lord Subramaniam, the original temple (built in 1860) was financed by local *chettiars*, or money-lenders. Rebuilt in 1984, the entrance features a typical South Indian *gopuram* (gateway), but its most unusual feature is a series of 48 glass panels in the ceiling engraved with images of the deities, which are designed to catch the light of the rising and setting sun. The temple is the end point for the Singaporean Thaipusam festival (*see pp26–7*).

15 Tank Road. Tel: 6737 9393. www.sttemple.com. Open: daily 8am–noon & 5.30–8.30pm. MRT: Dhoby Ghaut. Bus: 14, 32, 54, 65, 139 & 195.

Chinaman Scholar's Gallery

An interesting little museum assembled by antique dealer Vincent Tan, who has re-created a typical Cantonese scholar/merchant's house from the 1920s and 30s. The house contains a collection of embroidery, calligraphy and traditional Chinese stringed instruments. Mr Tan will demonstrate the instruments and perform a tea ceremony for groups.

14-B Terengganu Street. Tel: 6222 9554. Open: 9am–4pm, but call first. Admission charge. MRT: Chinatown.

Chinatown

Bounded by the Singapore River to the north and the financial district to the east, Chinatown is no longer the maze of crumbling façades and run-down shop-houses that used to exude such charm. Many areas have been painstakingly restored, and the new occupants are design consultants, software suppliers and architectural firms rather than the clog-makers and reflexologists who once lived here (and are now unable to afford to move back in). However, Chinatown still manages to convey some of the flavour of old Singapore and is well worth visiting (*see pp110–11*).

Chinatown Heritage Centre

This excellent joint venture between the Singapore Tourism Board and the National Heritage Board highlights the history of the early Chinese settlers and the development of Chinatown. The

premises, a splendidly restored old shophouse, has three floors. Entry to the first floor takes you into a typical Chinese retail shop and then into a *kopitiam* or traditional coffee shop where it's possible to sit and enjoy a very modern-day cappuccino. The second level explains the terrible conditions back in China that many of the migrants were fleeing. It also showcases the problems and temptations faced on arrival in Singapore, including opium, gambling, prostitution and the secret societies many of them were expected to join. The third floor highlights the 'Golden Age' of Singapore's Chinatown in the 1950s and the kinship between the different races living in the area, especially during festive occasions.
48 Pagoda Street. Tel: 6325 2878. www.chinatownheritage.com.sg. Open: daily 9am–8pm. Admission charge. MRT: Chinatown. Bus: 61, 80 & 197.

Chinese and Japanese Gardens

Linked by the 65m (213ft) Bridge of Double Beauty, these two gardens have been created on adjoining islands in the Jurong Lake. The Chinese Garden (Yu Hua Yuan), covering 13 hectares (32 acres), re-creates the exuberant style of the Sung Dynasty and Beijing's Summer Palace gardens, and includes the Penjing Garden (Yun Xiu Yuan), the largest Suzhou-style garden outside China, with over 3,000 bonsai specimens.

In contrast, the Japanese gardens are in a minimalist style, emphasising the spatial relationships between rocks, gravel, water, shrubs and a teahouse to create the calm, reflective atmosphere in keeping with its name, Seiwaen, the Garden of Tranquillity.
1 Chinese Garden Road, Jurong. Tel: 6261 3632. Open: daily 6am–11pm. Admission charge. MRT: Chinese Garden. Bus: 82, 154, 335 & 951.

Colonial Singapore

When Raffles first landed in Singapore, the only part of the island not then covered in swampy mangroves was a small area that became known as the Padang (Malay for 'open space'), and which eventually became the central focus of the colonial administration. The Padang is still the seat of judicial and parliamentary rule.

City Hall

Built in 1929, this imposing building housed the Municipal Offices until King George VI granted Singapore the status of a city in 1952, after which it became known as City Hall.
3 St Andrew's Road. Open: Mon–Fri 8.30am–5pm, Sat 8.30am–1pm. Free admission. MRT: City Hall.

Empress Place Building

This impressive neoclassical building was built in 1865 as the East India Company court house and was originally much smaller than it is now. Five different extensions were added to accommodate government departments, and fortunately none of these additions departed from the

original design. The whole building eventually fell into a state of considerable disrepair and has been painstakingly renovated. It is now a department of the Asian Civilisations Museums, focusing largely on Asian material, particularly Chinese culture. The museum has an agreement with China to feature a series of rotating exhibitions of priceless and rare artefacts from various Chinese dynasties, many of which have never been seen outside China before, combined with an extremely high standard of interpretative material.
1 Empress Place. Tel: 6332 7798. www.nhb.gov.sg/acm. Open: daily Mon 1–7pm, Tue–Thur 9am–7pm, Fri 9am–9pm, Sat–Sun 9am–7pm. Admission charge. MRT: Raffles Place.

SIR STAMFORD RAFFLES

The founder of Singapore, Stamford Raffles, was born in 1781 aboard the ship that his father captained off the coast of Jamaica. It was an auspicious beginning for the man who was to establish one of the world's greatest seaports.

At the age of 15, Raffles started work in the East India Company and rose up the ranks to become Lieutenant Governor of Java by the time he was 30. Posted to Sumatra, he chafed as he saw the Dutch based at Melaka take control of regional trade. He urged Lord Hastings, the Governor General of India, to establish a colony that could compete with the Dutch for supremacy.

He landed in Singapore on 29 January 1819, and negotiated a treaty with the Sultan of Johor, giving the East India Company permission to establish a trading post. Traders were soon attracted by the novelty of Singapore's free-port status.

Three years later, Raffles, returning from Sumatra, was dismayed to discover the ramshackle development of the port; he immediately drew up detailed plans allocating different areas for government offices and for the many ethnic groups who had settled there. Raffles left Singapore in 1823 and died soon after, but the legacy of his master plan is evident today in the communities of Little India, Chinatown and Arab Street.

Merlion Park

The mythical Merlion, emblem of Singapore, is half-lion, half-fish. In 2002, Merlion Park was moved to a new site overlooking Marina Beach from its old location by the Esplanade Bridge.
Open: daily.

Old Parliament House (The Arts House)

Originally a private mansion of 1827 designed by George Coleman, who stamped his mark on much of Singapore's colonial heritage, Old Parliament House was home to both the British colonial administration and the Singapore government. In 2004, after restoration, the building became The Arts House.
1 Old Parliament Lane. Tel: 6332 6900. www.theartshouse.com.sg. Open: Mon–Fri 10am–8pm, Sat 11am–9pm. Free admission. MRT: City Hall or Clarke Quay. Bus: 32, 51, 61, 63, 80, 103, 124, 145, 166, 174, 194, 197, 603, 851 & 961.

Padang

The cricket and parade ground is the traditional setting for ceremonies on

National Day (9 August). At one end lies the Singapore Cricket Club, at the other the Singapore Recreation Club. Cricket matches take place on the Padang at weekends between March and October.
MRT: City Hall.

Raffles Statue
Located near where Sir Stamford Raffles is thought to have landed in 1819, this is one of two Raffles statues: the original bronze cast (of which this is a replica) is in front of the Victoria Theatre in Empress Place.
MRT: City Hall.

St Andrew's Cathedral
Completed in 1861 by Indian convicts (*see p105*) who used a special plaster known as Madras Chunam (incorporating shell lime, egg white, sugar and coconut husk), St Andrew's withstood the elements for nearly 125 years before needing refurbishment. The neo-Gothic building, with a cool blue-and-white interior, has now been completely renovated.
11 St Andrew's Road. Open: daily. MRT: City Hall.

Impressive architecture – the Supreme Court building dazzles the neighbourhood at night

Supreme Court
Built in 1939 adjacent to City Hall, the classically-inspired Supreme Court occupies the site of the old Europe Hotel, a renowned watering hole for the colonial elite.
1 Supreme Court Lane. Open: Mon–Fri 8am–5pm. Tel: 6336 0644. Free admission. MRT: City Hall.

Victoria Memorial Hall and Theatre
Situated opposite Parliament House, this was once the Town Hall. It was later converted into a ballroom and theatre, and is now home to the Singapore Symphony Orchestra (*see p140*).
11 Empress Place. MRT: City Hall.

Fort Canning Park

Originally known as Bukit Larangan, or the 'Forbidden Hill', legend has it that the last Malay ruler of the kingdom of Singapura, Sultan Iskandar Shah, was buried here after his kingdom was destroyed by the Sumatran Majapahites in 1391. Consequently, Malays considered it sacred ground and access was banned long after the last Malay king had died. Ignoring this taboo, Sir Stamford Raffles built his own bungalow, Singapore's first Government House, at the top of the hill. Misfortune struck: Raffles lost three of his four children and was himself only 42 when he died of a brain tumour.

In 1859 the house was demolished to make way for Fort Canning. During the 1930s, an underground bunker system was built inside the hill, and it became the Far East Command and Control Centre during World War II. Said to be the largest underground bunker system in the world, it was from here that the British High Command made the decision to surrender Singapore. Although the British destroyed as much as they could before the Japanese arrived, old photographs of the interior survived and the bunker system has been re-created in authentic detail by the National Parks Board and named 'The Battle Box'.

On the east slope of the hill a Christian cemetery holds the weathered tombstones of many Singapore pioneers. Just above here is the Fort Canning Centre, home to the Singapore Dance Theatre and an art gallery. *Canning Rise. MRT: Clarke Quay.*

Harbour and river

A sheltered, deep-water harbour was one of the island's main assets when Raffles spotted its potential as a strategic trading post. Flowing into the natural harbour, the Singapore River soon became the commercial and historical hub of the new colony.

The low-slung, sturdy craft that plied back and forth were known as bumboats, traditionally painted with eyes on the bows to enable them to see the way ahead. Until just a few years ago hundreds of bumboats could be seen moored at Boat Quay in front of the business district. However, as part of a major programme to clean up pollution in the Singapore River, the bumboats were relocated to wharves west of the city centre. A few dozen can still be seen moored off Clifford Pier, from where they ferry crew to and from ships at anchor. You can also take a 30-minute bumboat cruise, with taped commentary on the historic sights of the river and its many bridges. An enormous range of tours is available, from basic trips round the bay to a full-blown dinner extravaganza on a Chinese junk. *Bumboat river cruises leave from the landing steps next to Parliament House at regular intervals between 9am and 7pm. Tongkang trips start around 10.30am and last approximately 2½ hours. Dinner cruises start at 6pm and last around 2–2½ hours. Contact Eastwind Organisation (tel: 6533 3432; www.fairwind.com.sg); Watertours (tel: 6533 9811; www.watertours.com.sg); or your hotel tour desk.*

Haw Par Villa (Tiger Balm Gardens)

The Haw Par brothers (Aw Boon Haw and Aw Boon Par) inherited a fortune based on the invention of Tiger Balm, a cure-all ointment still widely sold throughout Asia. Haw Par Villa was one of the Aw family's three residences in Singapore and originally had a zoo in the grounds until the government brought in licensing for zoos. The Haw Par brothers replaced the animals with over 1,000 statues depicting scenes from popular Chinese myths and legends.

By the 1980s, these gaudy displays had become tawdry and uninteresting, and in 1988 the park closed. It has now reopened as a Chinese mythological theme park, with its original statuary, covering five times its original size.

New attractions at the park include a flume ride, a large outdoor amphitheatre with dragon dances, acrobats and other performances, and three additional theatres with special-effect shows. A variety of 'fringe' performances take place throughout the park, among them a story-telling show at the Four Seasons amphitheatre where members of the audience help enact myths and fables.
262 Pasir Panjang Road. Tel: 6872 2780. Open: daily 9am–7pm. Admission charge includes all rides and shows.
MRT: Buona Vista, then bus 200.
Bus: 10, 30, 51 & 143.

Jurong Bird Park

Set in 20 hectares (49 acres) of grounds, the Bird Park houses one of the largest and most spectacular collections of exotic birds in the world, with over 8,000 birds from around 600 different species in spacious enclosures. You can walk around for a close look at their beautiful plumage in the larger aviaries, such as the Southeast Asian Birds enclosure (which simulates a rainforest environment, complete with rain showers) and the Waterfall Aviary (which has over 1,200 free-flying tropical birds and a 30m/98ft waterfall).

The park has a monorail that glides round at tree-top level and passes through the Waterfall Aviary. Other attractions include Pelican Lake, a Hornbill and Toucan exhibit and the Penguin Parade with an underwater viewing chamber. Shows staged at intervals throughout the day include a magnificent Birds of Prey show, penguin and pelican feedings, and the All Stars Birdshow.
2 Jurong Hill. Tel: 6265 0022. www.birdpark.com.sg. Open: daily 8.30am–6pm. Admission charge (does not include monorail charge).
MRT: Boon Lay, then bus 194 or 251.

Lau Pa Sat Festival Market (Telok Ayer Market)

This ornamental, Victorian cast-iron building, which used to be known as the Telok Ayer Market, had to be moved because the structure was unable to withstand the rigours of nearby work on the MRT (Mass Rapid Transport). It has been reborn as the Lau Pa Sat Festival Market ('Lau Pa Sat' means the 'old market' in Hokkien).

Built in 1894, the octagonal-shaped market was constructed using cast-iron frames specially shipped over from Glasgow, Scotland. The intricate filigree ornamentation and tall pillars supporting the roof have been restored and painted white, creating a sense of light and space within the structure.

A popular hawker centre for many years before renovation, it is now an up-market Food Hall. There are a number of craft stalls and regular performances by dancers, stilt-walkers, magicians and musicians.
18 Raffles Quay. Tel: 6222 9930. MRT: Raffles Place. Bus: 10, 70, 75, 97, 100, 107, 131 & 186.

Little India

Although not as extensive as Chinatown, Little India is an interesting area to explore on foot (*see* Little India walk, *pp114–15*). The central focus of Little India is Serangoon Road. Along here and in the streets off to either side, the sari-sellers, fortune-tellers and spice-millers evoke the sights and sounds of the Indian subcontinent. Although Indian traders had crossed the ocean to Malaysia over 1,000 years ago and founded coastal settlements, most of the Indians who arrived in Singapore in its founding years had little choice. The British East India Company in Calcutta decided Singapore was a convenient place to send convicts, and thousands were sent over to build roads and canals and clear the mangrove swamps. St Andrew's Cathedral and the Istana (home of the President) are among the buildings constructed by convict labour.

When a penal colony was built on the Andaman Islands in the 1860s, those with life sentences were transferred from Singapore, but many other prisoners were pardoned and given land around Serangoon Road, near their former prison.

Hindu priest, Little India

With the continuing influx of voluntary immigrants, the community expanded and developed, creating the basis for what is now known as Little India.
MRT: Little India. Bus: 64, 65, 92, 106 & 111.

Mandai Orchid Gardens

Covering 4 hectares (10 acres) of landscaped grounds, the Mandai Orchid Gardens are the largest on the island, with a huge variety of species to admire. A visit here can be combined with Singapore Zoo next door (*see p108*).
200 Mandai Lake Road. Tel: 6269 1036. www.mandai.com.sg. Open: daily Mon 8am–6pm, Tue–Sun 8am–7pm. Admission charge. MRT: Ang Mo Kio, then bus 138. Bus: 171 from Orchard Road or the Zoo Express shuttle bus, which picks up passengers from major hotels (tel: 6753 0506 for schedules).

National Museum and Art Gallery

Opened in 1887 in honour of Queen Victoria's Golden Jubilee, this splendid building was formerly the Raffles Museum. It now houses permanent exhibits, which include a series of 'dioramas' on the ground floor (with waxwork tableaux illustrating early lifestyles and historic scenes), the Straits Chinese Collection in the Sireh Gallery (first floor), and the renowned Haw Par collection of magnificent jade, agate, jasper and crystal carvings.

Temporary exhibits highlight a wide range of Asian arts and crafts. Daily multi-slide shows (between 10.15am and 3.45pm) focus on topics such as the Singapore River, Malay *kampungs*, Chinatown and the development of Singapore as a nation.

The adjacent Art Gallery features exhibitions of Singaporean and Asian artists drawn from their permanent collections, as well as local exhibitions.

Stamford Road. Tel: 6332 3659. www.nationalmuseum.sg. Open: daily 10am–6pm (Living Galleries until 8pm). Admission charge. MRT: City Hall or Dhoby Ghaut.

Peranakan Museum

This recently opened museum boasts the finest collection of Peranakan artefacts in the world. The ten galleries are entirely devoted to Peranakan culture and everyday life, and include a roll call of prominent Peranakans in history, a full scale 12-day Peranakan wedding and interactive exhibits to please the younger members of the family.

39 Armenian Street. Tel: 6332 2982. www.peranakanmuseum.sg. Open: Mon 1pm–7pm, Tue–Sun 9.30am–7pm (until 9pm Fri). MRT: City Hall. Bus: 7, 14, 16, 36, 97, 124, 131, 147, 162, 166 & 174.

Raffles Hotel and Museum

Between 1989 and 1991 the revered Raffles Hotel underwent a major face-lift and was extended to include the Raffles Arcade, with three floors of chic, up-market boutiques. The hotel rooms have been converted to suites, decorated in 1920s style; the famous Long Bar has been moved and now occupies two floors to accommodate the coachloads of tourists who pour in for their obligatory gin sling. Traditionalists will no doubt mourn the loss of the old-style Raffles, but if you haven't been there before you will enjoy the atmosphere in the Raffles Grill or the Tiffin Room.

One of the bonuses of the new Raffles is the intriguing and delightful Raffles Hotel Museum, where artefacts and memorabilia from the 'Golden Age of Travel' (roughly the period 1880 to 1939, which corresponded with the opening of Raffles and its rise to prominence as the 'Grand Old Lady of the East') are on display. As well as letters, postcards and photographs bearing witness to its many illustrious visitors, from Charlie Chaplin through to US presidents, there is also a collection of wonderful shipping and luggage labels, period photographs of Singapore and old travel guides.

Possibly Raffles' most famous patrons were writers such as Rudyard Kipling, Joseph Conrad and Somerset Maugham. The hotel's original owners, the Armenian Sarkie brothers, used these connections shamelessly, quoting Kipling in their advertising as having written: 'Providence led me to a place called Raffles Hotel, where the food is as excellent as the rooms are good. Let the Traveller take note: Feed at Raffles and Sleep at Raffles'. In fact, what Kipling actually wrote in *Sea to Sea* was: '. . . Raffles Hotel, where the food is as excellent as the rooms are bad. Let the Traveller take note: Feed at Raffles and sleep at the Hotel de L'Europe'!

1 Beach Road. Tel: 6337 1886. www.raffles.com. Museum open: daily 10am–7pm. Free admission. MRT: City Hall.

Sakya Muni Temple

This simple Buddhist temple, built in the style of a Thai *wat*, was constructed by a Thai monk, Vutthisasara, who came to Singapore in the 1880s determined to erect a monument to the Enlightened One. He built the entire temple with his own hands and died in the 1970s, aged 94, his task complete. It is also known as the Temple of a Thousand Lights, since the central 15m (49ft) high statue of a seated Buddha is surrounded by a halo of lights. Around the base of the statue scenes depict the life of Buddha.

366 Race Course Road. Tel: 6294 0714. Open: daily 8am–4.45pm. Free admission. MRT: Farrer Park. Bus: 64, 65, 106 & 111.

Sentosa Island

See pp122–4.

Singapore DIscovery Centre

With plenty of interactive exhibits for all the family, the SDC highlights Singapore's history and military capabilities. Visitors can design their own tanks, parachute from a plane (a virtual-reality experience) or become a modern fighter pilot in the state-of-the-art flight simulator.

510 Upper Jurong Road. Tel: 6792 6188. www.sdc.com.sg. Open: Tue–Sun 9am–6pm. Closed: Mon. Admission charge. MRT: Boon Lay. Bus: 182 or 193 from Boon Lay MRT.

Singapore Flyer

A newcomer to the Singapore skyline, the Flyer (a giant ferris wheel) presents the visitor with a stunning panoramic view of the city. At present it is the highest wheel of its type in the world, some 30m (100ft) taller than the London Eye.

30 Raffles Avenue. Tel: 6854 5200. www.singaporeflyer.com.sg. Open: daily 8.30am–10.30pm. MRT: City Hall and then bus 106, 111 or 133.

Singapore Science Centre

The Science Centre is a great place to let children loose to prod, poke, peer, press and play with everything in sight, which they can and will do – meanwhile, possibly learning a thing or two about the principles of flight, the workings of the human body, or computers and lasers.

Next door is the Omnimax cinema, where films are projected through a 180-degree fish-eye lens on to a huge domed screen, giving a complete wrap-around image. Film shows change regularly. *15 Science Centre Road, Jurong. Open: Tue–Sun 10am–6pm. Admission charge. Omnimax: Tel: 6425 2500. www.science.edu.sg. Screenings from 10am–8pm. Admission charge. MRT: Jurong East and then bus 335. Bus: 66, 178, 198 & 336.*

Singapore Zoo

Founded in 1973, the Singapore Zoological Gardens were designed to provide the animals with as natural a habitat as possible, keeping them in landscaped enclosures where different animals live together as they might do in the wild. The zoo says that the success of its breeding programme is proof that this has worked.

From their original collection of just 270 animals, the zoo has expanded to accommodate over 2,800 animals of nearly 216 species. The captive breeding programme of rare species has included polar bear cubs, orang-utans, Cape hunting dogs, Indian rock pythons, rhinoceros iguanas, ruffed lemurs, pygmy hippos, Malayan tapirs, oryx and Himalayan thars.

Animal feedings and shows are almost continuous throughout the day. Breakfast with Ah Meng, a Sumatran orang-utan, is particularly popular. There are also underwater viewing areas for polar bears, sea lions and penguins, crocodiles and pygmy hippos, as well as elephant, camel and pony rides. A recent addition is Children's World, with a miniature railway, play area and 'animal contact' area.

The zoo also operates a Night Safari, which gives visitors the opportunity to explore a tropical jungle at night. Over 1,000 nocturnal animals can be viewed thanks to state-of-the-art lighting. *80 Mandai Lake Road. Tel: 6269 3411. www.zoo.com.sg. Open: daily 8.30am–6pm (7.30pm–midnight for Night Safari). Admission charge. MRT: Choa Chu Kang, then bus 927; or Ang Mo Kio, then bus 138. The Zoo Express leaves twice daily from major hotels (tel: 6753 0506 for information).*

Siong Lim Temple

Built between 1898 and 1908, this is one of the largest Buddhist temples in Singapore and is now a National Monument. Thought to have been founded by a Seow family from China, the original construction was funded by two Hokkien merchants. It houses numerous shrines and works of religious art, including carved marble Buddha statues from Thailand. *184-E Jalan Toa Payoh. Tel: 6259 5292. www.shuanglin.sg. Open: 9am–5pm. MRT: Toa Payoh.*

Sri Mariamman Temple

The oldest Hindu temple in Singapore, originally built by Nariana Pillay, an early Indian pioneer who arrived with Raffles in 1819. The initial wood and *atap* (thatch) structure was replaced by the present building in 1843, which was extensively refurbished in 1984 by South Indian craftsmen. The South Indian Dravidian influence is evident in the colourful towering *gopuram* (gateway) with its mass of sculpted figures depicting mythological scenes. It is now a National Monument.

Early morning or early evening is the best time to visit, when devotees make their prayers to the accompaniment of temple music. The temple is also the setting for the annual Thimithi, or Fire-Walking Festival (*see p25*).

244 South Bridge Road. Tel: 6223 4064. Open: daily 6am–9pm. MRT: Chinatown. Bus: 103, 166 & 197.

Sri Srinivasa Perumal Temple

This Hindu temple, devoted to the worship of Perumal (better known as Vishnu), was first constructed in 1855. Although one of Singapore's oldest Hindu temples, the 20m (66ft) *gopuram* (entrance tower) was only begun as recently as 1966. This entrance tower is festooned in a colourful array of incarnations of Vishnu. Within the temple, statues of the blue Krishna, another incarnation of Vishnu, dot the area. The Sri Srinivasa Perumal Temple is the starting point for the annual Thaipusam Festival (*see pp26–7*). Early in the morning devotees gather to have their cheeks, tongues and backs pierced with a variety of skewers and metal hooks. Others support huge *kavadi* or heavy metal frames on their heads. All then process through the streets of Singapore, ending their ordeal at the Chettiar Temple on Tank Road.

397 Serangoon Road. Tel: 6298 5771. Open: 6.30am–noon & 6–9pm. Free admission. MRT: Little India. Bus: 23, 64, 65, 111, 130, 131, 139, 147 & 857.

Thian Hock Keng Temple

Completed in 1841, the Temple of Heavenly Happiness is one of the most ornate in Singapore, and the oldest Hokkien temple on the island. The present temple replaced an earlier josshouse (shrine) on the same site, then on Singapore's waterfront, which grew wealthy with the offerings of immigrants, grateful for their safe arrival. The shrine of Ma Chu Por, the Mother of Heavenly Sages and Goddess of the Sea, dominates the central courtyard.

158 Telok Ayer Street. Tel: 6222 8212. Open: daily 8.30am–5.30pm. MRT: Raffles Place. Bus: 124, 167, 174, 179, 182 & 190.

Siong Lim Temple

Walk: Chinatown

This walk encompasses many of the older streets in Chinatown, several temples, shrines and mosques, and the conservation areas with their pastel-coloured façades in the vernacular Singapore style.

Allow 2–3 hours.

From the Raffles Place MRT station, head north and turn left in Chulia Street, then take the first right which leads to Boat Quay.

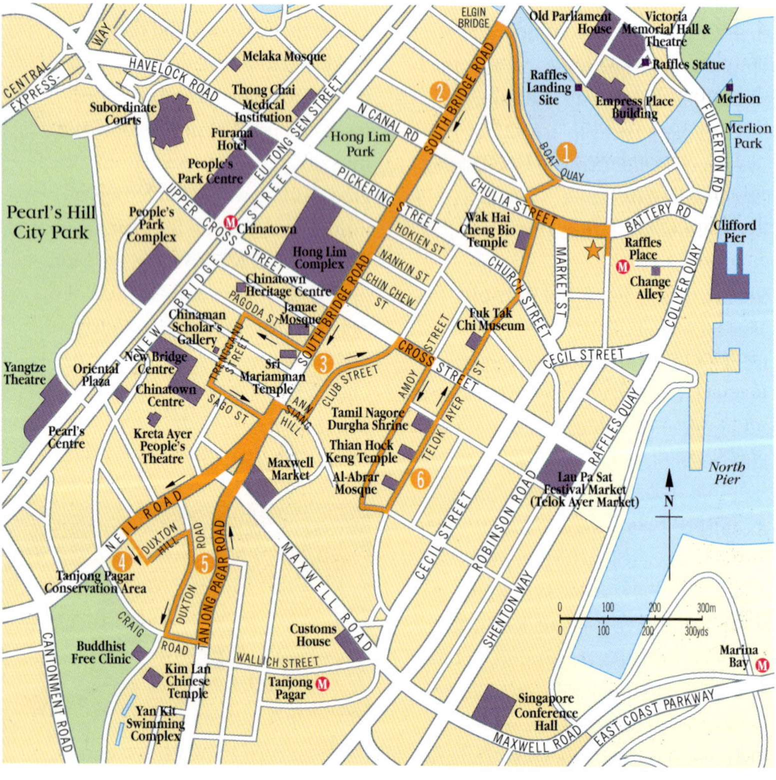

1 Boat Quay

This is a pleasant waterfront promenade with views of the Raffles Landing Site.
Walk along Boat Quay towards Elgin Bridge. At the bridge, turn left and proceed down South Bridge Road.

2 South Bridge Road

The side streets off to your left – such as Hokien Street, Nankin Street and Chin Chew Street – are worth exploring for their traditional Chinese houses.
Continue down South Bridge Road, across Cross Street, until you come to the Sri Mariamman Temple (see p109).

3 Sri Mariamman Temple area

Wandering around in the streets behind the temple you will come across some fine examples of restored Chinese town houses, resplendent in their pastel-coloured paintwork (*see p94*). Alongside the shops selling Chinese knick-knacks and souvenirs some old businesses still survive. Tucked away in Trengganu Street is the Chinaman Scholar's Gallery (*see p99*).
Re-enter South Bridge Road and head south, crossing over where it becomes Neil Road.

4 Tanjong Pagar Conservation Area

The area includes many old ornamental shop-houses with intricately decorated façades restored to their former vibrancy. At 51 Neil Road you will find what used to be Emmerson's Tiffin Room, a place made famous in Joseph Conrad's *The Rescue*. Originally the Tanjong Pagar area was a Malay fishing village.
Make your way up Duxton Hill, at the heart of Tanjong Pagar, and turn right down Duxton Road.

5 Duxton Road

Like Duxton Hill, Duxton Road has many exquisitely designed two and three-storey Straits Chinese residences. Before the arrival of the wealthy Straits Chinese, the area had a reputation for cheap brothels, opium dens and gambling parlours, mostly patronised by rickshaw drivers.
Turn left into Craig Road and left again into Tanjong Pagar Road. Cross Maxwell Road, then turn right up Ann Siang Hill and left into Club Street. At Cross Street, turn right and then right again into Amoy Street. Follow this to the end, doubling back down Telok Ayer Street.

6 Telok Ayer Street

Since Telok Ayer Street was once on the waterfront it was a natural site for places of worship, hence several mosques and Chinese temples were built here. The first mosque is the Al-Abrar Mosque, which began life as a thatched hut; the present building was erected between 1850 and 1855. Just past here lie the Thian Hock Keng Temple (*see p109*) and the Tamil Nagore Durgha Shrine. Beyond Cross Street is the Fuk Tak Chi Museum, once also known as the Temple of Prosperity and Virtue.
Continue to the end of Telok Ayer Street and turn right to return to Raffles Place.

Walk: Bukit Timah Nature Reserve

This walk links together several of the signposted trails in the reserve. It is an easy walk for most of the way, apart from one section of the aptly named Rock Path, where you have to scramble over boulders for a short way (this is easily bypassed if necessary). There are plenty of rest benches and hut shelters on the trails.

Allow 2–2½ hours.

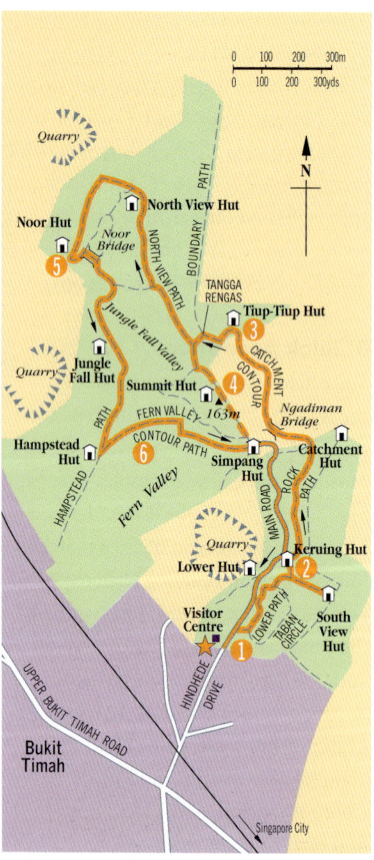

From the Visitor Centre, head uphill and take the first right-hand fork, marked Lower Path.

1 Dipterocarp Forest

The reserve is a good introduction to the ferns and trees of the dipterocarp or 'winged seed' forests characteristic of the region. Many of the more common forest trees along this track are labelled for easy identification. Of particular note are the towering seraya (*Shorea cutisii*), one of the most common dipterocarps. The older trees are supported by strong, thick buttresses at the base.

Keep straight on where the path forks right to the Taban Circle. At the top of the next gradient, you can detour right to South View Hut. Back at the junction, continue along Keruing Path.

2 Giant Keruings

This path is named after the typical dipterocarp species, the keruing. A commercially valuable species, keruings grow to great heights, like the seraya, with their topmost branches pushing out above the general forest canopy 50m (164ft) up. Another giant species seen along this path is the barking deer mango, so-called because barking deer are said to be partial to its fruits.

Where the path meets the road again at Keruing Hut, turn right where it is signposted Rock Path and Catchment Contour. For an alternative route and to avoid the Rock Path, keep on up the road towards the Summit Hut. Continue right along Contour Path. At the junction with Boundary Path follow the signs to Jalan Tiup-Tiup.

3 Ferns

The slopes leading off to the right of the path are typical of secondary forest, where clearings have been entirely colonised by a blanket of sun-seeking resam ferns (*Dicranopteris linearis*), preventing anything else from growing. Other secondary species to look out for include macaranga, which has ants living in hollows inside its leaf stems.

After 5 to 10 minutes, take the steps to your left signposted Tangga Rengas – Summit.

4 Summit

From the summit there are good views to the northeast across the Lower Pierce and Upper Pierce reservoirs that form part of the central water catchment area, one of the largest tracts of wilderness on the island.

Retrace your steps back down and follow the signs for North View Path. Take this all the way around the northern slopes of Bukit Timah to the Noor Hut.

5 Bird-spotting

The northern slopes are a good place to listen for the calls and songs of birds such as the short-tailed babbler (*Trichastoma malaccense*), which chatters away on the forest floor, or the stripe-throated tit-babbler (*Macronous gularis*), which sounds a loud and repetitive 'chonk-chonk-chonk' at mid-forest level. In the upper canopy, one of the easiest birds to spot is the greater racquet-tailed drongo (*Dicrurus paradiseus*) with its conspicuous racquet-tipped tail.

Immediately past the Noor Hut, take the right-hand track, crossing the small Noor Bridge, and turn right again at the next T-junction. At the junction with the Jungle Fall Path turn right, take the next right again down the Hampstead Path, and left at the Hampstead Hut to follow the Fern Valley Contour Path.

6 The Fern Valley Contour Path

This is one of the loveliest sections of track in the park, with views down the forest slope and through the trees at mid-forest level. Of the 100 or so species of ferns that still exist on the island, around 80 are now found only in the reserve.

At the Simpang Hut, take the road back down to the Visitor Centre.

Walk: Little India

While not as extensive as Chinatown or as distinctive architecturally, Little India is still an identifiable community where street life echoes the sights and sounds of the Indian subcontinent. This is an easy walk.

Allow 2 hours.

From Bugis MRT, head up Rochor Road, turn right into Jalan Besar and second left into Dunlop Street.

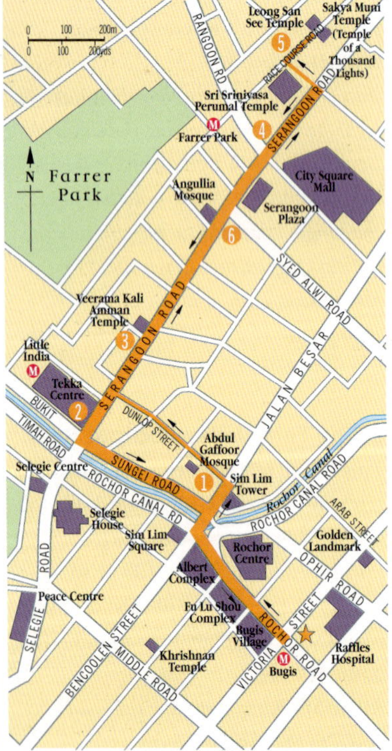

1 Dunlop Street

The beginnings of Little India become evident the closer you get to Serangoon Road. The covered walkways are strung about with glittering fabrics, luring customers inside where bolts of sari material line the shops almost up to the ceiling. Alongside, other stores are piled high with brass incense-holders, peacock feathers (considered lucky by Hindus) and 'tiffin' containers (the Indian equivalent of a lunch-box). Nearby, stallholders string together garlands of jasmine and marigolds, to be used for wedding celebrations or as daily offerings in the temple.

At the end of Dunlop Street, turn left and cross over Serangoon Road to the Tekka Centre.

2 Tekka Centre

This multi-purpose building comprising a wet market and food centre is a feast for eyes and appetite, serving not only the local community but also shoppers from further afield, drawn by the vast array of fresh produce. The Tekka Centre was closed for refurbishment at the time of writing but is expected to re-open mid-2009.

Turn up Serangoon Road and you will soon reach the Veerama Kali Amman Temple.

3 Veerama Kali Amman Temple

Dedicated to the Goddess Kali, this temple is at its busiest in the early evenings, when dozens of worshippers mill around outside waiting to perform their *puja* (prayers).

Continue up Serangoon Road. You will eventually reach the Sri Srinivasa Perumal Temple.

4 Sri Srinivasa Perumal Temple

The spacious interior courtyard of the Hindu temple houses numerous shrines, the main one being Lord Vishnu's, with others dedicated to Sri Anjanepar, Sri Vinayagar and Mahalakshmi. The original temple dates back to 1855, but it was completely rebuilt in the 1960s, with the towering *gopuram* (gates) only being completed in 1979.

Immediately after the temple, take a path to the left and turn right into Race Course Road. On your right is the Sakya Muni Temple (see p107), while facing it is the Leong San See Temple.

5 Leong San See Temple

Nestling incongruously beneath the apartment blocks behind it, this temple, dedicated to Kuan Yin (the Goddess of Mercy), houses some interesting frescoes, carved lions, and a splendid altar with carvings of birds and flowers.

Retrace your steps and proceed back down Serangoon Road on the opposite side.

6 Serangoon Road

Once past the Serangoon Plaza, it is rewarding to linger along this section of Serangoon Road and the side streets off to the left. Some of the old trades carry on regardless of your presence: a Tamil at his miller's wheel, for instance, grinds spices for his customers, sending aromatic clouds wafting into the air. Other traders have adapted to modern ways, such as the fortune-teller whose parrot, on being told your name, picks out a card with your future written on it. Although this is theoretically Little India, the Chinese influence is never far away, and you may well come across a fast and furious game of checkers on the sidewalk.

At the end of Serangoon Road, turn left into Sungei Road, and eventually retrace your steps back to Bugis MRT.

Painting of a deity, Veerama Kali Amman Temple

Getting away from it all

Malaysia's primary forests, lonely beaches and deserted islands provide the perfect terrain for those wishing to escape the rigours of the modern world. A stay in a Sarawak longhouse or a hike along one of Endau-Rompin's many trails will leave an everlasting impression. Singapore's status as a city state makes it a lot more difficult to find quiet, out-of-the-way places to relax, although Bukit Timah Nature Reserve in the north of the island provides a sanctuary for those seeking tranquillity.

MALAYSIA

Despite the destruction of large tracts of wilderness areas, Malaysia does have a network of protected areas, national parks and marine parks. The national parks are generally well managed, with dedicated rangers and staff who are knowledgeable about their domains and conscious of the need to preserve them.

Usually, a national park has a compound containing the headquarters building (sometimes with an interpretative centre) and a range of accommodation for all budgets from VIP chalets to student hostels, most of which have facilities for self-catering. Often there is a café (or canteen) on-site providing basic meals (national parks are one of the few places in Malaysia where you may have to do without the usual gourmet range of foods). Most have marked walking trails, some better maintained than others. There is almost nowhere in the country that you need worry about personal safety when off the beaten track, except from the point of view of weather conditions. Check the monsoon seasons (*see p179*), and make sure you are suitably equipped for heavy rainfall if you are travelling during this time.

National parks and nature parks

Bako National Park

See p76.

Endau-Rompin

One of the last remaining areas of protected lowland forest in Peninsular Malaysia, Endau-Rompin straddles the boundary between Pahang and Johor. This relatively undisturbed and lush region covers an area of 870sq km (340sq miles) and contains a wealth of endemic plants as well as hornbills, tigers, elephants, wild boar and tapirs. It is the last refuge on the peninsula for the rare Sumatran rhinoceros. Waterfalls, palm forests, highland swamps and visits to Orang Asli villages are all part of the Endau-Rompin experience.

The entry point for the park is Padang Endau, around 40km (25 miles) north of Mersing on the east coast. Boats can be chartered from here to go upriver; facilities for visitors are very limited. Permits must be obtained in advance from the Johor National Parks Corporation, JKR 475, Bukhit Timbalan, Johor (tel: (07) 223 7471). Day trips and longer treks are organised by My Outdoor: 15-01 Jalan Padi Emas, Bandar Baru UDA, Johor Bahru. Tel: (07) 235 1217. www.myoutdoor.com

Gunung Mulu National Park

See pp76–7.

Kampung Kuantan fireflies

Although not a protected area, Kampung Kuantan has recently become a popular place to visit, following the discovery that the riverbanks near the village are home to an unusual species of firefly that flashes in synchronised groups. Thousands of people have since descended on the village to take a night-time boat-trip down the river to witness this magical sight as the whole riverbank is lit up with millions of fireflies twinkling in the vegetation. The folded-wing fireflies (*Pteroptyx malaccae*) are the only fireflies that have developed this striking synchronised flashing. Sometimes only a dozen will flash at once, sometimes whole tree-loads will light up the riverbank. Sometimes, tree-loads that are close together may flash in time with each other. The fireflies only choose trees with open foliage, so their lights can be seen.

Flashing usually begins around an hour after sunset, and is at its height for the next two to four hours, diminishing towards dawn. The *kelip-kelip* (firefly) tours start from around 8pm through to midnight and last about 30–40 minutes. A jetty has been built with the help of nature groups and now, as the handout says: 'This blinking trees of Kampung Kuantan are well known among the worldwide'.

Kampung Kuantan is 20 minutes from Kuala Selangor. Driving west from Kuala Lumpur, turn right after 56km (35 miles) at Bukit Rotan and right again to Kampung Kuantan. The booking office is in a row of shops in the village; contact Mr Jalaludin, Kelip Kelip Trading, Kampung Kuantan, Batang Berjuntai, Selangor (tel: (03) 889 2403). Be warned that this boom has brought a certain degree of chaos, with over 30 boat trips per night going out, and reservations are not always honoured. The trip is not recommended on rainy nights or when there is a full moon.

Kinabalu National Park

See p86.

Niah Caves National Park

See pp78–9.

Taman Alam/Kuala Selangor Nature Park

On the west coast of the peninsula, the Taman Alam/Kuala Selangor Park covers 26sq km (10sq miles) of mangroves and wetlands. It is one of the most accessible places to see typical mangrove inhabitants such as the mangrove blue flycatcher, mangrove whistler, pied fantail and the elusive mangrove pitta. You are also likely to spot kingfishers, bee-eaters, kites, white-bellied sea eagles and grey herons.

At the entrance to the park there are chalets and an information centre, with short trails leading off to an artificial lake with purpose-built hides. Along the trails you will probably come across troupes of silver-leaf monkeys, an experience that is unlikely to be repeated elsewhere: silver-leaf monkeys usually live high up in the forest canopy, making them hard to spot, but those at Kuala Selangor have become used to people and are approachable. *65km (40 miles) from Kuala Lumpur, 1 hour by shared taxi or bus to Kuala Selangor Town. Open: 7am–7pm. Reservations for accommodation: Malayan Nature Society (Persatuan Pencinta Alam), Taman Alam, Kuala Selangor; tel: (03) 3289 2294. www.mns.org.my*

Taman Negara National Park

Malaysia's first national park, Taman Negara, covers 4,343sq km (1,677sq miles) spread over three different states (Pahang, Kelantan and Terengganu). It is the largest single area of protected tropical rainforest in the peninsula.

The park is home to some 250 species of birds and is rich in animal life, including elephants, Malayan tapirs, sambar and barking deer, tigers, otters and several species of primates. The typically dense rainforest foliage means that wildlife-spotting requires a great deal of patience, but there are numerous salt licks, some with observation hides, where you may have a better chance of seeing something.

The park headquarters at Kuala Tahan can only be reached by boat from Kampung Kuala Tembeling near Jerantut, from where it is a 2- to 4-hour journey up the Tembeling River. At the headquarters there are chalets and hostels for up to 200 people, and restaurant facilities. Camping and hiking equipment can be hired, and there are well-marked trails leading off into the jungle around the headquarters. Boat-trips further upriver and longer treks (for instance, to the summit of Gunung Tahan, which is a 9-day round trip) can also be arranged. *The park is closed during the monsoon (Nov–Jan). The gateway to the park is Jerantut, from where there are taxi and bus connections to Kota Bharu and Kuala Lumpur (change at Temerluh). From Jerantut, buses leave every 2 hours for the boat jetty at Kampung Kuala Tembeling; the park headquarters is a further 59km (37 miles) upstream.*

Advance bookings for transport to the park and accommodation are compulsory. The easiest place to make them is at the National Parks desk in the Malaysia Tourist Information Complex at 109 Jalan Ampang, Kuala Lumpur (tel: (03) 9235 4848).

Tawau Hills Park

The rugged volcanic terrain of the Tawau Hills Park lies north of Tawau in Sabah. Wildlife that you might spot here includes red-leaf monkeys, giant tree squirrels, macaques and hornbills. The park is also reputed to be home to clouded leopards. Vegetation ranges from dipterocarp forest in the lowlands to mossy forests on the upper reaches of Bombalai Hill (530m/1,739ft). From the top of the hill there are views across the rolling plantations of cocoa, palm oil and rubber trees on the coastal plains. The park is popular for weekend picnics, but a four-wheel-drive vehicle is essential.
24km (15 miles) north of Tawau. Open: 7am–6pm. No permits needed, but for further information contact either: Rangers Office, Tawau Hills Park, WDT 118, Tawau (tel: (089) 918 827), or Sabah Parks, Lot 1–3, Block K, G/Floor, Sinsuran Complex, Kota Kinabalu (tel: (088) 211 881).

Tunku Abdul Rahman Park

See pp90–91.

Turtle Islands National Park

See p91.

Marine parks

As well as the national parks, Malaysia also has a network of marine parks to protect the country's marine resources for the enjoyment of present and future generations. For most visitors, it is the mystery and beauty of coral reefs that provide the most compelling reason to explore the underwater world (*see pp72–3*).

With a mask and snorkel in your luggage, you will find plenty of opportunities to float in this watery realm and watch vividly coloured fish swimming among the corals and seagrasses. Snorkelling has many advantages over scuba-diving: it requires almost no training, it's free, you can jump in when and where you please, and a great deal of the life and colour on a reef is found within the top few metres of the water anyway.

If curiosity impels you to explore beyond the limitations of mask and snorkel, a scuba-diving course is the answer. Scuba-diving courses are available in most resorts near reef areas, with generally high standards of rental equipment and training. Before leaving home, get a medical check-up, and take the certificate with you.
A good mask and snorkel are sound investments if you plan to take a course, but you can always hire them if necessary. Qualified divers will need to

Orang Asli village, Taman Negara

bring proof of diver training from a recognised agency, and preferably also their log books.

In Peninsular Malaysia, the best reefs are on the east coast, most of them being patch or fringing reefs around the offshore islands. Owing to the turbidity of the water, reefs on the west coast are not so well developed except near Pulau Langkawi in the north.

Sarawak has virtually no reefs, since coral does not grow well where there is freshwater runoff from rainforests. In Sabah, fringing reefs occur around offshore islands on the north and northeast coasts. The best reefs in Sabah are those around the oceanic island of Sipadan off the coast near Semporna.

Coral reefs are fragile ecosystems, easily damaged by human activities. Like reefs elsewhere in the world, those in Malaysia have been subjected to destruction from pollution, coral mining and dynamite fishing. Within the marine parks they are generally in good condition, although not of the same calibre as more pristine reefs elsewhere in the Indo-Pacific region. The only exception to this is **Pulau Sipadan**, which is a world-class dive site and attracts serious sport-divers from every continent.

The best season for diving on the west coast is from December through to April/May, on the east coast from February/March through to September/October. The seasons in Sabah are similar to the east coast, the best diving being from February/March through to September/October, with top visibility from May/June onwards.

Snorkelling at Pulau Perhentian

Northwest coast

Off the Kedah coast, the **Pulau Payar Marine Park** encompasses a cluster of islands, foremost among them Pulau Payar itself. The other islands include Pulau Segantang, Pulau Kala and Pulau Lembu. The diverse and colourful reefs are known for a prolific variety of lionfish, feather stars, sea anemones and other creatures. The best diving is around the southwest tip of Pulau Payar and the north and northeast sides of Pulau Kala. *There is no accommodation on the islands, although camping is allowed. Permits are required to visit the Marine Park and a conservation charge will also be levied. Your local travel agent or the hotel where you stay will be able to arrange this. The islands are accessible from Pulau Pinang, although Pulau Langkawi is closer (1 hour by boat). Day trips are organised by: Langkawi Saga Travel, Lot 1–21, Jetty Point Complex, Langkawi. Tel: (04) 899 8822. www.langkawicoral.com*

Northeast coast
Off the shores of Terengganu, the **Pulau Redang Marine Park** includes Pulau Perhentian, Pulau Redang, Pulau Kapas, Pulau Tenggol and Pulau Lang Tengah. Reefs extend to around 20m (66ft) deep, with the best-developed corals on the north and east sides of the islands.
For accommodation and access details, see separate entries for Pulau Kapas, Pulau Perhentian, Pulau Redang and Pulau Tenggol (see pp68–9).

Southeast coast
The islands of the southeast coast form two marine parks: Pulau Tioman and its neighbouring islands (off Pahang), and the Pulau Sibu Archipelago (off Johor), which includes Rawa (*see p68*), Sibu, Besar, Tinggi and Tengah. On many of these islands the north and east sides have rocky cliffs dropping straight into deep water, with no reefs, but the more sheltered south and west sides have well-developed fringing reefs. The reefs are generally no more than 15m (49ft) deep and in variable condition, some good, some badly damaged. Pulau Tioman (*see p69*) has a good selection of dive sites around the coast and offshore islands such as Pulau Labas, Pulau Tulai and Pulau Chebeh; an artificial reef of concrete pyramids, recently built by the Fisheries Department, is now home to groupers, yellowtails, trevallys, batfish and moray eels.
There are PADI Dive Centres at the Berjaya Tioman Beach Resort, Lalang (tel: (09) 419 1000; www.berjayaresorts.com) and at Ben's Diving Centre, Salang Beach, Pulau Tioman.

Sabah

Pulau Sipadan
See pp88–9.

Tunku Abdul Rahman Park
Reefs around the five islands extend to depths of around 17m (56ft), with good diving and snorkelling around the southern tip of Pulau Gaya, the northeast tip of Pulau Mamutik (where there are extensive colonies of staghorn and plate corals), the east and west sides of Pulau Manukan and the southern side of Pulau Sulug (which has some of the best reefs in the park).

The islands of this marine park can be visited all year round, but between May and October storms may materialise in minutes, so care should be taken with boating arrangements. The heaviest rain falls during November to January; the driest months are February to May.
Diving trips can be booked through Sutera Sanctuary Lodges, Kota Kinabalu (tel: (088) 243 629; www.suterasanctuarylodges.com).
Day trips from Kota Kinabalu can be booked through Borneo Divers, 9th Floor, Menara Jubili, 53 Jalan Gaya, Kota Kinabalu (tel: (088) 222 226; www.borneodivers.info).

SINGAPORE

Sentosa Island

Just 0.5km (1/3 mile) offshore from the city, Sentosa Island is a popular recreation spot and attracts around 5.2 million visitors a year. The island is one of the largest in Singapore harbour and was converted from a British military base into a holiday resort in the 1970s. Cable cars (which run from Mount Faber or the World Trade Centre) are one of the most popular ways of getting there, with the added bonus of extensive views across the harbour. Alternatively, shuttle ferries operate regularly from the World Trade Centre; and with the completion of a bridge to the shore, Sentosa is now also accessible by bus, taxi, bicycle or on foot.

Scattered over Sentosa's 375 hectares (927 acres) is a wide variety of things to see and do for all age groups, including golf courses, three museums, nature trails, a butterfly park, musical fountains, a cycle track, monorail, roller-skating rink, a tropical-fish oceanarium and a range of restaurants.

On Sentosa's sea-facing coast the 3km (2-mile) beach-front has been upgraded and the two beaches (replenished regularly with sand from Indonesia) and swimming and leisure lagoons have facilities for aquabiking, windsurfing and canoeing. At one end of the beach is the Shangri-La Rasa Sentosa resort, Singapore's first 'beach hotel'; the island has one other hotel, the deluxe Sentosa, located near the golf courses and a luxury campsite, the NTUC Sentosa Beach Resort.

Further attractions include an Asian Village, a water theme park and various multimedia displays. Avoid weekends on Sentosa if you can, when there can be a crush on the ferries and at the attractions.

Butterfly Park and Insect Kingdom Museum

The collection includes over 2,500 live butterflies from 50 species and 4,000 mounted specimens of butterflies and insects from all over the world.
Open: daily 9am–6.30pm. Admission charge.

Fort Siloso

Originally built by the British in the 1880s, this 4-hectare (10-acre) complex of tunnels, bunkers and gun emplacements, Sentosa's only authentic site, also includes a display on the history of the fort.
www.fortsiloso.com. Open: daily 10am–6pm. Admission charge.

Images of Singapore

This three-part exhibition is a multimedia presentation of Singapore's history and culture.

The **Pioneers of Singapore** highlights the lives of the immigrant groups who helped build the colony, with dioramas (waxwork tableaux) illustrating historic moments and the day-to-day lives of Chinese coolies, colonial plantation owners and Indian merchants.

Siloso Beach, Sentosa

The **Surrender Chambers** continues the story, illustrating – with the addition of contemporary photographs and taped commentaries – the war years in Singapore from 1941 to 1945.

Festivals of Singapore re-enacts some of the customs of Singapore's multicultural society using animated models.
Open: daily 9am–7pm.
Admission charge.

Nature Walk/Dragon Trail
This is a 1.5km (1-mile) walk through forest foliage, with various dragon models, fossils and skeletal remains.
Open: all day. Free admission.

Sentosa 4D Magix
An amazing interactive theatre experience using the very latest in visual effects, motion-controlled seats and surround-sound technology. The viewer's senses are all fully engaged.
www.sentosa4dmagix.com.sg. Open: daily 10am–9pm. Admission charge.

Sentosa Orchid Gardens
An orchid theme garden with permanent exhibits, including a flower clock made from orchids, a carp pond and a Japanese teahouse.
Open: daily 9am–7pm.
Free admission.

Tiger Sky Tower
For stunning views of Sentosa, Singapore and close neighbour Malaysia, ascend the 110m (360ft) Tiger Sky Tower, Asia's tallest free-standing observation tower. It's situated next to the Sentosa cable car station.
Open: daily 9am–9pm.
Admission charge.

Underwater World
Underwater World is Southeast Asia's largest tropical oceanarium. The most

SENTOSA LEISURE GROUP

33 Allanbrooke Road. Tel: 1800–SENTOSA (736 8672). www.sentosa.com.sg
The majority of indoor attractions open between 9am and 10am and close between 9pm and 10pm, with varying admission charges. Basic admission charge includes bus transfers (Service A runs from the World Trade Centre; alternative service from Tiong Bahru MRT, 7am–11pm, daily) and monorail ride. If you walk or cycle across the causeway or take the ferry or cable car, admission charge includes free return bus transfer.
Ferries from the World Trade Centre at 15-minute intervals, 9.30am–9pm weekdays, 8.30am–9pm weekends & public holidays.
Cable Cars 8.30am–9pm, from either Mount Faber or the World Trade Centre.
Buses 10, 30, 61, 65, 84, 97, 100, 125, 143, 145, 166 & 167.

impressive feature is a 100m (328ft) long acrylic tunnel with a moving walkway running through it, which conveys you underneath two large marine aquarium tanks. The first of these is a coral-reef community tank, where typically colourful shallow-reef species such as parrotfish, angelfish, batfish and butterflyfish swim around and above you. The second tank contains carnivores and predators such as black-tipped and white-tipped reef sharks.

Other well-designed displays focus on tidal pools, schooling fish, sea sponges, hard and soft corals, cave habitats and poisonous marine creatures. There is also a turtle pool and a touch-pool, where you can handle sea cucumbers, starfish and other invertebrates. In the small theatre an audiovisual show (every 10 minutes) focuses on marine life and marine conservation. Feeding times are at 11.30am and 4.30pm.
www.underwaterworld.com.sg.
Open: daily 9am–9pm. Admission charge.

Pulau Sakijang Bendera (St John's) and Pulau Tembakul (Kusu Island)

The two most popular and easily accessible of the southern islands after Sentosa have regular ferry services from the World Trade Centre. The first ferry stop is Pulau Tembakul (Kusu Island), the smaller of the two, which has many myths and legends associated with it. Several of these involve rescues by turtles or tortoises ('Kusu' means 'place of the turtle' in Malay). In one, sailors shipwrecked at this spot were rescued by a giant turtle that turned itself into an island. Another relates how two fishermen were shipwrecked nearby, although this time it is a tortoise that becomes an island. In yet another, an Arab named Syed Abdul Rahman left Singapore with his wife and daughter in a sampan, which capsized in a storm. A giant tortoise spotted them and brought them to safety on the island. The Malay *kramat* (shrine) on the island commemorates this.

As well as the *kramat*, there is a Chinese temple (dedicated to Da Bo Gong, the God of Prosperity), a tortoise sanctuary, turtle pool and pavilion. During the Ninth Lunar Month (October/November) thousands of devotees make a pilgrimage to the island to pay homage to their deities.

The first recorded mention of the island dates from 1616, when Dom Jose de Silva, Spanish Governor of the

Popular for weekend picnics, St John's Island is one hour from Singapore by ferry

Philippines, ran aground on Kusu Reef while homeward bound with his fleet. Kusu was no more than two tiny outcrops on the reef until 1975, when it was filled in and expanded to its present size of 8.5 hectares (21 acres).

Pulau Sakijang (St John's) is another popular picnic spot at the weekends, with three swimming lagoons. Don't expect shimmering tropical sandy beaches with clear blue waters, though.

Both islands have grassed picnic areas, shelters, changing rooms and toilets. There is a canteen on St John's. *Ferries leave from Marina South Pier, taking 40 minutes to reach Kusu. They take a further 20 minutes to reach St John's. On Sundays and public holidays, more sailings and schedules allow both islands to be visited in the same day. www.islandcruise.com.sg*

Pulau Ubin

Ten minutes by boat from Changi Village on the northeast tip of the Singapore mainland, Pulau Ubin is a peaceful little island where life is closer in spirit to rural Malaysia than to Singapore, whose downtown skyscrapers can be glimpsed in the distance. It is best explored by bike or on foot.

The island is still home to agricultural and fishing communities – the latter mostly relying on traditional *kelongs*, the V-shaped fish traps that you can see strung out along the coast. Pulau Ubin ('stone island') is also an important source of granite. Some of the quarries are still being worked, but many of the disused quarries scattered around the island are now filled with water and overrun with jungle vegetation, providing picturesque settings for a spot of fishing or even canoeing.

Within a few metres of the jetty in the village are several hire shops renting out mountain bikes (and canoes), which is how most people choose to explore the island. The island is mostly flat, with very little traffic on its bumpy, potholed roads. The most popular route is over to the north coast, where there is an excellent seafood restaurant and a Buddhist meditation centre.

Just outside the village the road winds along with bananas, papaya and coco-palms crowding the verges. Elsewhere, there are extensive rubber and coconut plantations, with abandoned plantations providing a haven for wildlife. There are large areas of mangrove where monitor lizards are common.

Unlike the manicured resort islands to the south, Pulau Ubin has no swimming beaches, but is much more interesting if you want to experience a typical tropical island and the communities who live and work there. It is best explored on weekdays, when there are few other people about. There are a couple of basic guesthouses. *Take the MRT to Tampines and change to bus 29. Alternatively, take bus 2 (which goes past Changi Prison). From the jetty in Changi Village the small ferry boats leave roughly every 15–30 minutes, as soon as they fill up. Mountain bike hire is relatively cheap.*

Shopping

Shoppers should be prepared to return from both Malaysia and Singapore with their bank accounts considerably depleted! From the latest hi-tech products to the local crafts of the region, the most discerning buyer will find it hard to resist the temptation to shop endlessly.

MALAYSIA

Malaysia is trying hard to catch up with its neighbour to the south by promoting itself as a shopper's paradise. While it can never compete with Singapore in terms of convenience and the vast range of shops found there, it does have advantages if you're looking for handicrafts and other locally produced goods.

Malaysia is well known for its batik fabrics, pewterware, silverware, ceramics and rattan work. There are plenty of opportunities to buy direct from craftspeople and to visit factories or handicraft centres to see how things are made. Sports equipment is a good buy, and there are many bargains to be had in leatherwork belts and bags.

In the major cities and towns there are air-conditioned department stores and shopping malls (known as *kompleks*) where prices are fixed, but outside of these you are more likely to be buying from roadside stalls or in markets where bargaining is normal.

The islands of Langkawi and Labuan (off the coast of Sabah) are duty-free ports. Most shops accept credit cards.

Where to shop

KUALA LUMPUR

Antiques, arts and handicrafts

Artiquarium

This shop, in an unusual old mansion, is more of a gallery with a selection of modern Malaysian art, colonial and Chinese antiques, and tribal artefacts. *273A Jalan Medan Abdul Rahman. Tel: (03) 2692 1222.*

Central Market

A focal point for Kuala Lumpur's craftspeople, with numerous stalls selling hand-painted T-shirts, leatherwork, jewellery, batik, traditional Malaysian kites (*wau*), pewterware and silverware and a good selection of basketware and rattan. Several stalls specialise in tribal arts from the Asia-Pacific region. *Central Market, Jalan Hang Kasturi. Tel: (03) 2274 6542. www.centralmarket.com.my*

Karyaneka Handicraft Centre
A good place to get an idea of the range of handicrafts available from the different regions of Malaysia. Inside a series of individual houses you can see craftsmen at work and there is a showroom where the finished products can be bought.
Level 3, Bagunan Sri Anjung, KLCC, Jalan Conlay. Tel: (03) 2164 9907. www.karyaneka.com.my

Peter Hoe Evolution
This attractively laid out shop covering two floors specialises in Malaysian batik designs on dresses, sarongs and shirts. There is also an extensive range of Southeast Asian traditional clothes and jewellery, including silk scarves from Cambodia. Look out for the interesting kitchenware section.
2 Jalan Lekir. Tel: (03) 2026 0711.

Royal Selangor Pewter
Established in 1885, Royal Selangor Pewter is the country's biggest manufacturer and has a huge range of designs. Many out-of-town tours visit the factory where you can see the processes involved.
Main showroom: 4 Jalan Usahawan 6, Setapak Jaya. Tel: (03) 4145 6000. www.royalselangor.com

Shopping complexes

Kuala Lumpur has a number of air-conditioned shopping complexes scattered over the city. Some are fairly ordinary, catering more to local needs, while others house branches of chic designer-name boutiques. Among the major shopping centres are:

Avenue K
Avenue K is an up-market mall catering for a sophisticated crowd, with *haute couture*, jewellery, wicker furniture, oriental carpets, silks and handicrafts. Ampang Park, the city's oldest mall, is connected to it by a footbridge.
156 Jalan Ampang. Tel: (03) 2168 7888.

Berjaya Times Square
This vast mall is the largest in Southeast Asia and includes a branch of Malaysia's excellent Metrojaya department stores plus plenty of foreign designer names. There's also a branch of Borders Bookstore, reputedly the biggest of its kind in the world.
1 Jalan Imbi. Tel: (03) 2144 9821.

KL Plaza
Centrally located, with a good selection of jewellery shops and menswear (Christian Dior, Givenchy and Polo Ralph Lauren, as well as the local tailoring chain, Jim's Shop).
179 Jalan Bukit Bintang. Tel: (03) 2141 7288.

The Mall
This five-storey mall is the second largest in Kuala Lumpur. There is a wide variety of shops selling everything from carpets to cosmetics, as well as the Yaohan department store and a historic-looking hawker's centre, the Medan Hang Tuah.
100 Jalan Putra (opposite the Pan Pacific Hotel and Putra World Trade Centre). Tel: (03) 4042 7122.

Sungei Wang Plaza
Kuala Lumpur's largest shopping complex, with 550 shops, two cinemas,

department stores and food centres all under one roof. It is connected to the next-door Bukit Bintang Plaza on Jalan Bukit Bintang.
99 Jalan Bukit Bintang.
Tel: (03) 2148 6109.

Night markets

Kuala Lumpur's biggest and most colourful *pasar malam* (night market) takes place in the heart of Chinatown every evening, when Jalan Petaling and surrounding streets are closed off to traffic. Dozens of stalls spring up to create a noisy, crowded, brightly lit bazaar popular with locals out bargain-hunting. Keep a tight hold of your bag in the often congested lanes between the stalls.

The other main *pasar malam* is held on Jalan Tunku Abdul Rahman every Saturday night from 7pm to midnight.

PULAU PINANG

Georgetown on Pulau Pinang is the second major shopping centre after Kuala Lumpur and, while it doesn't have the same range of shops, it is much more compact and easier to get around. As well as the usual electronic and photographic goods, it is a good place for local handicrafts, T-shirts, antiques and sports equipment. Handicrafts from Thailand are also popular.

The main shopping malls are the Komtar and the Super Komtar, which are both in the massive Komtar Tower on the corner of Magazine Road and Pinang Road. There are three department stores within the tower, as well as the usual array of shops.

Most of the other shops in Pinang are concentrated along Jalan Pinang and Jalan Campbell. Within one block on Jalan Pinang are found most of the antique and curio shops, with a range of Chinese, Malay and Indonesian artefacts. Also on Pinang Road, the Piccadilly Bazaar and Chowrasta Market sell a wide range of goods.

Pinang's *pasar malam* is a moveable feast, changing locations every two weeks (call the Pinang Tourist Association to find out where it is currently being held). It is not always worth the effort since it can be a fair distance from the town centre, and is mostly geared to local needs.

MELAKA

Melaka is acknowledged as the main centre in Malaysia for antiques, which are to be found principally in the shops that line Jalan Hang Jebat. You are unlikely to find real treasures at bargain prices (collectors have long since scoured the shops), but many shops are piled high with fascinating curios of one sort or another, ranging from old tiffin boxes to pre-World War II electric fans, clocks, coins, lamps and Chinese lacquered furniture. With a dwindling supply of antiques, a lot of shops now stock handicrafts as well, and a few have workshops at the back where 'antiques' are manufactured.

KOTA BHARU

Undoubtedly, the best selection of traditional arts and crafts on the east coast is in and around Kota Bharu, state capital of Kelantan. Kelantan is renowned for pottery, silver, textiles (batik and songket), bamboo and rattan work, as well as kites (*wau*) and shadow puppets (*wayang kulit*).

A good starting point is the Kampong Kraftangan (Handicraft Village), which has a good selection of batik paintings, woodcarvings, songket, silver and pottery.

Also worth a look is the second floor of the Central Market, where a number of stalls sell clothes, brassware, songket and batik. The most interesting area is a 5km (3-mile) stretch of road on the way out to the Pantai Cinta Berahi, where you can visit numerous small workshops and watch songket-weaving or batik being made. The textile workshops are mostly clustered around Kampung Penambang, while further on you will find silversmiths, woodcarvers and several master kite-makers who proudly display their colourful wares.

EAST MALAYSIA

The best place for tribal arts and crafts is Kuching, the capital of Sarawak. An enormous variety of artefacts can be found here, ranging from colourful carvings to war shields, beadwork, baskets, charm sticks, spears and poison-dart holders. Look out particularly for Penan mats, Iban blankets (*pua*) and Bidayuh baskets and jewellery. Most of the tribal arts shops are concentrated along the Main Bazaar near Jalan Wayang. Be prepared to dig deep in your pocket if you want a genuine artefact.

Good-quality handicrafts at reasonable prices can be found at the Kampung Budaya Sarawak (*see p78*).

KELANTANESE CRAFTS

Many of the traditional arts and crafts for which Kelantan is famous were originally produced by craftsmen working for Malay royalty, and the relative isolation of the state from cultural influences that changed the pattern of life elsewhere in Malaysia ensured that many of the designs used remained unchanged for centuries.

Woodcarvers were employed in large numbers to decorate the magnificent wooden palaces of the nobility, creating ingenious decorative panels above the windows and doors with holes in the patterning to let in light and air. Many traditional Malay houses also display beautiful carved wooden panels in their interiors or on window shutters.

Songket-weaving is another skill that was largely fostered by royalty, who used the elaborately woven cloth for special occasions and weddings. Songket uses a specially dyed yarn of silk or cotton, into which gold and silver threads are woven in intricate patterns. The more threads used and the more intricate the design, the more expensive will be the songket. Traditional ceremonial costumes can use up to 9m (30ft) of this laboriously worked and richly coloured material.

Silverwork also owes its current prominence to royal commissions, with silversmiths in the past living and working inside the royal courtyards, producing exquisite items such as pendants, brooches and jewellery boxes. Silversmithing is still very much alive in Kelantan, with most of the work being produced by individual craftsmen using traditional methods.

SINGAPORE

Shopping has always been one of the major attractions of Singapore – there are thousands of outlets, ranging from small street-stalls to huge, air-conditioned shopping plazas. Shopping here is not just a necessity, it is a way of life. Shops are open at all hours – as much for the convenience of locals (who rate shopping as one of their favourite pastimes) as for tourists.

The variety of goods is enormous, ranging from the latest electronic gadgets, European designer clothes and American sportswear to Asian handicrafts and jewellery.

Value for money

Singapore claims to offer some of the best buys in the world at highly affordable prices. However, to make sure of getting your money's worth, some groundwork helps.

When you arrive, head for the department stores, where prices are fixed, to get an overview of what's available and roughly what the standard price might be. After that, browse around the big shopping malls to compare prices.

Bargaining is expected almost everywhere except in the department stores. Start off by asking the retailer for their 'best price' and then make an offer. It's difficult to say how much lower this should be than the initial price (it could be between 10 and 50 per cent), but be realistic. When bargaining you will get a better price for cash or traveller's cheques than credit cards.

Make sure you are comparing prices for exactly the same brand and model of photographic or electronic goods.

Consumer protection

Singapore has stringent laws to protect consumers, but this doesn't mean that all rip-offs have been eliminated. Check all guarantees and warranties issued with the product. Insist on a worldwide warranty.

Make sure that you get an itemised receipt with the shop's stamp on it, which you may need for insurance, customs inspection, or if you need to obtain a refund. Always check that your purchases are in working order before leaving the shop, and it is best to watch them being packed in case something is 'mistakenly' missed out. For very expensive items, consider paying by credit card if your card company offers some form of consumer protection.

Check the voltages on electrical and electronic goods to make sure they are the same as back home (UK, Hong Kong, New Zealand and Australia: 220–240 volts, 50 cycles; USA, Canada and Japan: 110–120 volts, 60 cycles).

Ignore the touts who will approach you in shopping malls. Touting is illegal and you will only end up paying commission on top of the price. Counterfeit goods are less common than they used to be, but there are still plenty of 'Rolex' and other copy watches on the streets: if you insist on buying a fake, bargain hard and don't expect it to last too long.

Most retailers are reliable and honest, but if in doubt shop with members of the Good Retailers Scheme; these shops display a white Merlion logo on a red background. If you have a complaint, you can either contact the **Consumer's Association of Singapore**, **CASE** (*tel: 6463 1811; www.case.org.sg*) or take action through a special Small Claims Tribunal.

Credit cards

All the major credit cards are accepted in most shops.

Shopping hours

Most shops open daily from around 10am through until 9–10pm at night. On Sundays some department stores and smaller shops may be closed.

Where to shop

The long, tree-lined boulevard of Orchard Road is Singapore's 'Golden Mile', lined with major department stores and multistorey plazas selling goods from every corner of the globe. Shopping here is simply a matter of hopping from one air-conditioned complex to the next. Just off Orchard Road is Scotts Road, which has another batch of big shopping malls.

Although it has the largest concentration of shops in the city, shopping doesn't stop beyond Orchard Road. To the south, there are plenty of opportunities for browsing in large malls such as Marina Square and Raffles City, as well as the up-market Raffles Arcade.

Many shopping malls have department stores occupying one or two floors. Locally owned stores such as Tangs, DFS and Metro (all of which have several branches) are good places to look for Singapore-made goods. Japanese goods are available at Isetan, French products are available at Carrefour in the Suntec City Mall, and European imports at the Robinson's department store.

Don't neglect the ethnic areas such as Chinatown, Little India and Arab Street, where you can often pick up some unusual bargains.

To help you find your way around, free shopping maps are available in hotel lobbies. The American Express Map of Singapore is very clearly laid out and one of the most popular.

SHOPPING MALLS

Orchard Road and Tanglin Road

Delfi Orchard

Fashions, jewellery, Waterford crystal, Wedgwood, rattan furniture; Meitetsu department store.

402 Orchard Road. Tel: 6877 1818.

The bright lights of Singapore's shops beckon

A saree shop in Little India

Far East Shopping Centre
Tailors, jewellers, computers, antiques.
545 Orchard Road. Tel: 6734 5541.

The Heeren
Sportswear, fashions and HMV, the largest music store in Southeast Asia.
260 Orchard Road. Tel: 6733 4725.

ION Orchard
All the world's best-loved brands in one intelligently designed shopping space.
2 Orchard Turn.

Lucky Plaza
Sporting goods, leather; Metro Grand department store.
304 Orchard Road. Tel: 6235 3294.

Ngee Ann City
Home to the largest bookstore in Southeast Asia.
391 Orchard Road. Tel: 6733 0337.

The Paragon
Quality fashions at Intermezzo, Dunhill, Gucci, Karl Lagerfeld, Lanvin, Offenbach; Metro department store.
290 Orchard Road. Tel: 6738 5535.

Plaza Singapura
Fashions, lighting, furniture, audio and video equipment.
68 Orchard Road. Tel: 6332 9298.

Tanglin Shopping Centre
Oriental carpets at Hassan's; antique maps and prints at Antiques of the Orient; pearls at CT Hoo.
19 Tanglin Road. Tel: 6737 0849.

Wisma Atria
Fashion boutiques, shoes; regional curios at Legaspi; Filippino leatherwork at Cora Jacobs; Isetan department store.
435 Orchard Road. Tel: 6235 2103.

Scotts Road

Far East Plaza
Electronics, sportswear, watches; fashion accessories at Coco; popular with students.
14 Scotts Road. Tel: 6734 2325.

Pacific Plaza
Quality fashions and furnishings. Australian designer clothes lines, Billabong, Mambo.
9 Scotts Road. Tel: 6733 5655.

Shaw Centre
Chinese and other exotic curios at Ming Blue and Singapore Woodcraft.
1 Scotts Road. Tel: 6737 9080.

Off Orchard Road

Funan Digitalife Mall
Computers and electronics.
109 North Bridge Road. Tel: 6336 8327.

Marina Square
Fashion at Tokyu, Export Shop and Stockmarket; sportswear; China Silk House; Habitat.
6 Raffles Boulevard. Tel: 6339 8787.

People's Park Complex
Gold and electronics.
101 Upper Cross Street. Tel: 6535 8888.

Raffles Arcade
Exclusive boutiques including Armani, Jim Thompson Thai Silk, Samsonite, Louis Vuitton, Lowe, Aquascutum and Tiffany.
1 Beach Road. Tel: 6337 1886.

Raffles City
Antiques, handicrafts, fashions, sportswear, watches; Robinsons department store.
250 North Bridge Road. Tel: 6338 7766.

Sim Lim Square
Electronics, stereos, televisions, videos, telephones.
1 Rochor Canal Road. Tel: 6338 3859.

Suntec City Mall
Numerous shops, restaurants and entertainment outlets.
3 Temasek Boulevard. Tel: 6825 2667.

VivoCity
One of Singapore's largest shopping malls.
1 HarbourFront Walk. Tel: 6377 6860.

DEPARTMENT STORES

China Square Central
18 Cross Street. Tel: 6327 4810.

DFS Galleria
25 Scotts Road. Tel: 6229 8100.

Far East Plaza
14 Scotts Road, Far East Plaza. Tel: 6734 2325.

Harbour Front Centre
1 Maritime Square. Tel: 6274 7111.

Isetan Orchard
435 Orchard Road, Wisma Atria. Tel: 6733 7777.

Isetan Scotts
350 Orchard Road, Shaw House. Tel: 6733 1111.

Jurong Point Shopping Centre
1, Jurong West Central 2. Tel: 6792 5662.

Marks and Spencer
68 Orchard Road, Plaza Singapura. Tel: 6835 9552.
252 North Bridge Road, Raffles City. Tel: 6339 9013.

Robinsons
176 Orchard Road, Centrepoint. Tel: 6733 0888.

Takashimaya
In Ngee Ann City, 391 Orchard Road. Tel: 6738 1111.

Tangs
320 Orchard Road. Tel: 6737 5500.
In VivoCity, 1 HarbourFront Walk. Tel: 6737 5500.

What to buy

Antiques, arts and crafts

Singapore offers a wide selection of items from all over the Asia-Pacific region. As well as Chinese porcelain, jade and silver, you can find Thai Buddha images, Burmese lacquerware, Indonesian masks and woodcarvings, and tribal art from the South Pacific.

Genuine antiques should be over 100 years old, and you should insist on a certificate of antiquity as well as a receipt.

Some of the best places to look are the Tanglin Shopping Centre, Raffles Arcade and Smith Street and Temple Street in Chinatown.

On the second floor of Marina Square there are several shops specialising in handicrafts with daily demonstrations.

For basketware, caneware, rattan and leather bags, try Arab Street.

Electronic goods

The range of high-technology goods available is mind-boggling. Prices are extremely competitive, but make sure TV/video systems and electrical supplies are compatible with your own.

Electronics shops are found almost everywhere, but two places that are worth checking out are Plaza Singapura and Sim Lim Square.

Computer peripherals and accessories are good buys, and all the big-name computer brands are available. Try Ultimate Lap Top Shop and others in Sim Lim Square.

Fashions and clothing

Singapore has a huge range of fashion, clothing, shoe and sportswear shops. International designers such as Ralph Lauren, Gucci, Versace and Issey Miyake are well represented, and as well as these Singapore now has a home-grown industry of designers. Look for Esther Tay, Celia Loh, Dick Lee, Arthur Yen, David Wang and others.

Tailoring and dressmaking services are widely available, and you will find most textile stores have a make-up service with good-quality workmanship. Be specific about design, cut and detailing and insist on fittings. Try any hotel arcade or Mode O Day in the Tanglin Shopping Centre, MaryJane in Far East Plaza, or Giordano in VivoCity.

For accessories, check out department stores such as Robinsons, Tangs and Isetan, or the Raffles Arcade. For bags, belts and leather goods from India and Indonesia, head for Arab Street. Countless shoe stores can be found in Far East Plaza.

Jewellery

The oriental love of ornamentation and fascination with precious gems, gold and pearls has not been swept away in Singapore, where there is a huge range of traditional and contemporary designs for all kinds of jewellery. Gold jewellery is sold according to weight, and is principally either 22K or 24K. Gold shops are found almost everywhere, with ethnic designs available in Serangoon Road in Little India and Arab Street; the People's Park Complex is another good place to look. Cultured and freshwater pearls, precious stones and jade can also be found in shops along Orchard Road.

Photographic goods

If you're looking for cameras and other photographic goods, decide on which model you want before leaving home and check out the price in discount stores, since European and North American prices often match those in the Far East. Camera stores are found all over Singapore, so shop around. Try Hoon Cheong at Sim Lim Square, Harvey Norman in Funan Digitalife Mall or Digital Foto at Lucky Plaza. If you haven't gone digital, film processing is very good value; for transparencies, a reliable lab is Albert Photo.

Night markets

The *pasar malam*, or night market, is an integral part of rural and urban life in Malaysia and you are bound to come across several in your travels through the country. Whether held in a narrow side street or in the town square, shortly after dusk it will be busy with people out for a stroll, browsing among the stalls, maybe stopping for a snack here and there, or simply chatting to friends.

It is a great place to try all the local specialities. You might find anything from delicious cinnamon rolls to sugar-cane juice or *won ton* (Chinese dumplings). Elsewhere, Malaysian satay, steamed corn on the cob, or *murabak pisang* (banana cakes) tempt the palate.

While some markets only sell food, in others you can find anything from cheap clothes to Asian pop cassettes or Chinese herbal medicines. For people working late, they are the only alternative once restaurants have closed, with many of the stalls staying open until 1am. When the shops have closed, locals can pop down for their necessities. It is, if you like, the Malaysian equivalent of the late-night supermarket and fast-food joint, all rolled into one.

Bead necklaces for sale at a night market

Entertainment

While the vibrant excitement of markets and shopping areas makes them major entertainment centres in both Malaysia and Singapore, there are a fair number of bars, clubs and karaoke bars for those looking for alternatives. Traditional dance and theatre are also very popular.

MALAYSIA

Entertainment and nightlife in Malaysia tends to be fairly low-key compared to neighbouring countries such as Thailand. Even Singapore has a huge choice of live music and discos by comparison. However, there are still a fair number of bars and nightclubs in major centres such as Kuala Lumpur and Pinang. Of course, the ubiquitous karaoke lounges are found in almost every town.

Cinemas in main cities and towns screen English-language movies as well as the Hindi, Malay and Cantonese films that predominate in smaller urban centres. Kuala Lumpur cinemas screen five shows daily, starting from around midday, with the last show around 9pm. Often the best evening's entertainment is simply to wander around the *pasar malam* (night markets – *see p135*). *Kuala Lumpur This Month*, available free from tourist offices, lists events and shows currently on in the capital.

KUALA LUMPUR

Bars and pubs

The Attic

A gallery bar with a range of fine cocktails.

61–2 Jalan Bangkung, Bukit Bandaraya, Bangsar. Tel: (03) 2093 8842. Open: Sun & Tue–Thur 5pm–1am, Fri–Sat 5pm–3am. Closed: Mon.

Ceylon Bar

With a terrace, bar and lounge, this is a great place to while away an evening.

20–2 Changkat Bukit Bintang. Tel: (03) 2145 7689. Open: Mon & Wed–Sat 5pm–1am, Sun 11am–1am. Closed: Tue.

Finnegan's

One in a popular chain of Irish pubs spread across the capital.

51 Jalan Sultan Ismail. Tel: (03) 2145 1930. Open: daily 10am–11pm.

Zeta Bar

Piano bar.

Kuala Lumpur Hilton, Jalan Sultan Ismail. Tel: (03) 2264 2264. Open: Mon–Sat 8pm–2am. Closed: Sun.

Cultural shows

Auditorium DBKL

Revue show of music and traditional dances at 8.30pm every Saturday.
Jalan Raja Laut. Tel: (03) 2699 3872. Free admission.

Central Market

The amphitheatre outside Central Market is one of the city's liveliest venues for a variety of performances ranging from Malay traditional dance to *silat* (martial arts) demonstrations, Indian drama, poetry readings, Balinese dance, and fringe theatre shows and street acts. A monthly calendar of events is available from the information desk.
Central Market, Jalan Hang Kasturi. Information counter open 10am–10pm. Tel: (03) 2274 6542. Free admission.

Malaysia Tourist Information Complex

Cultural performances in the mini-auditorium at 3.30pm daily.
Jalan Ampang. Tel: (03) 2164 3929.

Nightclubs

Aloha

Lot 924 Jalan P. Ramlee. Tel: (03) 2711 7266. www.alohakl.com. Open: daily 11.30am–3am.

The Disco

Central Market, Jalan Hang Kasturi. Tel: (03) 2026 5039. Open: daily 6pm–3am.

Funtheque

102 & 104, 1st Floor, Jalan Bukit Bintang. Tel: (03) 2144 3892. www.captainscabin.com.my. Open: daily 7pm–3am.

Maison

8 Jalan Yap Ah Shak. Tel: 2698 3328. www.maison.com.my. Open: Mon–Tue 5pm–1am & Wed–Sun 5pm–3am.

Orange Club

1 Jalan Kia Peng. Tel: (03) 2141 4929. Open: daily 7pm–3am.

Passion

18–1 Jalan Law Yew Swee, off Jalan P Ramlee. Tel: 2141 8888. Open: Mon–

TRADITIONAL MALAY DANCES

Among the many traditional dances that you will see performed at cultural shows, some of the more colourful include the **Kuda Kepang**, which originally came from the southern state of Johor. The dance re-enacts the story of the men who spread the Islamic faith, with performers riding two-dimensional 'horses' to dramatise the legends of battles waged.

A popular dance is the **Tarian Endang**, which portrays villagers cleaning up at the riverbank after a hard day's work in the rice-fields and symbolises the virtues of community life.

Also connected to the rice harvest, **Tarian Cangging** is usually performed during the harvesting season in the state of Perlis. Rice-planting and harvesting are likewise celebrated in the **Jong Jong Inai**, a joyous dance that is performed to celebrate a good season.

Tarian Cinta Sayang (meaning 'the loved ones' dance') is a romantic and lively folk dance from the state of Kedah, often performed as a gesture of bidding good luck to fisherfolk as they set off to sea. From Sabah in East Malaysia, the **Sumazu** is a rhythmic and graceful dance where the hands and limbs flap and flail in likeness of the flight of birds.

A popular east-coast dance is the **Tarian Wau Bulan** (moon-kite dance), which depicts the carefree spirit of the kite-flyer as he sends his *wau bulan* aloft.

Thur 4pm–2am & Fri–Sat 4pm–3am. Closed: Sun.

Ruums

Life Centre, Jalan Sultan Ismail. Tel: (03) 2162 8243. Open: daily 7pm–3am.

Zouk

113 Jalan Ampang. Tel: (03) 2171 1997. www.zoukclub.com.my. Open: daily 6pm–3am.

PULAU PINANG

Georgetown has several cinemas, karaoke lounges and bars, but the main form of entertainment in the evenings is browsing and sampling from the food-stalls on Lebuh Chuliah, the Esplanade or Gurney Drive. Clubs are mostly centred around the Batu Ferringhi beach resorts, but there are a few in Georgetown.

Borsalino

Park Royal Hotel. Batu Ferringhi. Tel: (04) 881 1133. Open: daily 7pm–2am.

Glo

A8, The Garage, 2 Penang Road, Georgetown. Tel: (04) 261 1066. www.glo.com.my. Open: daily 7pm–1am.

SINGAPORE

Much of Singapore's nightlife centres around Orchard Road and the Chijmes area, which have a host of bars, hotel cocktail lounges, discos and karaoke lounges. Some of the best entertainment is provided by street parades, open-air Chinese opera and other performances associated with Singapore's many festivals (*see pp24–5*). Both the *Straits Times* and the tabloid *New Paper* carry weekend supplements listing pubs, bars and lounges with live performances or other attractions. The listings magazine *Time Out Singapore* also has a good round-up of events.

Singapore has none of the raunchy nightlife of cities like Bangkok, although there are plenty of 'health centres' and escort services for the single male. The city's most notorious spot used to be Bugis Street, where flamboyant drag queens and transvestites paraded after dark around the cafés. The old Bugis Street was demolished to make way for the MRT and has been rebuilt on a new site across the road, complete with air-conditioned restaurants and a theatre-cabaret venue. However, since the transvestites have moved on elsewhere it is a shadow of its former self and no different from any other outdoor eating area with a small night market.

Bars and pubs

Prices for alcohol in Singapore are relatively high, owing to import duties on beers, wines and spirits; many bars have Happy Hours, with two drinks for the price of one, between around 5–7pm. Most open around noon and stay open until around 1am, extending to 2–3am at weekends. A lot of bars have live music, ranging from jazz to rock.

Alley Bar

Smart atmosphere (popular with ex-pats and airline crews), huge video

screen, live music and dancing.
180 Orchard Road. Tel: 6732 6966. www.pernakanplace.com. Open: daily 5pm–2am.

Brewerkz

Great handcrafted beers at this microbrewery overlooking Clarke Quay.
01-05 Riverside Point, 30 Merchant Road. Tel: 6438 7438. www.brewerkz.com. Open: Mon–Thur noon–midnight, Fri–Sat noon–1am, Sun 11am–midnight.

Eski Bar

The Arctic brought to the Tropics; as the name suggests it's cold inside, so cold you'll need a coat.
46 Circular Road. Tel: 6536 3757. www.eskibar.com. Open: Sun–Thur 4pm–1am & Fri–Sat 3pm–2am.

The Front Page

Situated in a beautifully restored Chinese shop-house, The Front Page has oodles of old world charm.
17 Mohammed Sultan Road. Tel: 6235 6967. Open: Sun–Thur 5pm–1am & Fri–Sat 5pm–3am.

Harry's Bar

One of Singapore's most famous venues, this long-running favourite serves a great nightly mix of blues, jazz and rock. Plenty of English-style pub food and tapas are served until 11.30pm. Can get very busy on a Friday evening.
28 Boat Quay. Tel: 6538 3029. www.harrys.com.sg. Open: Sun–Thur 11am–1am, Fri–Sat 11am–2am.

New Asia Bar

The highest bar in the city (with correspondingly high prices), on the 72nd floor of the world's tallest hotel. Fabulous views through the floor-to-ceiling windows. Dress code.
Fairmont, 80 Bras Basah Road. Tel: 6837 3322. Open: Sun–Wed 3pm–1am & Thur–Sat 3pm–2am.

Topps Lounge

Amusing bar where the waiters alternate with the live bands in providing entertainment and singing.
Copthorne Orchid, 214 Dunearn Road. Tel: 6250 3322. Open: Sun–Thur 7pm–1am, Fri–Sat 7pm–2am.

Chinese opera

Though not to everyone's taste, Chinese opera can be fun to see at least once in a lifetime. The costumes are usually sumptuous and the sets elaborate. Don't worry about not understanding what's going on, just soak up the atmosphere.

Chinese Theatre Circle

An easy introduction to Chinese opera can be found at this traditional Chinese teahouse. Shows can include either a dinner with specially brewed Chinese tea or just snacks. Occasionally shows are performed in English.
5 Smith Street. Tel: 6323 4862. www.ctcopera.com.sg. Open: Fri–Sat 7–9pm. Special arrangements can be made for performances outside official hours as long as there are more than ten people interested.

Cinemas

All the major international English-language movies reach Singapore,

The Victoria Theatre, Singapore

although they may be censored. Check the daily papers for listings. Cinemas are air-conditioned and clean. More serious art films are screened at the Jade Classics (Shaw Towers) or the Picturehouse (Cathay Building).

Classical music

When in session, the Singapore Symphony Orchestra holds concerts most Friday and Saturday nights at the Victoria Concert Hall, Empress Place. Details are advertised in the local press, or call the Victoria Theatre Central Booking Office (*tel: 6338 1230*).

Dance

Singapore's professional ballet group, the Singapore Dance Theatre, usually holds a season in June; performances are held at either the Esplanade Theatre, Fort Canning Park or University Cultural Centre.

Esplanade Theatre Booking Office. Tel: 6348 5555. www.esplanade.com.

University Cultural Centre. Tel: 6516 2492.

Drama

Amateur productions by local drama groups are usually staged at the **Drama Centre**, Canning Rise, or at the **Victoria Theatre**, Empress Place. Watch out for innovative and experimental performances by Theatreworks at the **Black Box** (*Canning Fort*), or **The Substation** (*45 Armenian Street*).

Karaoke lounges

As popular in Singapore as it now is all over the rest of Asia, karaoke is not everybody's idea of fun, but if you want to sing along to popular songs (with the lyrics often displayed over a video of the original singer), then there are plenty of places where you can have a go. The KJ (the karaoke equivalent of a DJ) will line up the tapes from a menu of songs in English, Mandarin or Japanese.

Nightclubs

Singapore has a young population and clubs are hugely popular, with plenty to choose from. Dress codes are usually 'smart casual' (no jeans, T-shirts or trainers). Outrageous dress is not part of the scene here, nor is overtly affectionate behaviour. Entry charges are high, although they include the first two drinks.

Bar None

In the heart of Orchard Road's tourist district, this dance club offers mostly rock and pop.

Marriott Hotel, 320 Orchard Road. Tel: 6270 7676. www.barnoneasia.com. Open: daily 7pm–3am.

Brix

Smart venue for the slightly older set, oriental décor, small dance floor.

Hyatt Regency Hotel, 10–12 Scotts Road. Tel: 6732 1234. Open: daily 8pm–3am.

Chinablack

Lavish, up-market, large and trendy.

Pacific Plaza Penthouse, 12th Floor, 9 Scotts Road. Tel: 6734 7677. Open: Wed–Sat 8pm–3am. Closed: Sun–Tue.

eM Studio

A big party destination for those looking for a boisterous night out. Large selection of drinks.

#02–05 Gallery Hotel, 1 Nanson Road. Tel: 6836 9691. www.em-n-em.com. Open: Mon–Thur 10pm–3am & Fri–Sat 10pm–4am.

Top 5

One of Singapore's hottest nightlife spots with pole, salsa and hip-hop dancers, and also cabaret shows once in a while. Plenty of great dance music and the occasional live band.

04-35/36 Orchard Towers, 400 Orchard Road. Tel: 6733 4666. www.top5.com.sg. Open: 7pm–2am.

Zouk

One of Singapore's trendiest venues, the Zouk complex incorporates a dance club, a pub, wine bar, café and restaurant. The sounds are predominantly house and world music.

17–21 Jiak Kim Street, off Kim Seng Road. Tel: 6738 2988. www.zoukclub.com. Open: Tue–Sat 6pm–3am, Sun–Mon 6pm–1am.

Theatre

Singapore's theatre scene now matches that of many of the world's other great cities. It is not unusual for a successful Broadway or West End show to make its way to one of the city's fine new theatre complexes. To find out what might be playing on your visit go to *www.singaporetheatre.com*

Esplanade – Theatres On The Bay

The space age-looking Esplanade houses a concert hall, theatre, recital studio, library and a number of other venues specifically designed for the performing arts. All programmes change frequently, so it's best to check their website or box office for performances.

Raffles Avenue. Tel: 6828 8377 (box office). Open: noon–8.30pm (box office). www.esplanade.com. MRT: City Hall. Bus: 36, 56, 70, 75, 77, 97, 106, 111, 133, 162, 171 & 195.

Malay pastimes

Many of the games and pastimes enjoyed by Malaysians originated on the east coast, particularly in the state of Kelantan, where old traditions are cherished in what has always been the Malay heartland. Although they have now caught on elsewhere in Malaysia, they are still most widely practised on the east coast. Most of the traditional games are normally held after harvests and on important state festivals, but regular events also take place at the Gelanggang Seni (Cultural Centre) in Kota Bharu (*see p67*).

Spinning tops in Kota Bharu

Top-spinning

With Kelantan tops weighing anything up to 5.5kg (12 pounds), top-spinning is an adult sport requiring considerable manual dexterity and strength. Neighbouring villages often challenge each other to a test of skill with the *gasing* (tops), sometimes with up to 500 people taking part. There are two types of contest, the striking match and the spinning competition. In the former, each team tries to topple the opposition's tops, while in the latter the winner is the one whose top spins the longest – experts claim to be able to set them going for two hours or more.

Kite-flying

Kelantanese kites (*wau*) come in all shapes and sizes, with the largest (measuring some 2m/6½ft across) being capable of soaring to great heights. Again, inter-village competitions are often held, with matches for the kite that flies the highest, the kite that sustains the best musical hum, the best-decorated kite, and the most skilful kite-flyer. One of the most popular designs is the *wau bulan* or moon-kite, which has a long, elaborate tail.

Silat

The Malay art of self-defence is characterised by highly stylised, graceful and disciplined movements. Now it is rarely used as a martial art, and demonstrations are more often given as part of dance performances, at ceremonies and at weddings, to the rhythmical accompaniment of gongs and drums.

Wayang Kulit

Malaysian shadow-puppet plays are similar to those found in neighbouring Asian countries. Puppets crafted from cowhide and mounted on rattan sticks are manipulated from behind a white screen by the *Tok Dalang* (Father of the Mysteries), who relates tales from the Indian classics of *Ramayana* and *Mahabharata*. Backed by a traditional orchestra, the performance may go on for several hours.

The *Wayang Kulit* shadow puppets

Rebana (giant drum) competitions

Found only in Kelantan, the *rebana* is an enormous drum weighing over 100kg (220 pounds), that can be heard several kilometres away. Teams comprising 12 men, with six drums between them, compete in the village fields from February to October (*see the Kelantan International Drum Festival, p23*).

A *rebana* drumming competition

Children

If the theme parks and hi-tech entertainment offered by Singapore to young tourists make it a fun holiday spot for families, the endless beaches and natural attractions of Malaysia prove equally compelling.

MALAYSIA

Malaysians love children and they are welcome everywhere. Although not as squeaky-clean as Singapore, Malaysia is less of a hygiene risk than many other Asian countries. Make sure that your children have all the necessary jabs and are protected from the sun.

Like Singapore, children are welcome in almost any eating place. They will probably love *satay*, and in larger towns and resorts you can nearly always find local or international fast-food chains.

One of the most popular family destinations in Malaysia is Pulau Pinang, where, in addition to the beach, there is the Butterfly Farm, funicular rides up Pinang Hill, parks and gardens (*see p54 and pp56–7*). Older children will appreciate the chance to observe wildlife – visit the Sepilok Orang-utan Sanctuary in Sabah (*see p90*) and watch turtles nest at Rantau Abang (*see pp70–71*).

In Kuala Lumpur the place for children is the Lake Gardens (*see p33*), with a boating lake and a Butterfly Park and Bird Park. Near Kuala Lumpur two major family attractions are:

Sunway Lagoon

A massive theme park with waterslides and other attractions.

3 Jalan PJS 11/11, Bandar Sunway, Petaling Jaya. Tel: (03) 5639 0000. www.sunwaylagoon.com. Open: Mon & Wed–Fri 11am–6pm, weekends & holidays 10am–6pm. Closed: Tue (except public and school holidays). Admission charge. Bus 252B or 51 from Klang bus station, Kuala Lumpur.

Wet World Water Park

A variety of wonderful water-related activities including the famous Monsoon Buster ride.

Persiaran Dato' Menteri, Shah Alam, Selangor. 26km (16 miles) from the city centre. Bus 222 or 338 from Kuala Lumpur's Klang bus station. Tel: (03) 550 2588. Open: Mon, Tue, Thur & Fri 1–7pm, Sat–Sun 10am–8pm. Closed: Wed. Admission charge.

SINGAPORE

Singapore is a great destination for families, with plenty of fun activities and festivals to amuse and entertain.

Singapore's clean and green environment poses few health risks, so apart from protection from the heat and the sun few precautions are necessary.

Eating out with children is never a problem (except in the most sophisticated establishments), and Singaporeans often dine out with several generations seated at the table. Some of the spicier foods may not be suitable for young palates, but there is nearly always something acceptable on the menu.

However, with children it can be expensive. Admission costs can add up, although some attractions (such as the Jurong Bird Park) have family packages that offer reductions.

Popular venues for children are:

Haw Par Villa
Children will particularly enjoy the flume rides, audio-visual shows and participation in story-telling (*see pp103–4*).

Jurong Bird Park
See p104.

Sentosa Island
Numerous attractions including roller-skating, Underwater World and the Dragon Trail with life-size dragons and skeletons (*see pp122–4*).

Singapore Discovery Centre
See p107.

Singapore Flyer
See p107.

Singapore Science Centre
Hands-on displays specifically aimed at youngsters, plus 'Crazy Rooms' with a weightless environment (*see pp107–8*).

Singapore Zoo
The 'open zoo' concept and lack of cages, animal shows and underwater viewing areas make this a favourite. **Children's World** has a farmyard, pet's corner, llamas, miniature horses, pony rides, a 'space walk' and a 1km (2/3-mile) miniature train ride (*see p108*).

Getting wet

Most hotels have swimming pools, but when children want to splash around to their heart's content, try:

Sentosa Island
Pedal-boats, aquabikes, fun bugs, canoes and surf boards for hire (*see p122*).
On Siloso Beach.

Wild Wild Wet
On the northeast coast, in the Pasir Ris district; a mix of exciting water slides and pools for all ages.
Downtown East, Pasir Ris.
Tel: 6581 9112. www.wildwildwet.com.
Open: Mon, Wed–Fri 1–7pm, weekends and public holidays 10am–7pm. Closed: Tue. MRT: Pasir Ris. Bus: 3, 5, 6, 12, 17, 21, 89, 354 & 358.

The view from the Singapore Flyer

Sport and leisure

There is lots that a sports fan can find of interest in both Malaysia and Singapore. The wide-ranging ethnic mix means that almost every sport is, at the least, represented. Even more fascinating are the traditional sports that are still enthusiastically played everywhere.

MALAYSIA

Malaysians are enthusiastic sports lovers and the country has a wide range of sporting opportunities for visitors. Soccer, badminton, tennis, squash and cricket are all popular sports. In addition, there are plenty of ways in which to experience the country's magnificent natural surroundings, such as white-water rafting, trekking or scuba diving.

Golf

Since British planters introduced golf to Malaysia over 100 years ago, golf courses have mushroomed and there are now more than 100, with many more planned. A detailed brochure, *Golfing in Malaysia*, is available from the Tourist Office.

Ayer Keroh Country Club

A challenging course near Melaka, host to many major tournaments.
Km 14.5, Jalan Ayer Keroh, Melaka. Tel: (06) 233 2000. www.akcc.com.my

Royal Selangor Golf Club

Less than 1km (2/3 mile) from Kuala Lumpur city centre, with the highest number of holes in the country. This course is the venue for the prestigious Malaysian Open and other tournaments.
Jalan Kelab Golf, off Jalan Tun Razak. Kuala Lumpur. Tel: (03) 9206 3333. www.rsgc.com.my

Saujana Golf Club

Noted for its challenging course.
Near Subang International Airport, Kuala Lumpur. Batu 3, Jalan Lapangan Terbang, Subang, Selangor. Tel: (03) 7846 1466. www.saujana.com.my

Scuba diving

See pp119–21.

Trekking

Malaysia's national parks offer some excellent opportunities for short treks, particularly in Taman Negara (*see p118*), and the Kinabalu National Park in Sabah (*see p86*).

More adventurous backpackers might like to consider tackling sections of the Roof of Malaya Mountain Trail (RMMT), which runs for 250km (155 miles) along the Titiwangsa Range, linking six of the highest mountains in the peninsula (all of which are above 2,500m/8,200ft). The RMMT consists of two parts: the east–west section that runs from Tanjung Rambutan in Perak for 33km (21 miles) to the Blue Valley in the Cameron Highlands; and the north–south corridor, which is still being charted.

Treks with knowledgeable guides are run by one of the country's leading ecotourism operators, **My Outdoor**. They offer small-group trips to Endau-Rompin on the peninsula, Kinabalu National Park and Mount Trusmadi (Sabah), Bako National Park, Gunung Mulu National Park and Batu Lawi and Murud (Sarawak).

Treks in the Central Highlands with Orang Asli as guides are organised by the **Green Park Adventure**. Two treks are available: a five-day trek, staying in Orang Asli longhouses (with traditional feasts and dancing in the evenings) with an average of three to four hours walking per day; and a seven-day trek, which is similar but also involves longer walks (up to seven or eight hours per day), as well as demonstrations on making bamboo rafts and a day's rafting on the Sungai Ulu Jelai.

Canoeing off the beach, Pulau Kapas

Association of Backpackers Malaysia
ABM Secretariat, Lot 6 553/33, Taman University. Tel: (03) 7875 6249.

Green Park Adventure
Green Park Jungle Lodge, Kuala Lipis, Pahang. Tel: (017) 975 8653. www.my-greenpark.com

My Outdoor
Unit L1-09, Level 1, Bangunan JOTIC No.2, Jalan Ayer Molek, Johor Bahru. Tel: (07) 227 2907. www.myoutdoor.com

Watersports

Resorts on the islands of Langkawi, Pangkor, Tioman and Pinang and beach resorts at Kuantan, Cerating and Tanjung Aru (Sabah) have excellent watersports facilities.

White-water rafting

In Peninsular Malaysia, white-water rafting and canoeing principally take place on the Tembeling River in the Taman Negara National Park, in the Endau-Rompin National Park, on tributaries of the Kelantan River, stretches of the Pahang River and on the Sungai Muda in Kedah. Canoeing expeditions lasting up to a week are occasionally organised by the Kuala Lumpur Canoe Sports Association.

In East Malaysia, the principal rafting location is the Padas River in Sabah, with day tours organised by Borneo Expeditions in Kota Kinabalu. Participants travel by train to Tenom. The 9km (6-mile) ride back down the rapids takes around 2 hours.

Nomad Adventure
525, Jalan 17/13, Petaling Jaya, Selangor. Tel: (03) 7958 5152. www.nomadadventure.com

Riverbug
Lot 227–229, 2nd Floor, Wisma Sabah, Jalan Tun Fuad Stephen, Kota Kinabalu. Tel: (088) 260 501. www.traversetours.com

SINGAPORE

From computerised bowling alleys to a remarkable number of golf courses, Singapore has a wide range of sports facilities to complement the swimming pools and fitness clubs found in most major hotels. For details on matches, fixtures or sports not listed here, contact the **Singapore Sports Council** (*tel: 6345 7111*). *www.ssc.gov.sg*

Bowling

Ten-pin bowling is a very popular local sport. Consequently, there are many bowling alleys in the city, most with excellent facilities.

Jackie's Bowl
542B East Coast Road. Tel: 6241 6519.

Kallang Bowl
5 Stadium Walk. Tel: 6345 0505.

Orchid Bowl
1 Orchid Club Road. Tel: 6759 4448.

Plaza Bowl
200 Jalan Sultan. Tel: 6292 4821.

Superbowl Marina South
6 Raffles Boulevard, Marina Square. Tel: 6334 1000.

Singapore Tenpin Bowling Congress
15 Stadium Road, National Stadium Kallang. Tel: 6440 7388.

Canoeing

The swimming lagoons of Sentosa Island and the inshore waters along the East Coast Parkway (the hire centre is near the Laguna Food Centre) both offer safe canoeing. (*See also p122.*)

Cricket

Matches are held on the Padang on weekends between March and October. For details of fixtures contact the **Singapore Cricket Club** (*tel: 6338 9271*). *www.scc.org.sg*

Golf

Singapore has a dozen courses but visitors are usually restricted to weekdays.

Changi Golf Club
9-hole, par-34 course.
20 Netheravon Road. Tel: 6545 5133. www.changigolfclub.org.sg

Jurong Country Club
18-hole, par-72 course.
9 Science Centre Road. Tel: 6560 5655. www.jcc.org.sg

Keppel Club
18-hole, par-72 course.
10 Bukit Chermin. Tel: 6375 1818. www.keppelclub.com.sg

Parkland Golf Driving Range
60 bays.
920 East Coast Parkway. Tel: 6440 6726.
Raffles Country Club
Two 18-hole, par-71 and par-69 courses.
450 Jalan Ahmad Ibrahim. Tel: 6861 7649.
Sembawang Country Club
18-hole, par-70 course.
249 Sembawang Road. Tel: 6751 0320. www.sembawanggolf.org.sg
Sentosa Golf Course
18-hole, par-72 course.
Sentosa Island. Tel: 6275 0022.
Singapore Island Country Club
Two 18-hole, par-72 courses.
180 Island Club Road. Tel: 6459 2222. www.sicc.org.sg

Horse racing

The Singapore Turf Club offers a year-round racing calendar. Visitors can join special tours of an afternoon at the races, which includes lunch (your hotel tour desk will have details).

Singapore Turf Club
1 Turf Club Avenue, Singapore Racecourse. Tel: 6879 1000. www.turfclub.com.sg

Polo

Played between February and October. Contact the **Singapore Polo Club** (*80 Mount Pleasant Road; tel: 6854 3999; www.singaporepoloclub.org*).

Scuba diving

Some of the best reefs are around Pulau Salu; Pulau Hantu and the Sisters' Islands are also popular with divers.

51 Scuba
195 Pearl's Hill Terrace, #02–38A. Tel: 6511 3237. www.51scuba.com
Dolphin Scuba
Block 10, North Bridge Road, 02–5101. Tel: 9190 4203. www.dolphinscuba.com.sg
Leeway Sub-Aquatic Paradise
Blk 115, 01–51 Aljunied Avenue 2. Tel: 6743 1208.
Planet Scuba
02–36 Tanjong Pagar Plaza, Tanjong Pagar Road. Tel: 6227 7561. www.planetscuba.com.sg

Snooker

Most snooker halls impose a dress code (long trousers and shoes). Contact **Cuesports Singapore** (*tel: 6345 3651*).

Tanglin Club
5 Stevens Road. Tel: 6739 4150.
YMCA of Singapore
1 Orchard Road. Tel: 6336 6000.

Water-skiing

Boat hire, driver and equipment is costed at an hourly rate.

Launch 2002 Wakeboard School
600, Ponggol 17th Avenue, Marina Country Club. Tel: 6581 2202. www.launch2002.com

Windsurfing

The **East Coast Sailing Centre** (*tel: 6441 3798*) hires out boards and offers beginner's courses.

Food and drink

The passion for food in Malaysia and Singapore is reflected in the vast number of cafés, restaurants and market stalls serving a wide range of flavoursome local dishes as well as tempting feasts from the provinces of China, the islands of Indonesia, the Indian subcontinent and other Far Eastern countries. This is especially true of Singapore, where eating out is probably the principal national obsession after shopping.

Visiting either country, it is almost impossible not to indulge to the full and find yourself among what the Hokkien call *yau kui* – those who love to eat.

The variety of eating establishments is almost as great as the range of foods, ranging from smart hotel restaurants to Chinese coffee-houses, from Malaysian *kedai makan* (eating houses) to Indian curry houses where your food comes served on a banana leaf. Roadside stalls or markets are a great place to try hawker food, which covers almost everything from *satay* cooked on charcoal to spicy fried noodles.

One of the most practical ways of sampling as many of these culinary delights as possible is to eat out in a group, so you can all share and taste different dishes. This is usually the best way to take advantage of the huge menus in Chinese restaurants and it is also a good way of tackling the unfamiliarities of hawker centres, where you can order any number of dishes from different stalls.

Although you can pay top dollar to eat in the smarter restaurants or hotels, everyday food is incredibly good value and won't put a large dent in your budget. In Singapore there are fast-food outlets and hawker centres within easy reach of the deluxe hotels, and in Malaysia likewise you only have to walk a few metres from the smartest hotel to find a cheap meal.

Tempting though it may be to rush out and try everything in sight, a few sensible precautions are necessary to make sure your trip isn't spoiled by tummy upsets or other health problems (*see p183*).

Chinese food

Cantonese

Regarded by many as one of the finest of Chinese regional styles, Cantonese food is enormously popular in Malaysia and Singapore. Food is usually prepared by stir-frying, roasting or steaming and is characterised by light, delicate flavours and subtle seasonings (normally with oyster sauce or soy sauce). Imaginatively cooked seafood is a Cantonese favourite. Other classics include roast suckling pig, crisp deep-fried chicken, deep-fried prawn balls and shark's fin soup. Another speciality is *dim sum*, which covers a whole range of steamed or deep-fried snacks served in bamboo containers or small bowls; popular for breakfast or lunch, *dim sum* are brought around the tables on trolleys or trays as fresh batches come out of the kitchen, with diners simply selecting the ones they want as they go by. At the end of the meal, your bill is added up according to the number of empty bowls on your table.

Chinese herbal

The Chinese attitude to food has always been linked to physical health, with many dishes carefully balanced to ensure the right combination of *yin* (cool) and *yang* (hot). These concepts are taken a step further in herbal food, where all the dishes are planned with their medicinal value in mind. Very little salt or oil is used, and flavours are generally subtle and delicate. In genuine herbal restaurants, a qualified Chinese physician presides over a huge wooden cabinet with numerous drawers containing herbs, roots and fungi. On request, he will check your pulse and tongue and decide what your body needs. After he has carefully weighed and mixed the desired ingredients, they are dispatched to the kitchen to be added to the dishes you have ordered. The food is delicious and even if you are already in good health, a herbal restaurant is a novel experience.

Herbs, roots and fungi contribute to the right balance of *yin* and *yang* in Chinese herbal cooking

Hokkien

The Hokkiens from Fukien province form the largest ethnic group in Singapore and have provided Singapore's most popular noodle dish, Hokkien fried noodles or *mee*, a tasty mixture of thick noodles fried with prawns, pork and vegetables. Hokkien dishes tend to be less sophisticated than food from neighbouring Canton, with robust, rich flavours based on garlic, soya-bean paste and soy sauces. Typical dishes include *poh piah* (soft spring rolls filled with prawns, cabbage, egg and sausage) and *khong bak* (a steamed bun containing pork).

Peking

The best-known of Beijing (Peking) food is of course Peking Duck, served in two or three separate courses (the crispy skin comes first, layered between pancakes with spring onions and plum sauce for seasoning; the meat is then stir-fried with bean sprouts as a second course, and, finally, the rest of the duck is served as soup). Lamb or mutton is a main feature of Beijing restaurants and baked freshwater tench is another popular dish.

Szechuan

Possibly the spiciest of Chinese foods, Szechuan (or Sichuan) cooking has a distinctive character, and as well as liberal doses of chilli paste or fried chillies it incorporates aromatic ingredients such as star anise, dried tangerine peel and Szechuan pepper. Don't be put off by the fiery reputation of Szechuan food – the chilli is not always that overwhelming and other, less strongly flavoured classics worth trying include duck smoked over jasmine tea leaves and camphor.

Hawker food

A *Bradshaw's Overland Guide* published in 1870 directs readers' attention to Objects of Notice in Singapore, which include 'Perambulating Restaurants'. In common with other Asian countries, Singapore and Malaysia have a long tradition of street vendors (hawkers) who wheel out their stalls every day to entice hungry passers-by with freshly cooked dishes.

In Malaysia, hawker stalls are still found on busy street corners, or sometimes grouped together at *pasar malam* (night markets). In Singapore, the government decided some time ago that street hawkers were cluttering up their vision of the perfect tropical city and encouraged them to set up permanently in purpose-built hawker centres where standards of cleanliness could be controlled.

Whether you are grabbing a quick bowl of *mee goreng* (fried noodles) fresh from the wok in the streets of Kuala Lumpur or enjoying charcoal-cooked fish in Marina Square in Singapore, hawker food is an essential part of the travel experience in these two countries. It is also exceptional value: if you're on a budget you could eat hawker food every day and still find there were dishes you hadn't sampled.

Whether it is in the air-conditioned comfort of a hawker centre in Singapore or the *pasar malam* of Malaysia, eating out follows the same pattern: find a convenient table and then wander round the stalls to see what's on offer. Once you have ordered, tell the stallholder where you are sitting and your food will be brought to you. You pay for each dish as it arrives (tipping is not expected).

The great thing about hawker food is that a group of people can each order exactly what they want from different stalls (no need to argue about whether to eat Indian or Chinese!). In Singapore, stalls often have menus, but if not simply ask what's on offer and choose something that looks good. Prices are so reasonable that it won't matter if you make the occasional mistake.

Most hawker centres will also have juice stalls or drinks (including beer), and these stallholders will often come to your table independently to see what you want. Hawkers almost everywhere are used to dealing with tourists, and most speak some English (if not, simply point – in Malaysia by using only the thumb).

Indian food

Northern Indian

This is generally not too spicy, relying more on subtly flavoured, creamy sauces. Many of the more popular northern Indian dishes are baked in a *tandoor*, or clay oven, with the meat or chicken often having been marinated previously in spices and yogurt. Indian breads such as *parathas* and *chapatis*

Chillies of various types are an essential ingredient in Szechuan cuisine

are more usually served instead of rice, with *naan* (baked in the *tandoor* with garlic and herbs) being popular.

South Indian

Tends to be highly seasoned, and is always served with rice. Many southern Indian and vegetarian restaurants serve rice dishes on a fresh banana leaf instead of a plate, with various curries and *dhals* (made from lentils) heaped up around the rice. This is always eaten with the right hand only (the left customarily being used for ablutions) and there are always washbasins provided if you want to have a go and end up making a real mess of it; of course, you can always ask for a spoon and fork. A Kerala dish, fish-head curry, is very popular in Singapore and tastes a lot better than it sounds (in fact, it is made from the top end of the fish, not just the head).

Indian Muslim

Centres around delicious snacks such as *roti paratha* and *murtabak* (similar to a *roti*, except filled with meat or vegetables), which you will see all over Singapore and Malaysia in cafés and street-stalls as the cook deftly swings the dough into bigger and bigger circles before slapping it on to a hot griddle plate. A popular staple is *biryani*, saffron-scented rice served with mutton or chicken.

Indonesian food

Indonesian food is more often found in Singapore than Malaysia, although Malaysian menus will often include items such as *gado-gado*, which is a vegetable and beansprout salad with peanut sauce. Other common Indonesian specialities are *nasi padang* (a rice dish with a selection of meat, chicken and seafood accompaniments) and *beef rendang* (hot, with a coconut sauce) from Sumatra.

International food

In Malaysia, most resort hotels feature western menus as well as local cuisine, and outlets such as McDonald's as well as local fast-food chains can be found in nearly every town or city. The same is true of Singapore, with the additional bonus of a wide range of top-class international restaurants with French, Swiss or Austrian chefs. Almost every national cuisine is represented in Singapore, from Mexican to Danish, Italian and Russian.

Japanese food

Sushi, *tempura*, *teppanyaki* and other classic Japanese dishes are all available in Singapore – at a price.

Malay food

Malay cuisine is very close to that of Indonesia, and is similarly rich in herbs, spices and coconut milk. Most dishes are rice-based, with the addition of chicken, fish, vegetables and meat (never pork, since Malays are Muslim). Fish (*ikan*) appears in many different guises, for instance as *ikan panggang* (baked in banana leaves),

Nyonya dishes, both savoury and sweet

ikan assam (fried in a tamarind curry sauce) and *ikan bilis* (anchovies, often sprinkled on top of other dishes). Chicken (*ayam*) is another widely served favourite, appearing on menus as, for instance, *ayam goreng* (fried chicken), or *ayam kapitan* (curried with chilli and lemon grass).

The most widely known Malay dish is *satay*, skewers of marinated beef or chicken grilled over charcoal and served with a tasty peanut sauce. It is usually eaten as a snack or starter. A popular breakfast dish is *nasi lemak*, coconut rice with peanuts, curry sauce and *ikan bilis*; visitors may find the strong flavours (particularly the anchovies) a little overpowering first thing in the morning.

Malaysians also eat a lot of noodle-based dishes, many of which are common to the rest of Asia, such as *mee goreng* (fried noodles). A dessert found nowhere else is *ali batu campur* (advertised simply as 'ABC'), a chilled mound of rice with beans, sweetcorn and palm sugar. Sickly and stodgy it may be, but you have to try it once.

Nyonya food

Like Peranakan (or Baba Nyonya) culture itself, Nyonya food is a unique crossover, involving combinations of Malay spices and Chinese sauces, Chinese-style soups with Malay herbs and other unusual dishes. The result is a piquant, spicy (but never fiery) cuisine with flavours provided by coconut milk, lemon grass, chillies and *belacan* (dried shrimp paste). One of the classic Nyonya dishes is *laksa lemak*, a sweet-sour noodle soup that is now eaten all over Malaysia. Other specialities include *otak otak* (spicy

Sacks full of dried produce at the grocer's

barbecued fishcakes) and *bakwang kepiting* (crabmeat and pork-ball soup). Cakes and desserts, which tend to be fairly heavy, include specialities such as *bubor terigu* (wholewheat porridge) and *gula melaka* (sago, palm sugar and coconut milk).

Seafood

The waters around Malaysia and Singapore produce an abundant harvest of seafood of every description, from gleaming snapper to mussels, lobsters, crabs, prawns and squid. In the quest for the freshest possible taste, many restaurants have fish tanks where live crustaceans, prawns and fish await the journey to the kitchen at the last possible minute.

As well as appearing in regional specialities such as baked fish in banana leaves or fish-head curry, seafood is often served using Chinese cooking methods. Fish is usually steamed, while prawns are either steamed or appear on the menu as 'drunken', in which case they are doused in Chinese wine or cognac and simmered in herbs. In Singapore, probably the most popular seafood dish of all is chilli crab, stir-fried with chilli, garlic, tomato and egg. Other favourites include fried squid in black-bean sauce, black-pepper crabs, seafood *dim sum* and baked mussels.

Vegetarian food

Vegetarians will have little difficulty in finding suitable food in either Singapore or Malaysia. One of the most popular options is Indian vegetarian food, which features plenty of vegetable curries, breads and *dhals* (lentil soups). Other vegetarian favourites include the southern Indian *masala dosa* (spicy vegetables inside a thin pancake, with *dhal* on the side), Indonesian *gado-gado*, and the Indian Muslim snacks *murtabak* and *roti paratha*. Sometimes the latter are served with meat, but you can simply ask for one without. In Singapore, there are a number of excellent restaurants serving all-you-can-eat salad buffets.

Drinks

As in most tropical climates, the most effective way of quenching your thirst and cooling off is – paradoxically – a hot drink such as tea. In Malaysia, tea in local cafés is usually served with dollops of sickly condensed milk, and if you would prefer black tea you have to ask for *teh-o* (without milk). Chinese restaurants and cafés serve refreshing and fragrant Chinese teas. Except in hotels, coffee is likely to taste fairly weak (the best beans go for export). Soft drinks such as Coca-Cola, Fanta and 7-Up are widely available in restaurants and supermarkets.

For visitors, one of the delights of the region is the enormous variety of fresh fruit juices, which can be found almost everywhere. Street stalls equipped with blenders will whizz up mango, watermelon, orange, starfruit or any other juice within seconds.

Alcohol is relatively expensive but is not always available outside tourist hotels in Malaysia (Muslims are forbidden to drink alcohol). Chinese restaurants and cafés usually have cold beer, with good local brands including Anchor and Tiger; bottled Guinness® is also surprisingly popular. Imported spirits are expensive, although local brandies and whiskies can be found at a fraction of the cost, usually in Chinese shops.

Brightly painted restaurant, Kuala Lumpur

Where to eat

MALAYSIA

As in Singapore, eating out in Malaysia is an adventure where even those on a tight budget will not find themselves constrained by lack of a credit card. Indeed, some of the best food in Malaysia is to be found at street-side food-stalls where fresh ingredients are thrown together to create mouth-watering dishes that cost no more than a few ringgit.

The following is, therefore, no more than a very broad sampling from the main tourist centres. There are many thousands of places where you can indulge in the culinary delights of the region.

The average cost per meal per person, not including alcohol, is indicated as follows:

★ up to RM20

★★ RM20–100

★★★ RM100+

KUALA LUMPUR

Chinese

Xin Cuisine ★★
Large restaurant popular for Cantonese food and *dim sum.*
Concorde Hotel, 2 Jalan Sultan Ismail.
Tel: (03) 2144 2200.
Open: daily 11.30am–2.30pm, 6.30–10.30pm.

Golden Phoenix ★★★
Traditional Cantonese dishes in a majestic setting.
Hotel Equatorial, Jalan Sultan Ismail.
Tel: (03) 2161 7777.
Open: daily noon–2.30pm, 6.30–10.30pm.

Ming Palace ★★★
Specialities include Szechuan dishes.
Corus Hotel, Jalan Ampang.
Tel: (03) 2161 1888.
Open: daily 11.30am–3pm, 6.30–11pm.

Shang Palace ★★★
A wide range of Cantonese cuisine prepared by Hong Kong chefs. Popular for *dim sum.*
Shangri-la Hotel, 11 Jalan Sultan Ismail.
Tel: (03) 2074 3904.
Open: daily noon–2.30pm, 6.30–10.30pm.

Indian

Annalakshmi ★
One of the best Indian vegetarian restaurants in Kuala Lumpur; excellent buffet.
44/46 Jalan Maroof, Bangsar Park.
Tel: (03) 2284 3799.
Open: daily 9am–10pm.

Bangles ★★
Reasonable, authentic North Indian food.
270 Jalan Ampang.
Tel: (03) 4252 4100.
Open: daily 10.30am–11pm.

Bombay Palace ★★
Good North Indian food in a traditional setting.
215 Jalan Tun Razak.
Tel: (03) 2145 4241.
Open: daily 11am–11pm.

The Taj ★★★
Award-winning Indian cuisine in stylish Anglo-Indian surroundings.
Crown Princess Hotel, City Square Centre, Jalan Tun Razak.
Tel: (03) 2162 5522.
Open: daily 11am–2.30pm, 5.30–11pm.

International

Coliseum Cafe ★★
A Kuala Lumpur institution, this old-fashioned café serves sizzling steaks on a platter, and other western foods.
98–100 Jalan Tunku Abdul Rahman.
Tel: (03) 2692 6270.
Open: daily 8am–10pm.

Hot-chestnut vendor in Chinatown, Kuala Lumpur

Top Hat ★★
Atmospheric old mansion serving a mix of European and Malay specialities.
7 Jalan Kia Peng.
Tel: (03) 2141 8611.
Open: daily noon–midnight.

Malay

Bijan ★★
Exquisitely presented dishes from the *kampung*.
3 Jalan Ceylon.
Tel: (03) 2031 3575.
Open: Mon–Sat noon–2.30pm, 6.30–10.30pm. Sun 4.30–10.30pm.

Seri Angkasa ★★
Excellent selection of Malay dishes with panoramic views of the city.
Menara KL, Jalan Puncak, off Jalan P Ramlee.
Tel: (03) 2020 5055.
Open: daily noon–11pm.

Seri Melayu ★★★
Exceptionally fine Malay cuisine with nightly cultural performances.
1 Jalan Conlay.
Tel: (03) 2145 1833. Open: daily noon–11.30pm.

Seafood

Eden@Chulan Square ★★
Large, seafood restaurant with an outdoor terrace. Dance show indoors.
92 Jalan Raja Chulan.
Tel: (03) 2141 4027.
Open: daily noon–3pm, 6.30–11.30pm.

MELAKA

Chinese

Hoe Kee Chicken Rice ★
Typical Chinese coffee-shop serving Hainanese chicken rice.
4 Jalan Hang Jebat.
Tel: (06) 283 4751.
Open: daily 7.30am–4pm.

UE Teahouse ★
Good *dim sum* at reasonable prices.
20 Lorong Bukit China.
Tel: (06) 282 3241. Open: daily 6am–noon, 7–10pm.

Indian

Banana Leaf ★
Very popular for *roti canai*, vegetarian curries and *biryanis*.
42 Jalan Munshi Abdullah.
Tel: (06) 283 1607.
Open: daily 11am–10pm.

Nyonya

Jonkers ★★
Pleasant restaurant in an old Nyonya house, excellent lunchtime menu.
17 Jalan Hang Jebat.
Tel: (06) 283 5578.
Open: daily 10am–5pm.

Nyonya Makko ★★★
Traditional Nyonya food.
123 Taman Melaka Raya.
Tel: (06) 284 0737.
Open: daily 11am–2.30pm, 6–9.30pm.

Restoran Peranakan Town House ★★★
Straits Chinese cuisine.
107 Jalan Tun Tan Cheng Lock.
Tel: (06) 284 5001.
Open: daily 8am–4pm.

International

Heeren House ★
Good breakfasts, sandwiches, cakes and excellent coffee.
1 Jalan Tun Tan Cheng Lock. Tel: (06) 281 4241.
Open: daily 7.30am–9pm.

Geographér Café ★★
A bar and café in an old colonial building.
83 Jalan Hang Jebat.
Tel: (04) 281 6813.
Open: daily 10.30am–1am.

PULAU PINANG

Chinese

House of Four Seasons ★★
First-class Sichuan and Cantonese fare.
Mutiara Beach Resort, 1 Jalan Teluk Bahang.
Tel: (04) 885 2828.

Open: daily 11.30am–2.30pm, 7–10pm.

Tai Tong ★★
Highly recommended for lunchtime *dim sum.*
45 Lebuh Cintra.
Tel: (04) 263 6625.
Open: daily 6am–noon, 6pm–midnight.

Indian

Dawood ★★
A popular spot for Indian Muslim food.
63 Lebuh Queen.
Tel: (04) 261 6223.
Open: daily 10.30am–10pm.

Kaliammans ★★
South Indian banana-leaf meals.
43 Lebuh Penang.
Tel: (04) 262 8953.
Open: daily 11am–10.30pm.

Malay

Kopitiam ★★★
Traditional Malay food with views over the sea.
Bayview Hotel,
25a Lorong Farquhar.
Tel: (04) 263 3161.
Open: daily 6.30am–1pm.

Seafood

Eden ★★
Reasonable prices for steaks and seafood.
11B Lorong Hutton.
Tel: (04) 263 9262.
Open: daily.

Jade Palace ★★
A great selection of Chinese seafood dishes.
3rd Floor Choo Plaza,
41 Lorong Abu Siti.
Tel: (04) 227 5758.
Open: daily 11am–11.30pm.

EASTERN MALAYSIA
KUCHING

Chinese

Mei-San ★★
Szechuan specialities and *dim sum* (good value set-price menu on Sunday).
Holiday Inn, Jalan Tunku Abdul Rahman.
Tel: (082) 423 111.
Open: daily 11am–2.30pm, 5.30–10.30pm.

Tsui Hua Lau ★★
Some excellent Cantonese and Shanghainese dishes, also a good selection of seafood – all served in sumptuous surroundings.
320–4 Jalan Ban Hock.
Tel: (82) 414 560. Open: daily 11am–10.30pm.

Indian

LL Banana Leaf ★
Vegetarian curries and various *dosai* served on fresh banana leaves.
7G Lorong Rubber 1, Jalan Rubber.
Tel: (082) 239 404.
Open: daily 7.30am–9pm.

International

Café Majestic ★★
International standards and Malay snacks.
Riverside Majestic, Jalan Tunku Abdul Rahman.
Tel: (082) 247 777.
Open: daily 11am–2.30pm, 6–11pm.

Steak House ★★★
Air-freighted sirloin steaks and western specialities.
Hilton Hotel, Jalan Tunku Abdul Rahman.
Tel: (082) 248 200.
Open: daily 6.30–10.30pm.

Malay

Hot and Spicy ★
As the name suggests, some of the dishes need handling with care.
Lot 303, section 10, Rubber Road.
Tel: (082) 250 873.
Open: daily 9am–10pm.

Jubilee ★
A choice of standard Malay dishes including

beef *rendang* and their very own Jubilee Biriyani Chicken.
49 Jalan India.
Tel: (082) 245 626.
Open: daily 8am–10pm.

SABAH

KOTA KINABALU

Chinese

Avasi Cafeteria & Garden Restaurant ⋆
Recommended for seafood and steamboat dishes.
41 Karamunsing Warehouse.
Tel: (088) 233 662.
Open: daily 11am–10pm.

Fook Yuen ⋆
Lots of great noodle dishes.
Damai Plaza, 4 Jalan Damai. Tel: (088) 232 794.
Open: daily 11am–9pm.

A selection of Indian snacks and sweets

King Hu Restoran ⋆
A great place for Chinese dumplings and Peking duck.
Lot 3, Pekan Tanjung Aru.
Tel: (088) 234 966. Open: daily 10.30am–9pm.

The Chinese Restaurant ⋆⋆
Dim sum and other Cantonese specialities.
Hyatt Kinabalu, Jalan Datuk Salleh Sulong.
Tel: (088) 221 234.
Open: daily 11am–11pm.

Indian

Bilal ⋆
Tasty Indian Muslim food.
Block B, Lot 1 Segama Kompleks.
Tel: (088) 253 075.
Open: daily 10am–9pm.

International

Peppino ⋆⋆
Very good but pricey Italian food.
Shangri-La Tanjung Aru Resort.
Tel: (088) 327 888.
Open: daily 6–10.30pm.

Tanjung Ria Café ⋆⋆
International and local dishes. Panoramic views across the harbour.
Hyatt Kinabalu, Jalan Datuk Salleh Sulong.
Tel: (088) 221 234.
Open: daily 11am–11pm.

Malay

Sri Melaka ⋆
A variety of tasty Malay dishes at exceptional prices.
9 Jalan Laiman Diki, Kampung Air.
Tel: (088) 224 777.
Open: 9.30am–9.30pm.

Sri Delima ⋆⋆
Excellent Malay dishes on offer, such as beef *rendang*.
Jalan Laiman Diki.
Tel: (088) 231 222.
Open: daily 10.30am–10pm.

Seafood

Port View ⋆⋆
Popular for chilli crab and other seafood specialities.
Jalan Haji Saman.
Tel: (088) 252 813.
Open: daily 11am–11pm.

Coco-Joe's ⋆⋆⋆
Expensive but good quality. Pleasant outdoor setting.
Tanjung Aru Beach Resort, Tanjung Aru.
Tel: (088) 327 888.
Open: daily 9am–10.30pm.

SINGAPORE

Eating out in Singapore can be as cheap or as expensive as you want it to be. On the one hand, you can get by very well eating from hawker centres, where basic dishes such as a bowl of tasty noodles costs as little as S$3 and more elaborate meals between S$10–20. On the other hand, you can spend upwards of S$100 or more for two people in any number of interesting and unusual restaurants.

The listings below represent a sample of the hundreds of restaurants in the city. The following symbols have been used to indicate the average cost per meal per person, not including alcohol.

★	up to S$25
★★	S$25–75
★★★	over S$75

A 10 per cent service charge and 6 per cent government tax is levied in all 'tourist class' restaurants (including all hotel restaurants). In coffee-shops and other simple eating places (including hawker centres) no charge is imposed, and a tip is not expected. Note that air-conditioned restaurants are non-smoking.

Cantonese

Fook Yuen Seafood ★★
Busy at lunchtimes for the popular *dim sum.*
252 North Bridge Road, 02–19 Raffles City. Tel: 6333 1661. Open: daily 11am–10.30pm.

Lei Garden ★★★
Classic Cantonese cuisine, rated among the best in Singapore. Huge selection of *dim sum* on Sundays. Reservations advisable.
01-24 Chijmes Centre, 30 Victoria Street. Tel: 6339 3822. Open: daily 11.30am–3pm, 6–11pm.

Chinese herbal

Imperial Herbal Restaurant ★★
Excellent food with medicinal herbs added to suit the requirements of individuals by a qualified Chinese herbalist.
#03–08, Lobby G, VivoCity, 1 HarbourFront Walk. Tel: 6337 0491. Open: daily 11.30am–2.30pm, 6.30–10.30pm.

Hokkien

Beng Hiang ★★
Serves traditional Hokkien specialities such as fried oysters and deep-fried liver rolls, in unpretentious surroundings.
112 Amoy Street. Off Maxwell Road. Tel: 6221 6695. Open: daily 11.30am–2.30pm, 6–9.30pm.

Peking

Prima Tower Revolving Restaurant ★★
Panoramic views of the harbour. House specialities include Peking duck and braised beancurd in claypot.
201 Keppel Road. Tel: 6272 8822. Open: daily 11am–2.30pm, 6.30–10.30pm.

Pine Court ★★★
Traditional Peking specialities such as duck and baked tench, in a palatial setting. Excellent lunchtime buffet.
Mandarin Hotel, 333 Orchard Road. Tel: 6831 6288.

Open: daily noon–2.30pm, 6.30–10.30pm.

Szechuan

Min Jiang ★★
Classic Szechuan cuisine such as camphor and tea-smoked duck and drunken chicken. Reservations essential.
Goodwood Park Hotel, 22 Scotts Road. Tel: 6730 1704. Open: daily 11am–2.30pm, 6–10.30pm.

Peony-Jade Restaurant ★★
Excellent Szechuan and Cantonese cuisine with fine views of the Singapore River.
Block 3A Clarke Quay, 02-02. Tel: 9633 9146. Open: daily 11am–3pm, 6–11pm.

Hawker centres

Lau Pa Sat Festival Market ★
Neat, clean food stalls serving a variety of cuisine amid lovely Victorian cast-iron work.
18 Raffles Quay.

Maxwell Road Food Centre ★
Good *dim sum* and Hainanese Chicken stalls.
Maxwell Road.

Newton Circus ★
The biggest in Singapore, with a huge choice.
Corner of Bukit Timah, Scotts and Newton, 10 minutes from Orchard Road.

Orchard Emerald Food Court ★
Local specialities as well as frozen yoghurts and fruit salads.
Basement, Orchard Emerald, 218 Orchard Road.

Northern Indian

Kinara ★★
Punjabi cuisine with lovely river views and Rajasthani décor.
57 Boat Quay. Tel: 6533 0412. Open: daily 11am–2.30pm, 6–10.30pm.

Colonial-style façades in Singapore's Chinatown

Moghul Mahal ★★
Plush surroundings with an excellent tandoori oven.
177A River Valley Road, #01–09 Clarke Quay. Tel: 6338 6907. Open: daily noon–2.30pm, 6–10pm.

South Indian

Banana Leaf Apollo ★★
Near Serangoon Road. Casual, canteen-type atmosphere. Famous for fish-head curry served on banana leaves.
56 Racecourse Road. Tel: 6293 8682. Open: daily 11.30am–10.30pm.

Bombay Woodlands ★★
Convenient location, set meals and a good range of desserts.
B1–12 Tanglin Shopping Centre, 19 Tanglin Road. Tel: 6836 6961. Open: daily noon–3pm, 6–10.30pm.

Indonesian

Tambuah Mas Café ★
Good-value Javanese and Padang dishes. Very busy at lunchtimes.
04–10 Tanglin Shopping Centre, 19 Tanglin Road. Tel: 6733 3333. Open: daily 11am–10pm.

The Rice Table ★★
One of a small chain of excellent *rijstaffel* restaurants (Indonesian 'rice table' buffet) to be found around the city.
#03–28 Suntec City Mall, 3 Temasek Boulevard. Tel: 6333 0248. Open: daily noon–2.30pm, 6–10pm.

International

Broth ★★
Good for lunches and dinners with a mix of Asian and Western cuisine.
21 Duxton Hill. Tel: 6323 3353. Open: daily noon–2.30pm, 6.30–10.30pm.

Hard Rock Café ★★
Good steaks and burgers; open till 2am.
02–01 HPL House, 50 Cuscaden Road. Tel: 6235 5232. Open: Tue–Thur 11am–1am, Fri–Mon 11am–3am.

Prego ★★
Cheerful Italian atmosphere, with home-made pasta.
Fairmont, 80 Bras Basah Road. Tel: 6431 6156. Open: daily 11.30am–12.30am.

Via Veneto ★★
Classic Italian dishes in an alfresco dining area.
Block E, 01-06, 3E River Valley Road, Clarke Quay. Tel: 6334 1983. Open: daily noon–3pm, 6–11pm.

Zouk ★★★
Greek, Spanish or Turkish dishes in a Mediterranean-style atmosphere.
17–21 Jiak Kim Street. Off Kim Seng Road. Tel: 6738 2988. Open: daily 7–11pm.

Japanese

Inagiku ★★★
Sushi counter, *tatami* rooms, quality service and a range of wines.
Fairmont, 80 Bras Basah Road. Tel: 6431 6156. Open: daily noon–2.30pm, 6.30–10.30pm.

Keyaki ★★★
Located in the middle of a beautiful Japanese rooftop garden.
Pan Pacific Hotel, 7 Raffles Boulevard, Marina Square. Tel: 6826 8240. Open: daily noon–2.30pm, 6.30–10.30pm.

Malay

Sabar Menanti ★
Typical, Malay-style coffee-shop, very busy at

lunchtimes, serving specialities such as beef *redang* and *ikan bakar* (barbecued fish).
48 Kandahar Street. Near Arab Street. Tel: 6396 6919. Open: daily 9am–6pm.

Tepak Sireh ★★
Daily buffet of classic Malay dishes and there's also a set menu.
73 Sultan Gate. Tel: 6396 4373. Open: daily 11.30am–2.30pm, 6.30–9.30pm.

Nyonya

Nyonya and Baba Restaurant ★
Authentic atmosphere with reasonably priced dishes such as *ayam buah keluak* (chicken with black nuts) and *otak-otak*.
262–264 River Valley Road. Tel: 6734 1382. Open: daily 11.30am–10pm.

Oleh Sayang ★★
Small restaurant with a wide selection of home-cooked Nyonya dishes.
Block 1018, 01–308 Woodlands Industrial Park D. Tel: 6368 6009. Open: daily 10.30am–8pm.

Seafood

Long Beach Seafood ★★
Long-established seafood restaurant with an outdoor section, famous for its very fiery black-pepper crab.
1018 East Coast Parkway. Tel: 6445 8833. Open: daily 11am–3pm, 5pm–12.15am.

Palm Beach Seafood ★★
Huge and popular place with good-value shellfish.
1 Fullerton Road. 01–08 One Fullerton. Tel: 6423 0040. Open: daily noon–2.30pm, 5.30–11pm.

Jumbo Seafood ★★★
A wide variety of seafood dishes; the chilli crab is particularly good.
#B1–48 The Riverwalk, 20 Upper Circular Road. Tel: 6442 3435. Open: daily noon–2.30pm, 6pm–midnight.

Café tables along Boat Quay

Vegetarian

Kingsland Vegetarian ★
Very popular Chinese vegetarian restaurant with an innovative menu.
121 Telok Ayer Street. Tel: 6535 0245. Open: daily 6am–7pm.

Original Sin ★★
Excellent selection of Mediterranean vegetarian savoury and sweet dishes all set in a quiet location.
01-62, 43 Jalan Merah Saga, Chip Bee Gardens. Tel: 6475 5605. Open: Tue–Sun 11.30am–2.30pm, 6–10.30pm, Mon 6–10.30pm.

Pete's Place ★★
'Pasta e Basta' buffet at lunchtimes with soups, 13 vegetable salads and pasta station with cooked-to-order dishes.
Hyatt Regency, 10–12 Scotts Road. Tel: 6732 1234. Open: daily noon–2.30pm, 6–10.30pm.

Tropical fruits

The hot, damp climates of Singapore and Malaysia are well suited to the cultivation of many exotic tropical fruits. If you haven't ventured beyond pineapples before, now is the time to indulge yourself and experiment. Street markets usually have fruit stalls where you can sample slices of a whole variety of fruits, temptingly laid out on ice, or they can make up fruit salads from any combination of your choosing.

The exotic rambutan

Apart from the more familiar fruits such as bananas, pineapples, coconuts, watermelons and oranges, others worth trying include the following:

Custard apple: squeeze the fruit to reveal soft, white flesh with a delicious, lemon-tinged flavour.

Durian: crowned the 'King of Fruits', this thorny, football-sized fruit has an overpoweringly pungent smell, principally reminiscent of open sewers, which is why it is banned on all airplanes and in hotel rooms. The flesh inside has a rich/creamy, strong/sweet flavour that is very hard to describe, but suffice to say that it is considered an aphrodisiac and connoisseurs are willing to pay top prices for wild fruits. You will either love it or hate it.

Succulent mangoes to tempt the taste buds

Try something new, such as a pomelo, at a street market stall

Guava: the raw fruit tastes nothing like the tinned version often sold in the west, and is usually served with a seasoning of ground sour plums from stalls. It is extremely rich in vitamin C.

Jackfruit (*or nangka*): an enormous fruit that opens up to reveal yellow, rubbery but sweet-tasting segments of flesh.

Mango: the appetising orange or yellow flesh of the mango varies in flavour between the huge number of varieties available.

Mangosteen: quite different from the mango, the mangosteen has a hard, purple skin, inside which are segments of white, juicy flesh with a sweet-sour flavour.

Papaya: the perfect breakfast fruit, served with a slice of lemon. The smooth, sweet flesh is rich in vitamins A and C.

Pomelo: resembling a pendulous grapefruit, the pomelo is not as tart. It is rich in vitamin C.

Rambutan: literally 'hairy fruit' in Malay, the red or yellow spines of the rambutan peel away to reveal sweet white flesh that tastes very much like the lychee.

Hotels and accommodation

From the most luxurious of international-class hotels to the basic facilities of a thatched hut – Malaysia and Singapore offer the entire gamut. There is no dearth of choice, though perhaps the range of accommodation available is a little wider in Malaysia.

MALAYSIA

Malaysia's range varies from simple thatch huts on the beach for a few ringgit a night to luxury hotels with swimming pools and full facilities. The international chains such as Hyatt, Hilton and Holiday Inn are well represented in major cities and in the larger resorts, with room prices that are generally lower than in Singapore. Local chains such as Sunway International Hotels (*www.sunway.com.my*) also offer high standards of accommodation in many locations throughout Malaysia (for more information visit *www.conferencemalaysia. com*). Other possibilities include government rest houses and youth hostels. National parks have a range of chalets and lodges; for bookings, see individual park entries in the Destination guide.

All hotels are subject to a service charge of 10 per cent and 5 per cent government tax (expressed as '++'). Cheaper hotels do not generally add service charges, and the price is usually quoted with tax included.

Deluxe accommodation

Kuala Lumpur has a range of international-class hotels, with rooms costing from between RM500–700++ in places such as the **Shangri-La** (*tel: (03) 2032 2388; www.shangri-la.com*), **Hilton** (*tel: (03) 2264 2264; www.hilton.com.my*) or the **Regent** (*tel: (03) 2141 8000; www.regenthotels.com*). These hotels offer all the amenities you would expect, such as air-conditioned rooms, IDD telephones and restaurants.

Outside Kuala Lumpur the cost of similar rooms tends to be less expensive (RM300–400++). At least two or three international-standard hotels can be found in major tourist centres such as Melaka, Pulau Pangkor, Kuching and Kota Kinabalu. For a taste of the South Pacific, Pulau Pangkor Laut has the exceptional **Pangkor Laut Resort** (*tel: 800 9899 9999; www.pangkorlautresort. com*), with water villas on stilts out over the sea. Pulau Pinang has a half-dozen good beach hotels, plus the venerable **E & O Hotel** (*tel: (04) 222 2000;*

www.e-o-hotel.com) in Georgetown if you want atmosphere and old-world charm (*see p171*).

In the hill resorts you will find local chains, such as the Merlin Hotels, with adequate, comfortable rooms. For colonial nostalgia there is **Ye Olde Smokehouse** (*www.thesmokehouse.com.my/ch.htm*) in both the Cameron Highlands and at Fraser's Hill (*see p171*).

Standard accommodation

In Kuala Lumpur, mid-price hotels tend to be fairly basic, offering clean, comfortable rooms with air-conditioning and a telephone, but otherwise very few frills. Hotels in this category include places such as the **Ancasa Hotel** (*tel: (03) 2026 6060*) and the **Hotel Malaya** (*tel: (03) 2072 7722; www.hotelmalaya.com.my*) in the downtown area, where rooms cost from RM100–250++. In most towns and cities outside Kuala Lumpur you can find similar-standard hotels.

Government rest houses (*rumah rehat*) are another option, often situated just outside town. The simple rooms cost, on average, RM60–100++.

National parks usually have a range of chalets and bungalows, with prices from around RM50 for a simple, twin-bed cabin with shower, up to RM400 for a deluxe cabin, sleeping four or more.

Budget accommodation

The standard budget accommodation in Malaysia is usually a Chinese-run hotel, often over a café or restaurant. Rooms are likely to be very basic indeed, with the minimum of furniture and probably just a washbasin – showers and toilets are normally shared. Sometimes they have air-conditioning, sometimes just a fan. Often the rooms have been partitioned off inside the house with thin walls, which can make them very noisy. Standards of cleanliness also vary widely. Rooms generally cost RM40–75.

Most of the islands (except Pulau Pinang) have one or more beaches where you can stay in simple, thatched A-frame huts for around RM35–65. Popular islands such as Pulau Tioman have the greatest choice at budget prices, while the other east-coast islands tend to be more expensive.

Kuala Lumpur is the most difficult place to find decent budget rooms. The Chinese hotels tend to be of a lower standard and costlier than elsewhere. However, there is a YMCA and a YWCA, which cost RM60–80 per person.

National parks almost invariably have dormitory accommodation with cooking facilities and communal bathrooms, generally costing around RM40–80 per person.

Where to stay

The accommodation prices are based on the cost per person for two people sharing the least expensive double room with en-suite bathroom and excluding breakfast.

★	Under RM100
★★	RM100–RM250
★★★	RM250–RM500
★★★★	Above RM500

KUALA LUMPUR

Ancasa Hotel ★★

Situated close to the Puduraya Bus Station, the Ancasa is a solid, good-value, mid-range place with 300 large rooms, each with its own en-suite bathroom, satellite TV, in-house movies and air-conditioning. There's a very good buffet breakfast on offer.

Jalan Tun Tan Cheng Lock, Chinatown. Tel: (03) 2026 6060. Fax: (03) 2026 8322. Email: jane@impianakl.udanet.com. www.kl-hotels.com/ancasa

Radius International Hotel ★★★

Well located in the heart of Kuala Lumpur's busy Golden Triangle area, this excellent mid-range hotel offers clean, comfortable air-conditioned rooms with in-house movie channels. Some floors have high-speed internet connections in rooms. Other amenities include an outdoor swimming pool and *kopitiam*, or traditional Malay coffee shop.

51A Jalan Changkat Bukit Bintang, Golden Triangle. Tel: (03) 2715 3888. Fax: (03) 2715 1888. Email: klsales@radius-international.com. www.radius-international.com

Hotel Istana ★★★★

One of the city's top properties, the Istana has long been a fixture in Kuala Lumpur's luxury accommodation scene. From the fabulous lobby to the immaculate bedrooms, this hotel radiates class. Rooms are spacious and decorated with traditional Asian fabrics. Fitness facilities include the Sompoton Spa specialising in traditional Malay rejuvenation treatments, gymnasium and whirlpool bath.

73 Jalan Raja Chulan, Golden Triangle. Tel: (03) 2141 9988. Fax: (03) 2144 0111. Email: rsvn@hotelistana.com.my. www.hotelistana.com.my

Mandarin Oriental ★★★★

Part of one of the world's finest hotel chains, the Mandarin Oriental exudes sophistication. Located close to the Petronas Towers, it offers a selection of apartments, suites and standard rooms, each with a choice of city view or park view. The park view is particularly attractive; you would hardly know that there was a large city surrounding you. Many rooms are decorated with beautiful Nyonya-style furnishings.

Kuala Lumpur City Centre (KLCC). Tel: (03) 2179 8818. Fax: (03) 2179 8659. Email: mokul-sales@mohg.com. www.mandarinoriental.com

MELAKA

Renaissance Melaka Hotel ★★★

Melaka's finest property is also the town's tallest with 24 floors. The Renaissance combines contemporary hotel design and the very latest modern amenities with the best in old-fashioned quality service. Rooms are large, all air-conditioned with luxurious bathrooms. The upper floors afford great views.

Jalan Bendahara. Tel: (06) 284 8888. Fax: (06) 284 9269. www.marriott.com

CENTRAL HIGHLANDS

Cameron Highlands

Ye Olde Smokehouse ★★★

This mock-Tudor, colonial-style hotel is probably the most famous hotel anywhere in Malaysia's highlands. The very British feel to the place is enhanced by all the exposed beams, large open fireplaces, and a restaurant that features roasts of all varieties and traditional English breakfasts.
Jalan Jeriau, Tanah Rata.
Tel: (05) 491 1215. Fax: (05) 491 1214.
Email: cameron@thesmokehouse.com.my.
www.thesmokehouse.com.my/ch.htm

Fraser's Hill

The Pines Hill Top Haven ★★★

Attractively located northeast of town, The Pines is a large apartment hotel offering many facilities including dry cleaning and laundry, medical services, a crèche for young families and currency exchange. Apartments are all kitted out with mini bars, satellite TV, and a kitchen and dining area. On site there are also banqueting and business services, as well as a coffee shop and restaurant.
Jalan Pecah Batu, Bukit Fraser.
Tel: (09) 362 2122. Fax: (09) 362 2288.
Email: thepines@tm.net.my.
www.thepines.com.my

PULAU PINANG

Cheong Fatt Tze Mansion ★★★

A hotel with a difference, 'the Blue Mansion', as it is sometimes known, is also one of Penang's star historical attractions. Guests stay in luxuriously appointed, individually designed suites, surrounded by period antiques. These suites are assembled around five separate and spacious courtyards. As with the E & O Hotel, personal butlers are on hand, and you can rent the entire mansion for RM6,000 a night!
14 Labuh Leith, Georgetown.
Tel: (04) 262 0006. Fax: (04) 262 5289.
Email: cftm@tm.net.my.
www.cheongfatttzemansion.com

Eastern & Oriental Hotel ★★★★

With a long and remarkable history dating back to 1884, the Eastern & Oriental has played host to the rich and famous over many of the intervening years. Old English writers seem to have loved the place, with Somerset Maugham and Rudyard Kipling amongst others making it home at one time or another. In 2001 it was completely renovated and is now probably Malaysia's finest colonial-era hotel. Facilities include six bars and restaurants, a fine swimming pool with sea views and an enormous garden containing Penang's oldest java tree.
10 Lebuh Farquhar, Georgetown.
Tel: (04) 222 2000. Fax: (04)261 6333.
Email: hotel-info@e-o-hotel.com.
www.e-o-hotel.com

Lone Pine Hotel ★★★

Run by the Eastern & Oriental Hotel group, this is Batu Ferringhi's oldest and most distinguished hotel. Established just after World War II, in 1948, the Lone Pine's colonial character makes a pleasant contrast to the rather soulless resorts that now populate Batu Ferringhi. The

emphasis here is on elegance and colonial charm, with fine views across the Straits of Melacca. The extensive facilities and services include a Chinese restaurant specialising, unusually, in Hainanese cuisine and a choice of watersports including water-skiing and parasailing.
92 Jalan Batu Ferringhi, Batu Ferringhi. Tel: (04) 881 1511. Fax: (04) 881 1282. Email: info@lonepinehotel. www.lonepinehotel.com

PULAU LANGKAWI

Meritus Pelangi Beach Resort and Spa ★★★★

A gorgeous spa and resort styled as a 'Malay village' with spectacular views across the Andaman Sea from Pantai Cenang. A host of facilities include health and fitness centres, tennis courts, squash courts and a variety of watersports. The stilted accommodation, approximating a traditional Malay village, contains deluxe air-conditioned rooms all with satellite TV and mini bar. Four good restaurants serve Malay, Chinese, Thai and Western cuisine. This family-oriented hotel includes babysitting services and a special club for children.
Pantai Cenang. Tel: (04) 952 8888. Fax: (04) 952 8899. Email: pelangi.pbl@meritus-hotels.com. www.pelangibeachresort.com

EAST COAST

Cherating

The Legend Resort ★★★

This large, comfortable resort surrounded by tropical gardens affords great views across the South China Sea. It has an elegant swimming pool, great choice of first-class restaurants and an outstanding choice of activities including waterskiing, snorkelling, sailing, tennis, squash, fishing and jungle trekking.
45km (28 miles) north of Kuantan, Cherating. Tel: (09) 581 9818. Fax: (08) 581 9400. Email: reservation@legendresort.com.my. www.legendsgroup.com

Kuala Dungun

Tanjong Jara Resort ★★★

Located about 10km (6 miles) to the east of Kuala Dungun on the South China Sea, this is both the best place to stay anywhere near the town, and one of the best resort hotels in Malaysia. Mainly chalet accommodation set in luxurious tropical gardens; the buildings are studiously Malay and very elegant. Three restaurants serve Malay, Chinese and International dishes.
Jalan Dungun, Kuala Dungun. Tel: (09) 845 1100. Fax: (09) 845 1200. Email: travelcentre@ytlhotels.com.my. www.tanjongjararesort.com

Pulau Redang

Coral Redang Island Resort ★★★★

An idyllic setting on remote Redang Island, this fun-filled, action-packed resort is the perfect place to chill out. Comfortable chalets offer either air-conditioned or fan rooms with lovely views of the South China Sea. Activities include diving, and the resort has its

own fully equipped dive shop plus well-qualified instructors for anyone who's never dived before.
Pantai Pasir Panjang, Pulau Redang.
Tel: (09) 630 7110. Fax: (09) 630 7112.
Email: crir@tm.net.my.
www.coralredang.com.my

Pulau Tioman

Berjaya Tioman Beach, Golf and Spa Resort ★★★★

The wide choice of accommodation at Tioman's only luxury resort includes villas, chalets and beautifully furnished suites. All this is sandwiched between a picture-perfect beach and a golf course. Other amenities include a spa, gym, pool and a number of restaurants catering to all tastes. They also offer an incredible variety of diving opportunities in the surrounding South China Sea.
3km (2 miles) southwest of Tioman Airport, Pulau Tioman.
Tel: (09) 419 1000. Fax: (09) 419 1718.
Email: reservation@b-tioman.com.my.
www.berjayaresorts.com

SARAWAK

Kuching

Hilton Kuching ★★★

Kuching's magical waterfront somehow looks even better from one of the Hilton's spectacular bedroom balconies. This excellent hotel dominates the Sarawak River and its surrounding sights. Facilities include some of the town's finest restaurants, an attractive outdoor pool and a children's playground.
Jalan Tunku Abdul Rahman, Kuching.
Tel: (082) 248 200. Fax: (082) 428 984.
Email: kuching@hilton.com.
www.kuching.hilton.com

SABAH

Kota Kinabalu

The Jesselton Hotel ★★★

Imbued with loads of character, including doormen kitted out in pith helmets and crisp white shirts and shorts, The Jesselton is Kota Kinabalu's oldest and most atmospheric hotel. It's a small place with only 31 rooms and one suite, but the service is excellent and heavy discounts can be had at most times.
69 Jalan Gaya, Kota Kinabalu.
Tel: (088) 223 333. Fax: (088) 240 401.
Email: jesshtl@po.jaring.my.
www.jesseltonhotel.com

Accommodation lines the river at Kuching, Sarawak

SINGAPORE

Singapore has an extremely high standard of hotel accommodation with dozens of international-class hotels offering every conceivable luxury and high standards of service. Unfortunately, where the city doesn't score so well is in the budget accommodation category. Although there are cheaper hotels, they are poor value compared to elsewhere in Asia.

With hotels now competing in terms of the services they offer rather than price, they are often in the process of upgrading or renovation. This can make for a very uncomfortable stay, so try and find out beforehand to avoid being disturbed by construction work.

All hotel rooms are subject to a 10 per cent service charge and government tax of 6 per cent (expressed as '++').

Deluxe accommodation

The majority of deluxe hotel rooms in Singapore come with all the standard facilities. Most hotels have 24-hour room service, hairdressing or beauty salons, news kiosks, and a travel desk for booking tours or entertainment.

In the standard deluxe hotels such as the Hyatt Regency, the Hilton, the Pan Pacific and the Mandarin Oriental, room rates hover around S$350–500++.

Apart from the normal deluxe hotels, there are several other options if you want somewhere with historic atmosphere. Foremost among them is the majestic Raffles Hotel, where all the rooms have now been converted into suites and furnished in colonial style. Rates start at around S$750++. Another elegant historic building is the Goodwood Park Hotel, built in 1900 (rooms cost S$400++). In complete contrast to the hi-rise hotels that predominate in Singapore, **The Berjaya** (*tel: 6227 7678; www.berjayaresorts.com*) is an intimate but luxurious conversion of former homes in the heart of Tanjong Pagar (from S$350++).

Standard accommodation

Just below the deluxe category there are plenty of options for mid-range hotels, with rooms costing S$150–250++. Most of these have clean, air-conditioned rooms with the usual facilities.

In this category are hotels such as the **Amara** (*tel: 6879 2555; www.singapore.amarahotels.com*) and the Copthorne King's, both near Chinatown and the business district. On Orchard Road itself, one of the better-value hotels is the SHA Villa. Over in Little India the Perak Lodge (*tel: 6299 7733; www.peraklodge.net*) and the Madras Hotel (*tel: 6392 7889; www.madrassingapore.com*) both offer good, mid-range value.

Budget accommodation

It is still possible to find somewhere to stay in Singapore for as little as S$25 per night, although this will certainly be in one of the 'crash pads' popular with backpackers. The main centre for budget accommodation is in the Bencoolen Street area. A notch above are cheap, Chinese-run hotels, where a basic room costs S$40–75 (inc. tax).

Where to stay

The accommodation prices below are based on the cost per person for two people sharing the least expensive double room with en-suite bathroom and excluding breakfast.

★ Under S$100
★★ S$100–S$200
★★★ S$200–S$400
★★★★ Above S$400

Colonial District

Gallery Hotel ★★★
Anybody interested in modern architecture will enjoy this post-modern Singaporean masterpiece. Everywhere you look there are exciting features, whether it be the cantilevered lap pool on the roof, or the photo and art gallery on the second floor.
1 Nanson Road, Robertson Quay, Colonial District. Tel: 6849 8686. Fax: 6836 6666. Email: general@galleryhotel.com.sg. www.galleryhotel.com.sg. MRT: Somerset or Clark Quay.

Grand Copthorne Waterfront ★★★
Overlooking the Singapore River, the Copthorne Waterfront attracts tour groups, mainly for its reasonable rates. All of the moderately sized rooms are equipped with cable TV, mini bar and high-speed internet access.
392 Havelock Road, Colonial District. Tel/Fax: 6733 0880. Email: enquiry@grandcopthorne.com.sg. www.grandcopthorne.com.sg. MRT: Somerset or Outram Park.

Swissôtel The Stamford ★★★★
An integral part of the Raffles City shopping complex, The Stamford is Singapore's tallest hotel, and with more than 1,200 rooms it must rank as one of the city's largest as well. Stunning views of the city from virtually every room, friendly service and a host of amenities.
2 Stamford Road, Colonial District. Tel: 6338 8585. Fax: 6338 2862. Email: singapore-stamford@swissotel.com. www.swissotel.com. MRT: City Hall.

The Fullerton Singapore ★★★★
Once a grand 1920s post office, and full of Doric columns and vaulted ceilings, this colonial jewel is one of Singapore's many great hotels. Each of the spacious bedrooms has its own high-speed internet connection, cable TV and mini bar. Facilities include The Asian Spa, boutique and gift shops, fitness centre and outdoor infinity pool.
1 Fullerton Square, Colonial District. Tel/Fax: 6733 8388. Email: info@fullerton.com. www.fullertonhotel.com. MRT: Raffles Place.

Mandarin Oriental Singapore ★★★★
The Oriental has stunning harbour-view rooms or ocean-view suites. The hotel is particularly child-friendly with amenities such as a children's outdoor swimming pool.
5 Raffles Avenue, Marina Square, Colonial District. Tel: 6338 0066. Fax: 6339 9537. Email: mosin@mohg.com. www.mandarinoriental.com. MRT: City Hall.

Raffles Hotel ★★★★

The Raffles Hotel is a tourist sight in its own right; the government declared it a National Monument in 1987 and since then it has undergone major renovations which have left it quite clearly in the very top rank of the world's hotels. Matchless facilities include the Raffles Amrita Spa, the Tiffin Room, the Empire Café, the Raffles Creamery and, of course, a fitness room and pool.

1 Beach Road, Colonial District. Tel: 6337 1886. Fax: 6339 7650. Email: singapore@raffles.com. www.raffleshotel.com. MRT: City Hall.

Chinatown and The Quays

Copthorne King's Hotel ★★

The Copthorne King's advertises itself as a business hotel, but in fact offers far more than business facilities. It's not badly located either, close to the Singapore River, Chinatown and the Central Business District.

403 Havelock Road, Robertson Quay. Tel: 6733 0011. Fax: 6732 5764. Email: rooms@copthornekings.com.sg. www.copthornekings.com.sg. MRT: Outram Park.

Miramar Singapore Hotel ★★★

A great location if you're interested in the bars, restaurants and nightlife associated with nearby Clarke Quay and Boat Quay. Tastefully decorated rooms include an elaborate satellite TV system. Other amenities include pool, gym and a 'reflexology path' in the garden.

401 Havelock Road, Robertson Quay. Tel: 6733 0222. Fax: 6733 4027. Email: miramar@pacific.net.sg. www.miramar.com.sg. MRT: Outram Park.

The Scarlet ★★★

A boutique hotel that puts the emphasis on classic design and personalised service. Some truly innovative furniture graces the various restaurants, bars and rooms and generally furnishings lean almost towards a Regency style.

33 Erskine Road, Chinatown. Tel: 6511 3333. Fax: 6511 3303. Email: enquiry@thescarlethotel.com. www.thescarlethotel.com. MRT: Chinatown or Tanjong Pagar.

Little India

Albert Court Hotel ★★

This superb Chinese shophouse redevelopment, at the edge of the lively Little India district, offers great service and comfort at attractive rates. All rooms are air-conditioned and have cable TV, coffee and tea-making facilities and broadband internet access. There's also a well-equipped gym.

180 Albert Street, Little India. Tel: 6339 3939. Fax: 6339 3253. Email: reseasy@fareast.com.sg. www.albertcourt.com.sg. MRT: Little India.

Orchard Road

SHA Villa ★★

This is the Singapore Hotel Association's training college, but don't let that put you off; standards are high here. The attractive old colonial building houses 40 immaculate air-conditioned rooms, all with attached bathroom, cable TV and internet access. The Rosette restaurant serves a good continental breakfast as well as a classic à la carte menu.

64 Lloyd Road, Orchard Road District. Tel: 6734 7117. Fax: 6736 1651. Email: shavilla@shatec.sg. www.sha.org.sg. MRT: Somerset.

Goodwood Park Hotel ★★★

Like the Raffles Hotel, the Goodwood Park has also been designated a National Monument. Built in 1900 for the German expatriate community, this rather odd-looking colonial building seems quite out of place in modern-day Singapore. However, a number of wings house some of the city's plushest accommodation.

22 Scotts Road, Orchard Road District. Tel: 6737 7411. Fax: 6732 8558. Email: enquiries@goodwoodparkhotel.com. www.goodwoodparkhotel.com. MRT: Orchard or Newton.

Regent Singapore ★★★

This huge luxury hotel just off Singapore's busy Orchard Road shopping area offers a tranquil hideaway from the hustle and bustle of the city. It's also good value considering the long list of facilities on site. These include a jazz bar, Cantonese restaurant, health and fitness centre, outdoor swimming pool and large, exquisitely furnished bedrooms.

1 Cuscaden Road, Orchard Road District. Tel: 6733 8888. Fax: 6732 8838. Email: reservation.rsn@fourseasons.com. www.regenthotels.com. MRT: Orchard.

Sentosa Island

Rasa Sentosa Resort ★★★

A member of the Shangri-la Hotel chain, the Rasa Sentosa sits overlooking the South China Sea on beautiful Siloso Beach. It's a very active, family-friendly resort organising cycling tours of the island and nature walks. Tropically inspired furnishings decorate the 459 large and airy rooms. Facilities include the Kids' Club, a children's pool and three restaurants including the popular Barnacles Restaurant and Bar.

101 Siloso Road, Sentosa Island. Tel: 6275 0100. Fax: 6275 0355. Email: sen@shangri-la.com. www.shangri-la.com. MRT: HarbourFront.

The Sentosa ★★★★

If you're a golfer then this place is perfectly located for the excellent 18-hole Sentosa Golf Course next door. Set atop a hill, this picture-perfect resort overlooks the Straits of Singapore and is just a short staircase away from Tanjong Beach. A vast array of facilities includes two floodlit tennis courts, a large outdoor swimming pool, a gymnasium and extensive gardens perfect for an early-morning jog. The grounds also contain Spa Botanica, a tropical garden spa – the first of its kind in Singapore.

2 Bukit Manis Road, Sentosa Island. Tel: 6275 0331. Fax: 6275 0228. Email: info@thesentosa.com. www.thesentosa.com. MRT: HarbourFront.

Practical guide

Arriving

For social visits of under three months to Malaysia or Singapore, no visas are required for citizens of most European and Commonwealth countries (with the exception of the Indian subcontinent), the USA or Japan. That includes Britain, Ireland, Canada, Australia, all EU countries and Switzerland. Other nationalities should consult their nearest embassy before departure. Visitors to Malaysia should ensure their passport is valid for at least six months beyond the period of intended stay.

By air

Malaysia's main gateway is the new Kuala Lumpur International Airport (KLIA) at Sepang, 75km (47 miles) from the city centre. KLIA operates the KLIA Ekspres, a high-speed train link between the airport and central Kuala Lumpur. Trains leave every 15 minutes and take 28 minutes to reach the city (RM35 one way, RM70 return), easily the fastest way to reach KL. KLIA also operates express buses to the city centre every 30 minutes (RM25 one way, RM45 return). The journey takes around one hour. The taxi fare to downtown KL is about RM90. Taxis operate on a coupon system. Coupons are available at the taxi counter at the exit from the Arrivals Hall. Many hotels provide a pick-up service. Major car rental companies also have offices in the arrivals concourse. Some international airlines fly direct to other Malaysian destinations, including Pulau Pinang, Kota Kinabalu and Kuching.

Singapore's Changi International Airport is generally recognised as one of the most efficient and well-equipped airports in the world.

Foreign exchange counters and telephone bureaux are open 24 hours. Disabled travellers are provided with adapted toilets and telephones as well as ramps and lifts for wheelchairs. The time taken from aircraft door to kerbside is swift (half-an-hour or less is normal), but don't neglect the duty-free arrival shops, which are located in the arrivals area.

Changi has two terminals connected by a monorail. Most international carriers use Terminal 1; the ten which use Terminal 2 include Singapore Airlines, Swissair, Air France and Malaysia Airlines. Transport from Changi Airport to the city is swift and efficient, either by taxi or by one of the three Airbus services which call at many major central hotels. The small military airport of Seletar, on the north coast of Singapore, is used for some local regional flights.

By train

The main railway route from Thailand runs down the west coast of Malaysia, connecting Bangkok with Butterworth and Kuala Lumpur, before terminating at Singapore's Keppel Road Station.

By road

Long-distance express buses link Kuala Lumpur and other destinations in Malaysia with Singapore. There are also frequent shuttle buses and shared taxis to and from Johor Bahru, across the causeway. Express buses and shared taxis also operate across the border between Thailand and Malaysia.

By sea

A high-speed catamaran links west-coast resort islands in **Malaysia** with Thailand and Indonesia. The ferry runs from Medan in Sumatra to Pulau Pinang, Pulau Langkawi and then on to Phuket in Thailand.

Ferries from the World Trade Centre link **Singapore** with the Riau Archipelago in Indonesia. Cruise ships arrive at the International Cruise Ship Terminal next to the World Trade Centre.

Timetables and further details of most of the above transport can be found in the *Thomas Cook Overseas Timetable*, published bi-monthly (*see p187*).

Camping

In Malaysia you can sometimes camp in national parks and nature parks. There is a campsite on Sentosa Island, with tents and camp beds for hire.

Children

Baby foods, nappies and so on are available in supermarkets and shops. Most tourist hotels have reliable baby-sitting services (24 hours' notice required). *See also pp144–5.*

Climate

Hot and humid all year round, average temperatures range from 23°C (73°F) to 33°C (91°F). It can rain at any time of year, usually in short, heavy downpours. In **Malaysia**, the west coast is affected by the southwest monsoon, which brings rainfall mostly between September and December. The northeast monsoon arrives on the east coast slightly later, from October through to February. The east coast should be avoided during this time, since roads can be flooded, ferry services stop operating and many island resorts are closed. Sarawak and Sabah are also affected by the northeast monsoon, but travelling is not usually restricted. **Singapore** has the most rain between November and January.

Conversion table/measurements

See page 181.

There are various sizing systems, depending on the origin of the item; in general, the terms S, M, L, XL are understood and used. As a foreigner, you are almost certainly an XL.

Crime

Malaysia is generally a safe destination for tourists. There have been occasional reports of bag-snatchers in Kuala Lumpur and Kota Kinabalu, but otherwise theft from tourists is unusual. Carry your own padlock if you are staying in beach huts or cheap Chinese hotels.

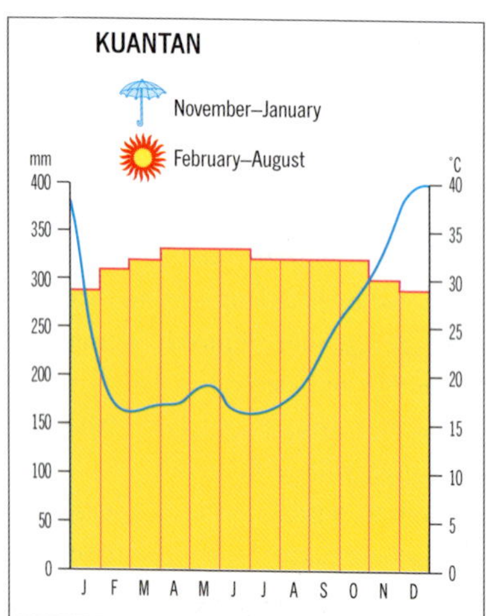

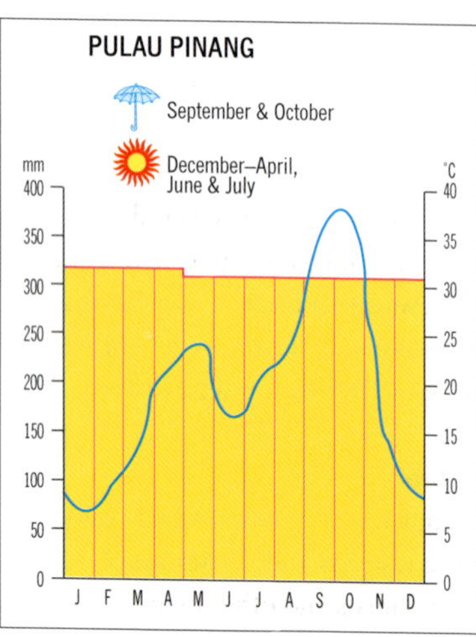

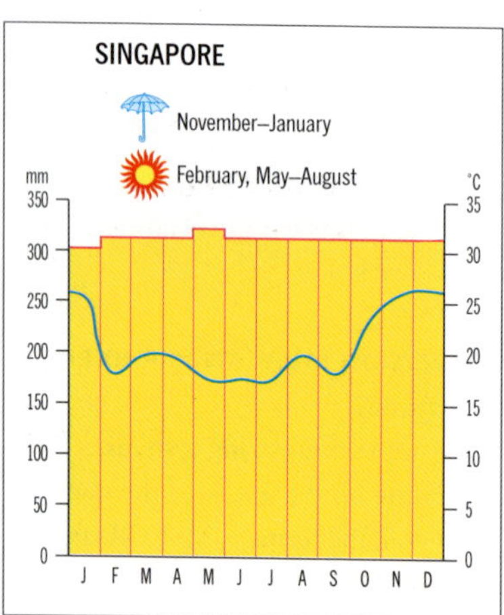

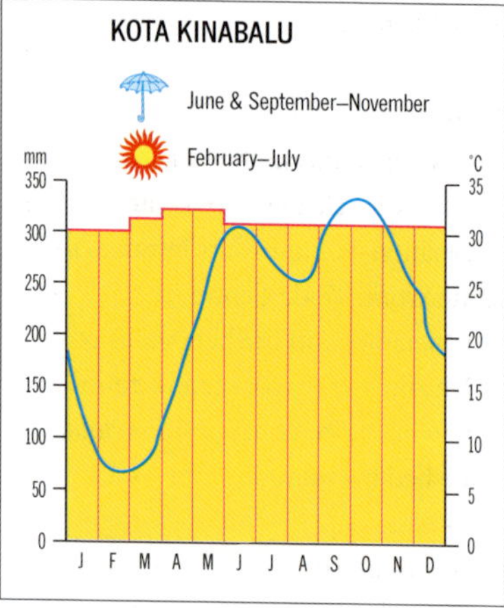

Singapore is one of the safest cities in Asia and crimes against tourists are rare; sexual harassment of women is likewise almost unheard of. However, take common-sense precautions.

WEATHER CONVERSION CHART

25.4mm = 1 inch
°F = 1.8 × °C + 32

Customs regulations

There are no restrictions on the amount of currency imported or exported from Malaysia and Singapore.

Travellers arriving in **Malaysia** can import 1 litre of wine or spirits, 200 cigarettes and perfume not exceeding RM200 in value duty free. Weapons and pornography are prohibited.

As the message on every tourist pamphlet and lurid billboard posted all over the country will remind you, the penalty for importing or dealing in *dadah* (drugs) in Malaysia is death. Severe penalties also apply in Singapore.

Travellers arriving in **Singapore** from countries other than Malaysia may bring in 1 litre each of spirits, beer and wine, free of duty. Controlled or prohibited items include pornography, weapons, endangered wildlife products, fire-crackers and chewing gum. Pirated tapes, videos and other material that infringes international copyright laws are liable to confiscation.

Driving

Peninsular **Malaysia** has a good network of well-maintained and usually well-signposted roads. If starting out from Singapore, it is cheaper to cross into Malaysia and hire a car from there.

Driving is on the left, with a speed limit of 110kph (68mph) on expressways, 80kph (50mph) on trunk roads and 50kph (31mph) in towns and cities. An international driving licence is required. Seat belts are compulsory for the driver and front-seat passenger.

There is very little point in hiring a car in **Singapore**, since taxis are relatively cheap and public transport is excellent.

Car rental

Avis *Angkasa Raya Building, Jalan Ampang, Kuala Lumpur. Tel: (03) 2144 4487. www.avis.com.my*

CONVERSION TABLE

FROM	TO	MULTIPLY BY
Inches	Centimetres	2.54
Feet	Metres	0.3048
Yards	Metres	0.9144
Miles	Kilometres	1.6090
Acres	Hectares	0.4047
Gallons	Litres	4.5460
Ounces	Grams	28.35
Pounds	Grams	453.6
Pounds	Kilograms	0.4536
Tons	Tonnes	1.0160

To convert back, for example from centimetres to inches, divide by the number in the third column.

MEN'S SUITS

UK	36	38	40	42	44	46	48
Rest of Europe	46	48	50	52	54	56	58
USA	36	38	40	42	44	46	48

DRESS SIZES

UK	8	10	12	14	16	18
France	36	38	40	42	44	46
Italy	38	40	42	44	46	48
Rest of Europe	34	36	38	40	42	44
USA	6	8	10	12	14	16

MEN'S SHIRTS

UK	14	14.5	15	15.5	16	16.5	17
Rest of Europe	36	37	38	39/40	41	42	43
USA	14	14.5	15	15.5	16	16.5	17

MEN'S SHOES

UK	7	7.5	8.5	9.5	10.5	11
Rest of Europe	41	42	43	44	45	46
USA	8	8.5	9.5	10.5	11.5	12

WOMEN'S SHOES

UK	4.5	5	5.5	6	6.5	7
Rest of Europe	38	38	39	39	40	41
USA	6	6.5	7	7.5	8	8.5

Hertz *Lot 214A Kompleks Antarabangsa, Jalan Sultan Ismail, Kuala Lumpur. Tel: (03) 2148 6433. www.hertz.com.my*
Magic Green *58 Jalan Mayang Pasir, Bandar Bayan Baru, Pulau Pinang. Tel: (04) 643 7603. www.magicgreen.com.my*
Mayflower *Mayflower Building, 18 Jalan Segambut Pusat, Kuala Lumpur. Tel: (03) 6252 1888. www.mayflower.com.my*

Electricity

The voltage is 220–240 volts AC. Hotels can supply transformers or adaptors to reduce the voltage if necessary.

Embassies and consulates

Australia *6 Jalan Yap Kwan Seng, Kuala Lumpur. Tel: (03) 2146 5555.*
25 Napier Road, Singapore. Tel: 6836 4100.
Canada *17th Floor, Menara Tan & Tan, 207 Jalan Tun Razak, Kuala Lumpur. Tel: (03) 2718 3333.*
1 George Street, 11–01 Singapore. Tel: 6854 5900.
Ireland *The Amp Walk, 218 Jalan Ampang, Kuala Lumpur. Tel: (03) 2161 2963.*
541 Orchard Road, 08–00 Liat Towers, Singapore. Tel: 6238 7616.
New Zealand *8 Jalan Sultan Ismail, Kuala Lumpur. Tel: (03) 2078 2533.*
391A Orchard Road, 15–06 Ngee Ann City Tower A, Singapore. Tel: 6235 9966.
UK *185 Jalan Ampang, Kuala Lumpur. Tel: (03) 2170 2200.*
100 Tanglin Road, Singapore. Tel: 6424 4200.
US *376 Jalan Tun Razak, Kuala Lumpur. Tel: (03) 2168 5000.*
27 Napier Road, Singapore. Tel: 6476 9100.

Emergency telephone numbers

Malaysia
Police, Ambulance & Fire *999*
Singapore
Police *999*
Ambulance and Fire *995*

Etiquette

In **Malaysia**, pointing with the forefinger (or any finger) is considered rude. This applies to animals, inanimate objects and especially to people. The polite way is to point with your whole hand or with the hand loosely fisted with the thumb sticking forward.

Touching people is definitely not acceptable, particularly if they are of the opposite sex.

Singapore takes great pride in the cleanliness of the city. There is a hefty fine of up to S$1,000 for littering. Smoking in public buses, taxis, lifts, theatres, cinemas and government offices is also banned (punishable by a S$500 fine). Smoking in many private offices is usually frowned on – always ask first. Smoking in restaurants is also banned.

Eating, drinking and smoking are prohibited on the whole of the MRT system. Crossing roads except where marked is theoretically an offence within 50m (55yd) of a pedestrian crossing, underpass or bridge, but this is rarely enforced. Chewing gum is banned outright.

Health

No vaccinations are required to enter either Malaysia or Singapore, unless you have visited an area where cholera or yellow fever is endemic within the previous six days.

In **Malaysia**, water is safe to drink in major towns and cities, but elsewhere ensure that it has been purified.

Singapore is one of the healthiest cities in Asia. Tap water is safe to drink.

One major hazard is dehydration from the tropical heat. Make sure you drink plenty of fruit juices and water to compensate for fluid loss.

Another common health problem is an upset stomach. In general, choose restaurants or cafés that look clean and are busy. Avoid food-stalls or restaurants where there are flies near the food. Avoid undercooked meats. Wash fruit in purified water and peel it yourself. Never eat raw seafood.

Medical facilities in clinics and hospitals are of a high standard with well-qualified, English-speaking medical personnel.

In Peninsular **Malaysia**, malaria exists in limited pockets only in the deep hinterland; if exploring rural areas, anti-malarial precautions are advisable. In Sarawak and Sabah (except in the coastal areas of Sarawak) there is an all-year malarial risk and precautions are recommended. Precautions should also be taken against typhoid, polio, tetanus and hepatitis A.

There is no risk of malaria in **Singapore**. Dengue fever is known to occur – this is mosquito-borne and there is no vaccine, so take care to avoid insect bites.

Hitchhiking

In Malaysia hitchhiking is acceptable, and it is usually fairly easy to get rides as long as you look presentable. There are few dangers involved, although women should not hitchhike alone.

Insurance

Comprehensive insurance covering medical expenses and theft or loss and damage to your belongings is recommended.

Lost property

In both countries, report lost property to the hotel management and the police, and obtain a copy of the report if you need to make a claim on your insurance. In Singapore you have a good chance of recovering lost items.

Media

The main national English-language newspaper in **Malaysia** is the *New Straits Times*. Other national papers include the *Star*, *Business Times* and the *Malay Mail*. In East Malaysia, regional papers include the *Borneo Post* and the *New Sabah Times*.

Singapore's leading English-language newspapers are the *Straits Times* and the *Business Times*. There is one afternoon English-language paper, the *New Paper*. Singapore also provides Chinese, Malay and Tamil daily papers.

Language

There are four official languages in Singapore (English, Mandarin, Malay and Tamil), although English is the most widely used and understood. The official language of Malaysia is Bahasa Malaysia, although you will also come across a multitude of other languages in the country that reflect its ethnic diversity. English is widely spoken, and even in remote areas you will be able to find someone who knows a few words and can help you out. However, even a smattering of Bahasa Malaysia will prove useful.

BASIC

good morning	selamat pagi
good afternoon	selamat petang
good night	selamat malam
please	silakan
thank you	terima kasih
sorry	maaf
excuse me	maafkan saya

QUESTIONS

How much?	berapakah harganya?
What is this?	apa ini?
What is your name?	siapa nama awak?
How are you?	apa khabar?
Where is . . . ?	di mana . . . ?
When?	bila?
Why?	mengapa?

TIME

today	hari ini
tomorrow	esok
yesterday	semalam
hour	jam
week	minggu
month	bulan
year	tahun
weekend	hujung minggu

PLACES

airport	lapangan terbang
beach	pantai
hill	bukit
island	pulau
mountain	gunung
lake	tasik
river	sungai
road	jalan
town	bandar
village	kampung

USEFUL WORDS

good	bagus
bathroom	bilik mandi
drink	minuman
eat	makan
expensive	mahal
hot water	air panas
room	bilik
shop	kedai
sleep	tidur
toilet	tandas

FOOD AND DRINK

beef	daging lembu
chicken	ayam
coffee	kopi
drinking water	air minuman
egg	telur
fish	ikan
pork	daging babi
rice	nasi
fried rice	nasi goreng
fried noodles	mee goreng
tea	teh
black tea	teh-o
vegetables	sayur

NUMBERS

1	satu
2	dua
3	tiga
4	empat
5	lima
6	enam
7	tujuh
8	lapan
9	sembilan
10	sepuluh
50	lima puluh
100	seratus
1000	seribu

Money matters

In **Malaysia**, the unit of currency is the Malaysian ringgit, until recently symbolised by a dollar sign '$'. You may still see '$' used to denote ringgit, but the official symbol is RM, for Ringgit Malaysia. The ringgit is divided into 100 sen, with notes in denominations of RM1, 2, 5, 10, 50, 100, 500 and 1,000. Coins are in denominations of 1 sen, 5 sen, 10 sen, 20 sen and 50 sen. All major credit cards are widely accepted.

In **Singapore**, the unit of currency is the Singapore dollar. Coins are issued in denominations of 5, 10, 20, 50 cents and S$1, notes in units of S$2, 5, 10, 20, 50, 100, 500, 1,000 and 10,000.

Shops and restaurants in the main cities in Malaysia and in Singapore will accept traveller's cheques denominated in any major currency, and they can be cashed commission-free at the following banks: Overseas-Chinese Banking Corp, United Overseas Bank, Chung Khiaw Bank, Far Eastern Bank.

National holidays

1 January New Year's Day
January/February Chinese New Year
March/April Hari Raya Puasa
1 May Labour Day
27 May Vesak Day
5 June Birthday of the Yang Di-Pertuan Agong (Malaysia)
July/August Hari Raya Haji
9 August National Day (Singapore)
31 August National Day (Malaysia)
October/November Deepavali
17 December Birthday of the Prophet Mohammed (Malaysia)
25 December Christmas Day.

During national and school holidays in **Malaysia**, hotels in resort areas are likely to be heavily booked, so make sure you have a reservation before you arrive.

In **Singapore**, offices and government departments are closed on national holidays, but many shops stay open.

Opening hours

Government offices in **Malaysia** are open on weekdays from around 8.30am–12.30pm and 2–4.30 or 5pm, and on Saturdays from 8.30am to 12.30–1pm. Shops open from around 9–10am to 6–7pm, with department stores and supermarkets in cities often open until 10pm. Chinese shops and those in tourist areas are also often open until 9pm or later. Banks are open Monday–Friday 10am–3pm, Saturday 9.30–11.30am.

In Johor, Kedah, Perlis, Kelantan and Terengganu, shops, banks and offices are closed on Thursday afternoon and all day Friday. In all states, the lunch hour on Friday lasts from 11.30am–2.30pm.

Official hours for government offices in **Singapore** are 8am–5pm weekdays, 8am–1pm Saturday. Shops are open from around 10am to 8–9pm, many until 10pm or later. Most banks are open from 10am–3pm weekdays, 9.30am–1pm Saturday (some banks in

Orchard Road are also open from 9.30am–3pm on Sunday). Money-changers are usually open from 10am–10pm daily.

Pharmacies

Western medicines are widely available in pharmacies (found in most shopping malls and department stores).

Places of worship

Visitors are welcome in Chinese, Buddhist or Hindu temples and in mosques outside prayer times. There are Christian churches in most large towns and cities in Malaysia and several Christian churches and a synagogue in Singapore.

Police

In case of trouble in **Malaysia**, contact any police station, or in Kuala Lumpur one of the numerous *Pondok Polis* (mini police stations). Kuala Lumpur has a special Tourist Police unit (*tel: (03) 2149 6593*). **Singapore** has no separate tourist police force (dial *999* for emergencies).

Post offices

In **Malaysia**, post offices are open from 8am–5pm Monday–Saturday, closed on Sunday. The cost of a postcard to anywhere in the world is 50 sen. In Kuala Lumpur, the central post office is on the second floor of the huge Dayabumi complex (*tel: (03) 2274 1122*).

In **Singapore**, post offices are located in several shopping malls (such as Raffles City, Specialists Centre), open 8.30am–5pm weekdays, 8.30am–1pm Saturday. Twenty-four-hour facilities are available at the General Post Office, Fuller Building, Fullerton Road and the Comcentre, 31 Exeter Road.

Public transport

Malaysia

Air

Malaysia Airlines (MAS) operate a network of domestic flights. Special fares are available on some routes for night flights and 14-day advance purchase. MAS and Singapore Airlines operate a joint shuttle service between Kuala Lumpur and Singapore. Domestic flight tickets are available at travel agents or MAS booking offices.

Bus

The country has a huge network of long-distance and local buses, providing a cheap, fast and fairly reliable service.

Ferries

Regular ferries operate between the mainland and offshore islands.

Taxis

One of the best ways to travel between major towns is by long-distance taxi.

Trains

Malaysian Railways (KTMB – Keretapi Tanah Melayu Berhad) operates two main lines. The west-coast line runs down from the Thai border to Kuala Lumpur's new KL Central Station and Singapore. The other line branches off from this one south of Kuala Lumpur and travels up through the centre of the country to Kota Bharu on the east coast. For overseas visitors, a Railpass is available.

Up-to-date information for Malaysian trains, long-distance buses and ferries can be obtained in the bi-monthly *Thomas Cook Overseas Timetable.* It can be purchased online at *www.thomascookpublishing.com*, or from branches of Thomas Cook in the UK (*tel: 01733 416477*).

In the US contact: SF Travel Publications, 3959 Electric Road, Suite 155, Roanoke, VA 24018 (*tel: 1800 322 3834; www.travelbookstore.com*).

Singapore

MRT (Mass Rapid Transport)

The fastest way to get around is on the MRT, with trains operating from 6am to midnight. The easiest way to use the MRT is to buy a TransitLink Farecard. This has the additional advantage of being valid for Singapore Bus Services (SBS) and SMRT Buses Ltd (SMRT).

Farecards can be obtained from TransitLink counters in MRT stations and at bus interchanges.

Buses

Bus services are frequent and fares cheap. The exact fare must be paid. You can use a TransitLink card on some buses, or a Singapore Explorer ticket.

Taxis

Fares are metered, and surcharges apply for journeys between midnight–6am, those starting at Changi Airport, for telephone bookings, and for trips to

Mass Rapid Transport, Singapore

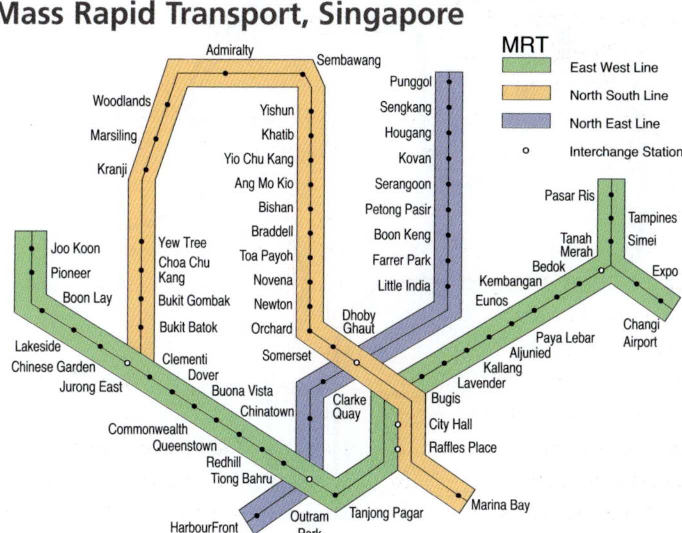

Kuala Lumpur Rapid Transit

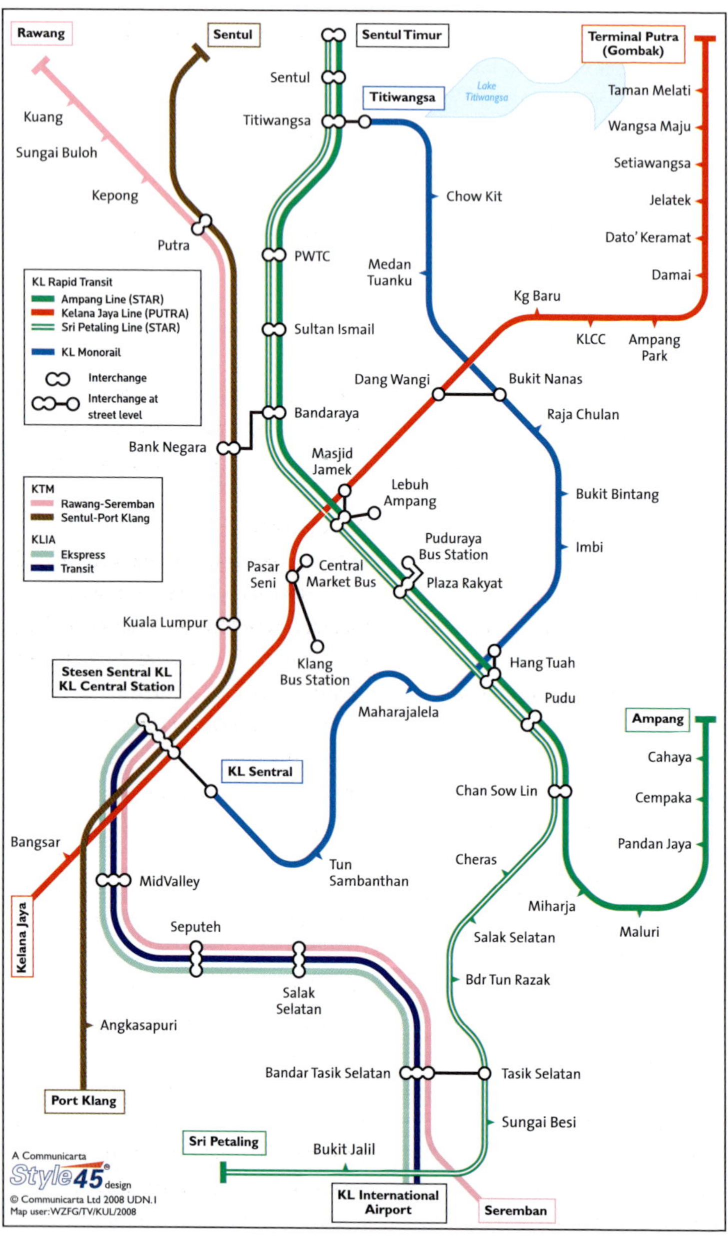

and from the Central Business District during peak hours.

Sustainable tourism

Thomas Cook is a strong advocate of ethical and fairly traded tourism and believes that the travel experience should be as good for the places visited as it is for the people who visit them. That's why we firmly support The Travel Foundation, a charity that develops solutions to help improve and protect holiday destinations, their environment, traditions and culture. To find out what you can do to make a positive difference to the places you travel to and the people who live there, please visit *www.thetravelfoundation.org.uk*

Telephones

Public pay-phones in **Malaysia** accept coins or phonecards. International calls can be made from any Kedai Telecom.
Enquiries *102*
Directory *103*
International *108*
International Access Code *00+*

Public pay-phones in **Singapore** accept either coins or phonecards. For overseas phone calls, all major hotels provide IDD facilities, but the costs will be much higher than calling from a public phone. IDD calls can be made from phone booths or Telecom centres (open 24 hours) such as those in the GPO on Fullerton Road.
Directory Enquiries *100*
Overseas Operator *104*
International Access Code *001+*

International dialling codes

Australia *61*
Canada *1*
Ireland *353*
New Zealand *64*
UK *44*
US *1*

Time

Australia (east coast) +2; Canada –13 to –16; Ireland –8; New Zealand +4; UK –8; US (EST) –13; US (WST) –16.

Tipping

This is not expected at hotels and restaurants that levy a service charge. Taxi drivers will expect to keep the change.

Tourist offices

In **Malaysia**, local and regional MTDC offices provide the usual services.
Kuala Lumpur *Head Office: 17th Floor, Putra World Trade Centre, 45 Jalan Tun Ismail. Tel: (03) 2615 8188. www.tourismmalaysia.gov.my*
Singapore
Head Office: Tourism Court, 1 Orchard Spring Lane. Tel: 6736 6622. www.visitsingapore.com

Travellers with disabilities

In **Malaysia**, very few tourist attractions cater for wheelchairs. However, lift services are available in major hotels.

Singapore has excellent facilities. A detailed guide to easily accessible attractions, *Access Singapore*, is available from the **National Council of Social Services**, *170 Ghim Moh Road* (more information on *www.ncss.org.sg*).

Index

A
accommodation 168–77
air travel 178, 186
antiques 128, 133
architecture 33–4, 35, 40, 42, 58, 100–101, 102, 105, 109, 111, 175
Armenian Apostolic Church of St Gregory 96
Asian Civilisations Museums 101
Astana 74

B
Baba Nyonya Heritage Museum 40
Bajau culture 85
Bako National Park 76, 80–81
Batu Caves 37
Batu Ferringhi Beach 56
beaches 52, 53, 56, 64, 65, 66, 68–9, 71, 79, 122
Beserah 66
Bidayuh culture 75
Bird Park (Kuala Lumpur) 33
birds 33, 53, 92, 97–8, 104, 113, 118
bird's-nests 79, 86
boats 23, 43, 71, 79, 103, 117, 118
Buddhism 15, 25
Bukit Bendera 56
Bukit China 41
Bukit Fraser 46–7
Bukit Timah Nature Reserve 98–9, 112–13
buses 178, 179, 186, 187
butterflies 33, 49, 56–7, 122
Butterfly Farm (Pulau Pinang) 56–7
Butterfly Park (Kuala Lumpur) 33
Butterfly Park and Insect Kingdom Museum 122

C
Cameron Highlands 46, 48–9, 50, 51
camping 179
cathedral (Singapore) 102
caves 37, 76, 78–9, 86
Central Highlands 28, 46–9, 50, 51, 147
Cerating 66
Chan See Shu Yuen Temple 32
Changi Prison Chapel and Museum 99
Cheng Hoon Teng Temple 41
Chettiar Temple 99
children 108, 144–5, 179
Chinaman Scholar's Gallery 99
Chinatown (Georgetown) 61
Chinatown (Kuala Lumpur) 32
Chinatown (Singapore) 99–100, 110–11
Chinatown Heritage Centre (Singapore) 99–100
Chinese culture 12–13, 15, 20–21, 22, 24, 32, 40–41, 55, 58, 61, 99–100, 101, 104, 106, 110–11 *see also* food and drink
Chinese and Japanese Gardens 100
Chinese opera 139
Christ Church (Melaka) 41
churches 41, 43, 60, 96
cinema 108, 136, 139–40
City Hall (Singapore) 100
clan-houses 55, 58
clan piers 54–5
climate 16–17, 18–19, 46, 116, 121, 179, 180
climbing 86
Confucianism 5
consulates 182
conversion measurements 179, 181
coral reefs 68–9, 72–3, 88, 119, 120, 121, 124
cricket 101–2
crime 130–31, 179–80, 181
culture 5, 14–19, 25, 31, 65, 66–7, 102, 137 *see also* architecture; ethnicity; museums; religion
customs 180–81

D
dance 137, 140
Dhammikarama Burmese Temple 58
disabilities 189
diving 68, 88, 119–20, 121, 149
documents 178
dress 18–19
driving 62–5, 71, 181–2
drugs 181
drum competitions 143

E
E & O Hotel 61
east coast 29, 66–71, 121, 129, 172–3
electricity 182
electronic goods 134
embassies 182
Emerald Bay 53
emergencies 182
Empress Place Building 100–101
Endau-Rompin 116–17
entertainment 104, 108, 123, 136–41, 143
ethnicity 4, 5, 10, 12–13, 14, 23, 24, 40, 74, 78, 84–5, 87, 94, 122, 123, 126, 139–40 *see also individual cultures*; food and drink
etiquette 16, 17, 182

F
fashion and clothing 134
fauna 49, 69, 76, 81, 82, 83, 90, 113, 116, 118, 119 *see also* birds
feng shui 5
festivals 22–7, 123
fireflies 117
fish 72–3
fishing 66, 68
flora 33, 49, 54, 69, 71, 76, 80–81, 82–3, 86, 92, 93, 96, 98, 105, 112–13, 123
food and drink 5, 16, 22, 23, 49–51, 75, 114–15, 135, 145, 150–67, 183
Forest Recreation Park 63
forests 49, 63, 80, 82–3, 88, 90, 92–3, 112–13, 116, 118, 123
Fort Canning Park 102–3
Fort Cornwallis 55
Fort Margherita 75
Fort Siloso 122
funicular railway 56

G
gardens 33, 56–7, 93, 96, 98, 100, 105, 123
Genting Highlands 47
Georgetown 54–6, 60–61, 128, 138
golf 146, 148–9
Gomantong Caves 86
granite quarrying 125
Gunung Berembun 49
Gunung Mulu National Park 76–7

H
handicrafts 66–7, 126–7, 129, 133
Haw Par Villa 103–4
hawker food 152–3, 163
health 151, 183
Hinduism 14, 24, 25, 26–7, 37
history 8–9, 10, 11, 30–31, 40, 45, 54, 78, 84, 105
hitchhiking 183
hornbills 53
hot springs 65, 88

I
Iban culture 13, 77
Images of Singapore 122–3
Independence Memorial Hall 41–2
Indian culture 13, 14, 22, 105, 114–15 *see also* food and drink
Indonesian food 154
Insect Museum 57
insurance 183
Islam 4, 14, 22
Istana Balai Besar 67

J
jewellery 134
Jurong Bird Park 104

K
Kadazan culture 85
kampungs 63, 78, 117
Kapitan Kling Mosque 61
karaoke 140
Kek Lok Si Temple 58
Khoo culture 55
Kinabalu National Park 84, 86, 92–3
kite-flying 142
kongsi 55, 58
Kota Belud 87
Kota Bharu 66–7, 129
Kota Kinabalu 87, 161
Kuala Lumpur 28, 30–35, 37, 126–8, 136–8, 158–9, 169, 170
Kuala Terengganu 67
Kuan Yin Temple 61
Kuantan 67–8
Kuching 74–5, 129, 160–61

L
Lake Gardens (Kuala Lumpur) 33
language 184
Leong San See Temple 115
Little India 105, 114–15
logging 82
longhouses 74, 77
lost property 183
lotuses 71

M
Makam Mahsuri 65
Malaysia 4–5, 6–7, 28–9, 116–21 *see also individual terms*
Mandai Orchid Gardens 105
Marang 68
Masjid Jamek 33–4
Masjid Kampung Kling 42
Masjid Negara 34
MRT 187
Mausoleum of Hang Jebat 42

Melaka 8, 40–45, 128, 159
Melaka River 43
Merlion Park 101
Miri 78
money 185
mosques 18, 19, 33–4, 42, 61, 96, 111
Mountain Garden (Kinabalu) 93
Murut culture 85
museums
 Kuala Lumpur 34–5, 37
 Melaka 40, 41–2, 43
 northwest coast 55–6, 56–7, 63
 Sabah 87
 Sarawak 75
 Singapore 99, 101, 106, 107, 108, 111, 122–3
music 140
Muzium Budaya 42
Muzium Negara 34

N

National Art Gallery (Kuala Lumpur) 34–5
national holidays 185
National Monument (Kuala Lumpur) 33
National Museum and Art Gallery (Singapore) 106
newspapers 183
Niah Caves 78–9
Niah National Park 78–9
night markets 128, 135
night safari 108
nightlife 136, 137–9, 140–41
northwest coast 52–65, 120, 128, 138, 159–60, 171–2

O

oceanarium 123–4
Old Parliament House 101
opening hours 131, 185–6
Orang Asli culture 37, 38–9, 147
Orang Asli Museum 37
orang-utans 90
orchids 92, 105, 123

P

Padang (Melaka) 45
Padang (Singapore) 100, 101–2
palaces 67, 74
Pangkor Laut 53
Pantai Damai 79
Pantai Kok 64
Pantai Rhu 65
parks, gardens and reserves 116–19, 147, 169
 east coast 68, 121
 Kuala Lumpur 33
 northwest coast 56–7, 63, 120
 Sabah 84, 86, 90–93, 119, 120, 121
 Sarawak 76–7, 78–9, 80–81
 Singapore 96, 98–9, 100, 101, 102–3, 105, 112–13, 123
pastimes 142–3
Perak 52
Peranakan Museum 105
Petronas Towers 35
pharmacies 186
photographic goods 134
Pinang Museum and Art Gallery 55–6
places of worship 186 *see also individual terms*
police 186
politics 10–11
porcelain 20
Porta de Santiago 42–3
post 186
prehistory 78
Princess Hang Li Poh's Well 45
proboscis monkeys 81
public holidays 185
public transport 56, 122, 123, 178–9, 186–9
Pulau Gaya 90
Pulau Kapas 68
Pulau Langkawi 58–9, 64–5
Pulau Manukan 91
Pulau Pangkor 52–3
Pulau Payar Marine Park 120
Pulau Perhentian 68
Pulau Pinang 52, 54–8, 60–63, 128, 138, 159–60
Pulau Rawa 68
Pulau Redang Marine Park 68, 121
Pulau Sakijang Bendera 124–5
Pulau Sibu Archipelago 121
Pulau Sipadan 88–9
Pulau Tembakul 124–5
Pulau Tenggol 69
Pulau Tioman 69, 121
Pulau Ubin 125

R

Raffles Hotel 106–7, 176
Raffles Hotel Museum 106–7
Raffles statues 102
rail travel 56, 178, 186–7
Rantau Abang 70–71
religion 4, 14, 15, 22, 24–5, 26–7, 37
reserves 90, 98–9, 112–13
rubber trees 98

S

Sabah 6, 13, 29, 84–93, 119, 120, 121, 147–8, 161
Sabah State Museum 87
safety 17–18, 56, 116, 179–80, 183
St Andrew's Cathedral 102
St George's Church 60
St Paul's Church 43
Sakya Muni Temple 107
Sandakan 89–90
Sarawak 6, 13, 29, 74–81, 129
Sarawak Museum 75
sea travel 179, 186
seasons 120, 121, 179
Semporna 90
Sentosa Island 122–4
Sentosa Orchid Gardens 123
Sepilok Forest Reserve 90
Sepilok Orang-utan Sanctuary 90
shadow-puppet plays 143
shopping 31, 67, 75, 87, 96, 105, 114, 126–35, 185–6
siamangs 49
Sibu 79
silat 142–3
silver-leaf monkeys 118
Singapore 5, 7, 29, 94–115, 122–5 *see also individual terms*
Singapore Discovery Centre 107
Singapore Flyer 107
Singapore Harbour 103
Singapore River 103
Singapore Science Centre 107–8
Singapore Zoo 108
Siong Lim Temple 108
smoking 182
Snake Temple 63
snorkelling 119
sport and activity 48–9, 68, 69, 71, 86, 88, 101–2, 119–20, 121, 146–9
Sri Mahamariamman Temple 35
Sri Mariamman Temple (Georgetown) 61
Sri Mariamman Temple (Singapore) 109
Sri Poyyatha Vinayagar Moorthi Temple 45
Sri Srinivasa Perumal Temple 109, 115
Stadthuys (Melaka) 43
Sultan Abdul Samad Building 35
Supreme Court (Singapore) 102
sustainable tourism 189

T

Taman Alam 117–18
Taman Negara National Park 118
Tanjong Pagar 111
Tasik Chini 71
Tawau Hills Park 119
taxis 178, 179, 186, 189
tea 50–51, 156–7
Telaga Air Hangat 65
Telaga Tujuh 65
telephoning 182, 189
Teluk Cempedak 71
Temple of Admiral Cheng Ho 43
Templer's Park 37
temples 18, 19, 32, 35, 41, 43, 45, 58, 61, 63, 99, 107, 108, 109, 115
ten-pin bowling 148
textiles 96
theatre 123, 140, 141
themed attractions 94, 103, 104, 144, 145
Thian Hock Keng Temple 109
Tiger Sky Tower 123
time differences 189
tin mining 30–31, 52
tipping 189
top-spinning 142
tourist information 189
tours 62–5, 103
Tunku Abdul Rahman Park 90–91, 121
Turtle Islands National Park 91
turtles 70–71, 88–9, 91

U

Underwater World 123–4

V

Veerama Kali Amman Temple 115
Victoria Memorial Hall and Theatre 102

W

walks and treks 44–5, 48–9, 60–61, 69, 80–81, 88, 92–3, 110–15, 123, 146–7
Wat Chayamangkalaram 58
waterfalls 65
white-water rafting 147–8

Z

zoo 108

Acknowledgements

Thomas Cook Publishing wishes to thank the following photographers, libraries and associations for their assistance in the preparation of this book.

AA PHOTO LIBRARY/KEN PATERSON 38, 39a, 39b, 43, 51, 69, 83a, 83b, 124, 131, 147, 151, 153, 161, 166a, 166b, 167
ARDEA LONDON LTD 72, 73a, 73b
DAVID HENLEY/CPA MEDIA 7, 12, 15, 16, 17, 18, 19, 21, 26, 27, 29, 35, 41, 47, 50, 53, 59, 70, 74, 76, 77, 79, 84, 86, 87, 89, 91, 98, 102, 105, 109, 115, 123, 132, 135, 142, 143a, 143b, 155, 156, 157, 158, 173
DREAMSTIME.COM 145 (Pavol Kmeto)
THOMAS COOK 13, 57, 67
US DEPT OF DEFENSE 11
WORLD PICTURES/PHOTOSHOT 1, 49, 119, 120, 140, 163, 165

For CAMBRIDGE PUBLISHING MANAGEMENT LTD:
Project editor: Karen Beaulah
Typesetter: Paul Queripel
Proofreader: Kevin Parnell
Indexer: Karolin Thomas

SEND YOUR THOUGHTS TO
BOOKS@THOMASCOOK.COM

We're committed to providing the very best up-to-date information in our travel guides and constantly strive to make them as useful as they can be. You can help us to improve future editions by letting us have your feedback. If you've made a wonderful discovery on your travels that we don't already feature, if you'd like to inform us about recent changes to anything that we do include, or if you simply want to let us know your thoughts about this guidebook and how we can make it even better – we'd love to hear from you.

Send us ideas, discoveries and recommendations today and then look out for your valuable input in the next edition of this title.

Emails to the above address, or letters to Travellers Series Editor, Thomas Cook Publishing, PO Box 227, Coningsby Road, Peterborough PE3 8SB, UK.

Please don't forget to let us know which title your feedback refers to!